WHO DO YOU THINK YOU ARE?

A leader's guide to what the mirror doesn't show you

ADAM QUINEY

Contact the author
adam@adamquiney.com
https://adamquiney.com/

Edited by Steve Voien
Designed by Danielle Baird
Author photo by Trevor Ball

Cover illustration source material by Meranna/Shutterstock.com and kersonyanovicha/Shutterstock.com

Interior illustrations by iStock.com/AlexSukhoterin

ISBN: 978-1-7782071-0-5

First Edition

This book is dedicated to all those who yearn for the life that lies beyond "good enough." For all those souls who thirst for what's possible, and are committed to the sacred journey of transformation.

Through your courageous work, we find our own courage.

Thank you.

TABLE OF CONTENTS

SECTION TWO (CONTINUED)

INTRODUCTION

IN YOUR HANDS you hold the key to all that ails you as a leader and manager. A book that can revolutionize your approach to your relationships, your leadership, and the those you support at work. *Who Do You Think You Are?* is a model for how people operate in the world, how we ended up being "the way we are," and how to get back to seeing and working with people as they truly are.

Most approaches to management and leadership largely tackle the surface by focusing on behaviour and habits rather than going deeper into *being* and transformation. Some approaches are focused on the potential of those you lead, but that potential is limited by the narrow perspective through which we relate to the person in front of us. Alternatively, these approaches explain why things happen, without offering effective tools to bring about deeper, transformational change.

You're left frustrated, trying your best and implementing approach after approach, only to conclude that the problem isn't the approach—it's the person. Ironically, this is accurate, though not in the way we usually think. The problem isn't that someone is unleadable or uncoachable—it's that you're unable to get truly present to the human in front of you. Until you can see the depth below the surface, your attempts to support someone will be stuck at your current level of consciousness.

Common symptoms of this flavour of being stuck include: A growing frustration with your staff and those you are leading, a reduction in the amount of time before you notice people's flaws show up and sabotage what you aim to create, disappointment in those you lead and their inability to address what gets in their way, creating inspiring visions and great plans only to have them fall off the rails, and a slow-growing sense of disillusionment.

Who Do You Think You Are? aims to help you make real, lasting changes in your leadership approach and relationships, and in how you live your life. This book is for leaders, aspiring leaders, and leadership coaches. Many readers will also find it to be a useful guide for deepening personal relationships and self-awareness.

Who Do You Think You Are? is a model for relating to people, and how people got from where they started, to how they're showing up today. By learning what lies underneath the obnoxious or frustrating tendencies we *all* have in moments of confrontation, you're provided with the opportunity to see past the surface and to the gift that lies at the heart of each person.

Who Do You Think You Are? explains why you seem to continually run into the same kind of problematic personality types and why your attempts to resolve this kind of dysfunction on your teams don't seem to work (and if anything, become less effective as time wears on). In addition to providing the altitude needed to understand what's really going on with you and your team members, *Who Do You Think You Are?* lays out a path to the heart of the matter—to forging truly powerful teams and growing the seed of leadership that exists in every human being.

HOW THIS BOOK IS LAID OUT

THIS BOOK HAS three main sections.

The first section describes the foundation and underlying context for the model that is used throughout. I'll talk about how this model was created, how it works, how it pertains to leadership, and some examples of how you can put it to work. The first section is meant to be a bit of a primer for the rest of the content. Once you've read this (and you may even choose to skip it if it doesn't interest you), you will probably not come back to it.

The second section of the book details the twenty-five qualities of being I've laid out and distinguished in this book. This section is **not** intended to be read all the way through. This section is intended to be something you can come back to every time you notice you're up against your own leadership or that of someone else. When you find yourself frustrated with someone or annoyed by a particular way someone is showing up, it can be helpful to grab this book, reference the quality in Section Two, and refresh yourself to better understand where they are coming from, who they truly are, and how you might work with them to expand their leadership.

On the right side of the page, you'll notice tabs referencing the "the gift" of each of the qualities of being, along with the two aspects of their shadow. For each of the qualities laid out in this section, I provide a number of practises designed to open up and support someone on the path of breakthrough, possibility, and leadership. Finally, there's a reference page at the start, as well as an index at the end of the book to make it easier to reference whatever is showing up.

The third section of the book provides a guide to how you can put what you've learned into practise in the real world with a set of eight practical How-To chapters. Leadership grows when we attach action and embodiment to insight. If all you do with this book is read it and gain some interesting insight, I have failed in my mission to support you in deepening your leadership. So don't let me fail you — put this work into practise.

WHO I AM AND HOW THIS BOOK WAS CREATED

I'VE BEEN WORKING as an executive coach for over a decade now. Before this, I had careers as a software developer, project manager, and lawyer.

My work in those previous careers was efficient, effective, and tidy. I was very good at identifying all of the variables in any particular situation I found myself in, and then managing those variables to ensure I arrived at the desired result with as little deviation as possible.

This approach was not limited to my career. It was the lens through which I related to and experienced *all* of my life. My relationships and friendships were neat and tidy. My life looked well put together, and just the right amount about me was revealed to give you a sense of how interesting and polished I was without giving you anything deeper (no need to look too deeply beneath the cover—I certainly wasn't interested in doing that).

I believed that I was deeply invested in my personal growth.

I read a lot of books about personal development, watched and listened to a lot of content about how to be a better person, and took on practises in service of bettering myself.

Most of this work was done inside the safety of the world I knew and had created. Even though I would read about things like the importance of practising vulnerability, I had already precluded the possibility of any vulnerability in my life (because that was a variable I had figured out how to control and eliminate—vulnerability is not particularly efficient). Consequently, I would take on practises like vulnerability inside of the perfectly safe world I had created.

If you asked me whether I was doing my own work to grow myself, I would point to all of the stuff I was doing as evidence that I was. At the same time, I was completely oblivious to the fact that I was safe inside the known, comfortable world I had created.

This is the way our shadows work. Operating at its very best, our ego keeps us safe while simultaneously fooling us with the belief that we are courageously forging into the vast unknown. By doing this, the ego ensures that we don't get too crazy about this idea of "growth." The need, fed to us societally, to always be growing is appeased while we are simultaneously kept safe. The best of both worlds (...ish).

About a decade ago, I was ready to change careers again and discovered coaching. Originally, I got into this work to help other people become more like *me*. I thought that was what coaching was about: Me, having figured out the pinnacle of how to be, helping other people achieve the lofty heights I had.

A lot of my early training and work as a coach (including the work I did with my own coach at the time) was fairly facilitative and superficial. Helping people do exactly what I thought this work was about. Here's a life wheel. Rate the areas of your life on a scale of one to ten, and then we'll figure out what you need to do to move them to a ten. Plenty of process, loads of tools, but not a lot of real transformation. Of course, I couldn't see this; I was more present to a growing sense of boredom as I went through the motions.

Eventually, by good fortune and a lot of support from people much deeper in their work than myself, I found my way into a coach training program that truly made a difference for me (Accomplishment Coaching—mentioned in the Acknowledgments chapter at the end of this book). In this line of work, I was exposed to a deep ontological model, shown who I truly was, and shown everything I was putting in the way of that.

When I talk about an ontological model, I'm referring to an approach that looks below the level of what I am *doing*, and instead, puts attention on who I am *being* underneath it. Rather than be distracted by the well-articulated dialogue, nice suits, and professional success I presented, those working with me reflected back who I was *being* underneath all of it.

All of my strategies were laid bare in front of me. All of the clever commentary, incessant pursuit of knowledge, fancy words, witty repartee—and everything else I was doing to ensure you liked me and thought I was fun—was pointed out to me, so I could see how it was getting in the way of my possibility on this planet.

For the first time since beginning this line of work, I actually got a glimpse of who I was, and all of the sophisticated work I was doing to keep that from coming to light (because that was safer than having my whole self expressed). I saw that despite all the books I had read, all the videos I had watched, and all the earnestness with which I believed I was deep in my work—my work was just beginning.

At the end of the first weekend (in what would be a year of deep, uncomfortable, and transformational work), I drove the four hours back to my brother's house where I was staying and cried the entire way. My heart, for the first time in thirty some-odd years, had been opened.

As I deepened through this year of training, I slowly learned, and then even more slowly came to embody, a deeper truth: That coaching was not about helping other people be more like me. It was about helping other people be more like *themselves*—the person they had always been but had learned to cover up. And before I had any hope of helping people do that, *I* needed to become more like myself.

After completing my year of training, I stayed on and led Accomplishment Coaching's work in various capacities, learning about what it is to *be* a leader, as opposed to *talking about* leadership. I received feedback and training in the moment on who I was being as a leader, as I was leading (*not* a comfortable experience but a transformative one), and then, over time, provided this same feedback and training to those I was developing as leaders.

After I left Accomplishment Coaching's leadership team, I continued my own work—with clients, coaches, and teachers—writing about what I learned in their company.

Much of the work in this book is *discovered*. This is not a compendium of knowledge and information I learned from researching and reading a bunch of other books. That doesn't mean I haven't read a bunch of books (part of my essential nature is Brilliance, and people that possess the quality of Brilliance tend to be voracious consumers of information).

More importantly, in learning to let go of my need to continue finding knowledge *out there*, and beginning instead to trust the Brilliance within, this book began to assemble itself. I would work with my clients, supporting them in the path they wished to walk. And, as I continued to do so, I would see patterns emerge. I would reconcile those patterns with the models I had already learned, and as I did so, *Who Do You Think You Are?* slowly started to emerge.

I didn't set out to create a model for ontology and how humans operate, and you don't need to worry too much about the model to make it work. Those of you with the trait of Brilliance will likely be curious about it because that is innate to the gift of Brilliance—the insatiable desire for more knowledge. If this describes you, then be sure to check out the section on Brilliance, and feel free to explore the model itself as a whole. If it doesn't describe you, don't worry about it.

The real point of this book and work is to support you in embodying who you are at your core, and to support others in doing the same. Understanding the inner workings of a particular model is just icing on the cake.

SECTION ONE

Setting the Foundation

WHO DO YOU THINK YOU ARE?

CAROL WAS FRUSTRATED. Her staff were struggling, and she didn't understand why she couldn't seem to motivate them. When she had initially hired Brent, he had been committed and a true believer in the product line Carol had brought him on to manage. Brent had been devoted to the work in front of them and put all of himself into the project.

However, as time wore on, Carol noticed that Brent started to become flakier with his time. He seemed to alternate between rigid, almost tyrannical adherence to project timelines (including what he demanded of his team) and bailing out of commitments and deadlines he had promised. When Carol tried to help him set up systems to make sure that he stayed on track and on target, Brent got frustrated and angry with Carol.

Carol's other team lead, Doris, was a brilliant engineer. Carol had initially hired her because of how sharp her mind was. She had already seen the possibilities available for the product Carol was launching, and before the end of her first week, Doris had contributed in some significant ways. In fact, Doris had helped them see the potential to launch their product through a vastly different approach than what they had originally planned and had helped them avoid a costly re-engineering process that would have slowed them down and cost a great deal. Throughout all of this, Doris had been an ocean of calm—her staff had been deeply appreciative of Doris's ability to provide them the answers they needed to keep moving forward while keeping things easy and peaceful regardless of the steps they were walking through.

Doris was indisputably brilliant and one of the smartest people Carol knew. But as time went on, Carol had noticed that Doris had become harder and harder to work with. While her initial plan to re-engineer and relaunch their product had been spot-on and perfect, at times she had other ideas that simply weren't feasible given other factors in the company. Rather than remain peaceful and easy-going through these conversations, Doris would get condescending and outright nasty. Instead of the peaceful presence Carol (and Doris's team) had come to rely on, Doris would get frenetic with her energy. She would end up dividing her time between the task at hand and other tasks devoted to proving why her ideas simply *had* to be implemented. The diffusion of her energy this way was causing problems not only for Carol and the rest of the executive team but also for Doris's direct reports.

WHAT DIDN'T WORK:

- 360-reviews for the executive team
- More check-ins
- Trying to solve the problems for them
- Micromanaging
- Fantasizing about firing everyone

Finally, Carol herself was wondering if she had made the right decision in founding this company. While Carol had originally felt like being an entrepreneur and forging into the unknown was the reason she was on this planet, as things had moved forward, she'd started to find herself more worried and continually concerned about the impact her decisions would have on the rest of her employees. Decisions stopped being fun sorties into the unknown and became moments she learned to dread. Carol found herself less able to make decisions on her own and noticed that she was leaning on the members of her executive team more and more to make decisions for her.

What frightened Carol most of all was the amount of judgment she was present to during her workday. While Carol knew herself to be kind and inclusive, she found herself operating with a shorter and shorter fuse. Carol was regularly thinking about firing people for the slightest provocations and noticed that she was labelling certain members of her staff and fantasizing about throwing them out on their ear. Carol had always been willing to do the hard work of leading, including letting people go, but she noticed that this felt different. This felt cold-hearted.

Carol wasn't sure what had gone wrong. While things had started out so promising, they had slowly devolved into a mired-down, unpleasant work environment. Something needed to shift, and Carol could not seem to find the right actions that would make the difference. She had tried instituting performance reviews and regular check-ins. She had tried 360-reviews for her executive team and set up regular meetings for them to provide each other with feedback for how they were doing with the changes they were trying to make.

Carol had also tried to handle this with her own ingenuity, sitting down and figuring out what she felt would resolve the issues for each of her executive team. More structure and ongoing check-ins for Brent, Doris staying focused on the task at hand and watching her condescending tone, and for Carol, making decisions regardless of the consequences and reminding herself that she knew best on some level.

Carol was at her wit's end. If she couldn't solve this, she concluded it was time to exit the company.

None of these choices had worked. They'd created temporary changes and left the team feeling better for a while, and then, when things reverted back to what seemed to be their default, left the team feeling more disillusioned than ever.

Carol was at her wit's end. If she couldn't solve this, she concluded it was time to exit the company.

—

Where Carol finds herself is characteristic of most leaders in most organizations after a certain point. Carol has started a company and hired great people, based on the strengths and qualities she saw in them and in herself.

While at first, these qualities lend themselves beautifully to the entrepreneurial process, over time, Carol, Brent, Doris, and the rest of their team start to develop friction with one another. This friction is a natural result of humans working together to build beyond what is predictable. As Carol and her team push beyond the boundaries of their comfort zone, their truest nature—the qualities for which they were brought together—starts to get clouded by their shadows. These shadows are the tendencies that show up when we are confronted.

While Carol is noticing Doris's arrogance and condescension and trying to resolve this behaviour on the surface, what she is unable to see is that these traits are exactly how we would expect someone with the quality of Brilliance to show up when they're feeling afraid. Perhaps Doris is left feeling stupid or like her opinion is no longer valued. Maybe Doris feels like she's been eclipsed and no longer has a place on the team. Whatever it is that's triggering Doris and her shadow, Carol's attempt to control and manage these aspects of her being are missing the mark. Before Carol can really get a hold of what is going on, she needs to get to the root of the issue.

Many leaders believe the only solution is to fire someone or leave the company entirely.

Even more problematic, Carol's earnest attempts to move Doris out of her fear-based patterns actually reinforce the fear. Rather than get at the heart of the matter, Carol's directive that Doris stop focusing on other things and look only at what she has been tasked with is likely to perpetuate Doris's concerns of becoming irrelevant, further driving up her fear and re-triggering her shadows.

Carol, like so many leaders on so many other teams, is trying to address the patterns that show up on the surface because that is what is immediately apparent. Like trying to shift an iceberg by applying pressure only to the part that lies above the water (because that is what we can see), the impact tends to be minimal and only seems to keep the same problems present.

As time wears on, Carol's efforts to address the dysfunction on her team prove fruitless, and Carol reaches the conclusion that many leaders arrive at: The problem is either an employee or the job itself. It's time to fire someone or leave the company entirely and do what's next.

Although these solutions will create a shift, they do nothing to deepen Carol's ability to lead nor to draw out the leadership in her team. Instead, Carol will create a new circumstance, free of the dysfunction she is stumped by, until enough time passes and she ends up recreating the same issues.

Carol will create a new circumstance, free of the dysfunction she is stumped by, until enough time passes and she ends up recreating the same issues.

What Carol is unable to see is that these shadows are a fundamental aspect of the light that casts them. If Carol wishes to work alongside Brilliance, she will need to develop the ability to work with the shadow that shows up along the way: Arrogance, Condescension, and what might occur like Stupidity. Absent taking on this work, Carol's employees will have a diminishing half-life. They will be hired on and do great work, until, inevitably, the friction of being in relationship with other humans starts to trigger their shadows. As Carol's ability to work with these shadows atrophies further, she'll have less and less patience before she ends up making a new round of firings.

HOW YOU WOUND UP HERE

"HOW DID I end up here?"

Have you ever wondered that question? In this case, *here* happens to be wherever it is you currently find yourself. If you look back, you can see a series of logical decisions that have led you to this point in your life, wherever this point currently happens to be.

Here isn't even a bad place to be—it's probably gotten you a lot of benefits, friends, and joy. But *here* also brings with it a set of consequences, disappointments, and letdown.

Everyone ends up *here*. The benefits are different for each person, as are the consequences, but for most of us, there are points throughout life where we look up and wonder, "How did I get here?"

At first, we may have a vague sense of the direction we're traveling in. We might, in a moment of lucidity, realize that some things about ourselves seem a little more ingrained than they used to be. As time wears on, we might start to relate to ourselves through the fixed lens of "Well, this is just the way I am." But if we look back to when we were younger, that wasn't always the case. When did we start to get fixed into these patterns?

Maybe you started to notice that you have some tendencies that really mirror those of your parents. Growing up, you swore you would never be like them, but as time has worn on, you've noticed that it turns out you're quite a bit like them.

Or maybe you view things from the other direction, remembering a level of freedom or way of being that seemed so present for you in your childhood, but these days seems distant and far away. Wondering when you gave that up or questioning whether things were really quite as vivid as you remember them, it becomes easier to shrug your shoulders and simply chalk it up to "youth."

Either way, regardless of what you notice about where you are now versus how you remember being, the question remains: How did I end up here?

Before We Get Started...

A couple of notes before we get started: Throughout this book, I will use your "light" as shorthand to refer to the particular qualities that you *are*. As you read through these examples, the light I refer to is a reference to the qualities described in Section Two.

Whenever I'm referring to one of the qualities I've described in Section Two, it will be denoted with a capital letter. This is to help you differentiate when I am talking about a particular quality of being versus an action you may take or something else.

For example:

> *You possess the quality of Connection. When you are sitting with people, connecting with them, practise noticing when Connection is present, and when it's not.*

Now, without further ado...

QUICK TIPS

- Your "light" refers to the particular qualities that you *are*.
- This is a reference to the qualities described in Section Two.
- It will be denoted with a capital letter.

IN THE BEGINNING, THERE WAS LIGHT

WHEN FIRST BORN, we are simply the full expression of our own particular light.

Babies don't come out of the womb with stories about what is acceptable and what isn't. They don't yet know who to fear, who to hate, who is likely to hurt them, situations that are safe, or any of the other social rules that we slowly but surely put together as we mature into adults.

As babies and toddlers, we simply are.

You can see this by spending any amount of time with young toddlers. They don't spend time questioning whether or not they should express what they are feeling—they simply do. When they're angry, they throw a tantrum. When they are happy, they laugh joyously. When they are sad, they cry—loudly. This is part of what makes babies such a delight, and part of why it's so annoying that most major airlines seem to have a policy of booking them directly behind me on long flights.

While everyone begins life as a being of fully expressed light, we very quickly receive feedback from the world around us about how we *should* and *should not* be. This feedback comes from parents, teachers, guardians, friends, and the world at large and is a function of everyone else's created stories about the right way to be.

If your mother was raised with a story that expressing her Brilliance was arrogant, it's quite likely she will raise you the same way. Alternatively, your mother may have been raised with this story and conclude that there was no way her children were going to operate under the same disempowering story. And so, in this second case, you were raised to know, excel with, and rely on your Brilliance.

When first born, we are simply the full expression of our own particular light.

For some of the stories you are fed, you will accept them and follow along, operating in line with what is appropriate, right, or correct. In other situations, you will rebel against the story you are fed, rejecting it and refusing to fall in step with this particular belief. In these latter situations, we end up doing the opposite. If you noticed your parents playing very safe and being unwilling to take risks, you may have decided "I'll never be like that!" and chosen to live a life of adventure, freedom, and out on the edge.

While it seems like we've overcome our childhood conditioning, we're still every bit as imprisoned by it as the person that has learned to accept and march along in step with it. Doing the opposite of something grants no more freedom than doing the same thing. Whether we follow the rule or violate it, our actions are still ultimately a function of the underlying rule we were taught.

Hopefully it's clear that there's no way of escaping how this goes. Whether it's aligning with or rebelling against the story about ourselves, either way we grow up learning to overemphasize or underemphasize certain parts of who we naturally are.

Most people have trouble coming to terms with and accepting this truth, especially in areas that are tender and lie in our blind spots. We want to believe that we are *not* (said emphatically) like our parents and that we have overcome their defunct ways. But the more we insist that their approaches are wrong and ours are not, the more binary we become and the more locked into these patterns we get stuck. If we cannot distinguish something, we have no access to it (that is, we have no ability to do anything about it). Consequently, the places where you notice an insistence that this isn't the case for you are often the best places to practise softening and really taking a look.

It's important to note that this tendency to grow into the stories we were told as children isn't a *bad* thing (although people will tend to relate to it this way). This is simply the journey that we take as we grow up. Despite our parents doing their very best to raise us with the tools they had available, we're going to learn that some parts of ourselves are exceptional and some parts of ourselves are bad.

This learning as we grow up leads to two fundamental approaches to altering our natural expression.

In situations where we are trained to *dim* our light (perhaps because who we are was deemed too much, made us a target, intimidated others, got us laughed at, etc.), we will aim to *under-express* that part of our being. If you are told that you are being arrogant or are a nerd for expressing your Brilliance, you may try to diminish it. You may practise speaking with simpler words or keeping your intellect to yourself. You may underperform on exams and tests so that you can alleviate the expectations and pressure your family puts on you to be smart.

We've been trained to dim or emphasize our light, depending on the situation.

Consequently, in the situations, circumstances, and around people that look like the times when your light needed to be underemphasized, you learned to diminish or hide these parts of yourself. This creates what we call the *under-expressed* aspect of your shadow.

In other situations, we were trained to *emphasize* our light (perhaps because we didn't feel seen or because that was what got us noticed, earned us love, left us feeling valued, or kept us safe). If you *feel*[1] dismissed for being stupid or are surrounded by a bunch of brilliant people and are worried about looking dumb, you may work extra hard to demonstrate your intellect. You may use large words or speak in long sentences. You may argue and debate with people or attempt to prove them wrong and yourself right.

As a result, in the situations, circumstances and around people that look like the times when your light needed to be overemphasized, you

1 **NB:** It doesn't matter whether or not someone is actually intended to dismiss you as stupid — all that matters is how you feel.

learned to trumpet your being loudly into the space. This creates what we call the *over-expressed* aspect of your shadow.

A Caveat About Asking "Why?"

You could look at your childhood upbringing, and who your parents were for you, or remember a story about a teacher doing something to you in the fourth grade, and it will leave you a little clearer on *why* you arrived at this particular configuration you find yourself in today. While looking at *why* you are the way you are can be a satisfying itch to scratch, it rarely leads to transformation. Everyone comes by their shadow honestly. The simplest approach is to trust you put together the system and shadows you have because that was what was necessary in childhood to get you here today.

Knowing more about how you arrived here can certainly be interesting, and at times helpful. But more often than not, it's a digression that keeps you safe from the real work in front of you.

Knowing more about how you arrived here can certainly be interesting, and at times helpful. But more often than not, it's a digression that keeps you safe from the real work in front of you: Taking the courageous action of embodying and expressing your qualities more fully. We will talk more about this later. For now, let's look at what happened as you kept practising and developing these parts of your shadow.

The Vicious Cycle

At first, learning to build your shadows was practising something new. Like a child exploring a new game, you practised different approaches and strategies to life and the circumstances you encountered and learned what worked and what did not. This is part of what makes our shadow so effective—the world around us has trained us that these approaches work.

Each time your shadow earned you the result you wanted in the moment (love, attention, safety, etc.), you were left with more evidence that this was the appropriate way to show up in this situation and stored that memory away for future use.

For example, if your insecure father showed you more love when you dimmed your light around him, your brain will store this memory and access it for future use anytime you find yourself around someone that presents in the same way your father did. These situations begin to represent an automatic stimulus-response pattern for you. When you see insecurity, you no longer have to think about it. You already know how to be. Show up smaller than you are, dim your light, and you will receive love and appreciation from the person in question.

Each time you store and retrieve the behaviour of your shadow from memory, it moves further into the realm of the automatic. At first you may need to recall what happened in the past and how you overcame this situation, but, over time, you learn simply to respond automatically to the stimulus presented. Eventually, and with enough practise at this, you stopped *using* these approaches to the circumstances you encountered in life and started being *used by* them.

Polishing and Honing Your Shadows

Over time, your shadows moved from something you may have been consciously aware of into the automatic realm of the unconscious. At this point, we're beyond the realm of creating your shadows and into the realm of polishing and honing them.

> Both the under- and over-expression of your qualities are a product of your fear and a function of having learned that some part of yourself is either *too much* or *not enough.*

The issue with these shadows is they are incongruous with who you truly are, and so it requires work and energy to maintain these states. When you are in situations for which you feel the need to express a shadow, you are left feeling tired, depleted, and, over time, burnt out.

Because this now happens below your level of consciousness, you're left concluding that the problem is outside of you. That it lies in the situations, people, and circumstances in which you feel unconsciously compelled to run your shadows. Because you are unable to see the *choice* actively being made into a shadow-based way of showing up, you have no ability *but* to conclude that the issue is something external rather than internal. As life travels on, you make decisions that allow you to avoid, leave or suffer through the circumstances that trigger your shadows.

You will also tend to thrive in situations where your shadows are particularly well-suited. For example, if you learned that, contrary to your natural state of Peace, there were times when being extremely belligerent (an under-expression of Peace) got you what you wanted, you will naturally find yourself gravitating towards careers and situations where this shadow aspect of yourself is rewarded.

As time goes on all of this becomes part of who you relate to yourself as. You no longer think, "In these situations, I've got fear, and from my fear, I tend to show up a certain way that is not quite who I really am." You simply think, "This is just the way I am."

Because your shadows become a part of who you relate to yourself as, you naturally structure your life around them. You choose careers where your shadows are especially valuable. You avoid the people that trigger the parts of your shadows that you don't like and spend time with people that share similar aspects to your own shadows.

Think of this like a series of drills you've been practising all your life. If you had been practising kicking objects off your foot into a rectangular net since you were about four years old, you would naturally find your way into the sport of soccer. You've been practising for it all your life!

This tendency to avoid the people, situations, and circumstances in life that drive up our shadows and lean further into the aspects of life that reward our shadows is what we would call polishing and honing your shadow. This is the act of navigating around some part of yourself you've learned to relate to as "who you are."

Where You're Left

As we move beyond the point of assembling our shadows and into our twenties, these strategies and patterns tend to really be working for us. As with any kind of pattern, it takes time for us to see what it's costing us. At first, our shadows don't occur like they have a cost. They occur like they really benefit us. They move us towards what we want and when they don't, we devise new strategies and "lifehacks" so as to avoid the thing in the way, or better use our shadows to get what we want.

Our shadows are like a collection of fixed stimulus-response pairs. As a result, they represent areas in life where we lose the ability to choose. When a particular stimulus presents itself, the choice is already made for us.

Consequently, our shadows are like a river rushing across rock. At first, there's little impact to the rock, but, over time, the water wears down the rock. It creates grooves and ruts, and those changes to the rock also dictate the path that the water may flow.

In our early days, we're more present to the short-term payoffs our shadows are providing us than we are to the long-term costs.

In our early days, we're more present to the short-term payoffs our shadows are providing us than we are to the long-term costs. And to be really clear here, our shadows absolutely do provide us with short-term payoffs. Your shadows are not bad—they are simply automatic and *using* you rather than the other way around. A lot of personal development in our twenties tends to be about optimizing and making our existing patterns more efficient. At this age, it's challenging to see the cost of our shadows because it hasn't really had the time to really show up yet. (And thus, why would we do anything about them?)

As we move out of our twenties and into our thirties, the long-term cost of our shadows starts to become more apparent. Our lives start to seem like there's less choice available. While we remember a time during our early years that was filled with joy, discovery, play, and exploration, we notice that life has started to take on more of a gray pallor. When we try to consider how to shift the way life seems to be going, we find that we have a lot of valid reasons why the options presented won't work with us. Friends, trying to support us, may offer suggestions, but we already have answers as to why those suggestions wouldn't work for us. ("It's just not who I am.")

Finally, because our careers are often a built on top of the short-term payoffs created by our shadows, even where we are thriving, we are doing so out of a mechanism designed to protect us from what we are afraid of. The impact is that we may well have money, results, promotions, power, and whatever else seems to matter—all of this is being created out of avoiding our fear.

The life we're left with is one built on top of managing and avoiding our fears rather than one in which we are going after what we truly desire. Put slightly differently, we discover that are lives end up being the expression of playing to avoid losing rather than to win.

Burnout is a common symptom of succeeding through our shadows.

You've probably already felt the impact this has on your life. When we are resisting or avoiding our fear, we tend to feel burnt out. While initially we may have felt frustrated and then angry, a lot of the times we are left resigned, the end result of continually suppressing the truth we feel in the moment. We no longer feel anger, and so on some level, people around us are safe, but the life around us feels ho-hum. When people ask you if you love your life, you can probably answer with a good deal of articulation about why you do while at the same time missing the part of life that would leave you so giddy with love that you were unable to articulate anything at all.

Burnout is a common symptom of succeeding through our shadows. Because our shadows are ultimately rooted in resisting some aspect of ourselves and/or life, they demand effort. Over time, and especially when we try to pour more enthusiasm, passion, and urgency on top of our already-taxed survival system, we're left "efforting" more and more of our lives.

Burnout is inevitable. While the obvious path seems to be taking time away from work and reducing "how much you care," this is just another version of polishing your shadows. Instead, the real work might be developing the capacity to sit with the very thing your perfectionism is designed to avoid (disappointment, heartbreak, let down, upset, and so on.)

A life lived from our shadows can look incredibly successful on the outside and leave us feeling ever emptier on the inside. The trappings of success only serve to hide from ourselves, and others, the fact that we're not fully actualizing the person we're on this planet to be. Over time, we chase after the temporary reprieve that money, promotions, sex, new relationships, travel, and anything else external provide us. We become increasingly addicted to the short-term high and numbing these opportunities provide, and increasingly resigned to the long-term experience of something being missing.

Some of the Symptoms

A life functioning at the effect of your shadows tends to create a paradoxical experience, and these are often great diagnostics for identifying where we might be able to create transformation. Here are some of the paradoxical symptoms you might be experiencing as a result of operating at the effect of your shadow.

- Feeling increasingly frantic *and* bored in your life.
- Feeling both impatient *and* listless.
- Having more of everything you've ever wanted in your life while simultaneously never having felt emptier.
- Feeling surrounded with more people than ever while never having felt more lonely or disconnected.
- Having more money in the bank than ever before while feeling less and less secure.

Other tell-tale signs of opportunities for transformation include increasing "bad habits," addictions, resentment, frustration, grief, rage, resignation, and, over time, a *graying* of your experience of life.

The Promise

Where we ended up is simply that: The place we currently find ourselves. Although the strategies of our shadows feel hardwired and like an inextricable part of our personality, the good news is that they aren't! They are simply habits we have learned to adopt and represent particularly efficient ways of showing up in any given moment. By efficiency, I mean these tendencies are practised, nuanced, and immediately available. They don't require a lot of thinking or effort to conclude they are the approach to take; they're almost tied to the stimuli they are designed to address.

Efficiency is a good thing in times of danger but becomes problematic when we want to create choice and transformation for ourselves. *Who Do You Think You Are?* is designed to provide access to what lies beneath our automatic patterning. By distinguishing our habits from who we truly are, we can see new ways to work with ourselves and those we lead.

The good news: ***Although the strategies of our shadows feel like an inextricable part of our personality, they aren't! They are simply habits we have learned to adopt.***

Getting clear that someone's franticness is not who they are, but a function of how they show up when afraid helps us hold our direct report with a little more compassion. Rather than get frustrated with how frantic they are being and trying to address that, we can start by acknowledging the fear that lies beneath and check in with ourselves. "Who would I need someone to BE for me when I'm feeling afraid?"

When we acknowledge the underlying fear rather than the symptom presenting on the surface, the door is opened to create actual transformation, as opposed to short-term change. If the only thing you started doing was noticing when those you lead are struggling in their fear and brought compassion to that, your leadership would shift. *Who Do You Think You Are?* provides access not only to that compassion but also to opportunities for transformation and leadership through the breakthrough paths and practise opportunities available to each person struggling with their own particular flavour of fear—yourself included.

By using this book to shift the way you relate to yourself and the people around you, you will discover a radically different life than the one you thought had been chosen for you. A life made rich by *being* that which you already are and always have been, regardless of the circumstances in which you find yourself.

DISCOVERING WHO YOU ARE

ONE OF THE most fascinating aspects of our own particular qualities of being is that they are immediately present for everyone around us and almost completely invisible to ourselves. In the paragraphs below, imagine the lightbulb and the color it shines as a metaphor for the qualities of being you were born with.

Imagine that everyone is born with a lightbulb floating behind their head. Everyone's lightbulb is always on and shines a uniquely colored light into the space. The color of your light is a function of the qualities of being that you embody. Your light is uniquely yours, and my light is uniquely mine. People may have similarities or overlaps in their lightbulb's particular color, but no two lightbulbs are the same. Your lightbulb shines its unique color from the moment you are born until the moment you die. You cannot see your lightbulb—it remains forever just behind your head (and it's also invisible in mirrors and photographs, etc.)

Let's imagine that your lightbulb is a beautiful color of indigo. When you enter a room, everyone in that room gets the immediate experience that the room just got a little more shaded with this color of indigo. Even if they can't distinguish this using the words, "Oh, the

Trying to see your light is like trying to see your eyeballs. It is almost impossible.

room is now colored with a little more indigo," they still have this experience when you enter the room. When you leave the room, people notice that the room has now gotten a little less indigo.

Everywhere you go, that color of indigo follows you. Every space you enter gets the gift of a little more indigo. Every space you leave becomes a little less indigo.

Everyone else gets the benefit of seeing your light because they get the experience of being in the room when you are not there and remaining in the room when you have left. They can perceive the difference between a room or space with you present and that room or space when you are absent.

You never get this experience. Everywhere you go, from the moment you were born to the moment you will pass on, your light is shining with you. Trying to see your light is like trying to see your eyeballs. It is almost impossible. You are trying to see the thing you see the world *through*—like a fish trying to see water.

As a result, it can be incredibly challenging to see the qualities of being that we embody. When we ask ourselves questions like, "What's my Zone of Genius?", we inevitably miss the mark because we cannot *see* the mark. Instead, we put our attention on the actions we take, the things we do, or the habits we seem to have gotten used to—all of which are, at best, like looking at a single piece of the puzzle and thinking it's the entire picture, and at worst, confusing our shadows with the qualities that we are innately.

Great. So, Now What?

The upshot of all of this is that you may be wondering about your particular light and finding it challenging to identify who you are, as expressed by the qualities listed in this book.

I'll talk first about how someone's light is reflected through these qualities, and then how you may go about distinguishing the essential nature that is uniquely yours.

Human beings represent an infinite possibility for expression. Each of us has the capacity for the expression of all the qualities listed in this book, along with every other quality you could come up with. You could begin writing a much larger volume called *Who Do You Think You Are Even More? (Now With More Awesome)* that distinguishes fifty-thousand different qualities of being, and you would still have room for an infinite number of other ways people can show up.

The qualities of being listed in Section Two of this book are not exhaustive—the aim is to provide a bit of a spectrum on which you can begin to distinguish particular ways you and others show up, and then begin to refine from there. So, if you start to feel like Unity/Oneness somewhat captures a particular way of being, but that there might be something more nuanced, that's okay. Just like a sommelier begins by distinguishing a tobacco-like flavour on their palate from a straw-like flavour, I'm not trying to be exhaustive. My aim is to support the development of your palate for distinguishing the qualities of being in humans and developing the ability to lead and work with people embodying those qualities.

While humans have the capacity for infinite expression, each of us tends to embody particular qualities of being to a greater extent than others. While I can certainly be generous at times (embodying the quality of Generosity), people are much more present to the qualities of Brilliance, Connection, and Wit when they are with me. That isn't to say that I'm never generous—rather that I have "strong suits" in those other three qualities.

While humans have the capacity for infinite expression, each of us tends to embody particular qualities of being to a greater extent than others.

Again, like that sommelier tasting wine, we are often able to distinguish more than a single type of flavour. A good wine will have a number of notes to it, such as tobacco, blackberry, and a hint of spice. Just like a good wine, humans have more than one strong suit. In order to avoid getting overwhelmed by the infinitude that is human expression, it can be helpful to narrow down the particular qualities you're present to in someone to between three and five. This gives you a nice range to work with without creating so much information that it's the same as having none at all.

Getting Clear On Your Light

Notwithstanding that our qualities of being can be difficult to distinguish, there are a couple of approaches that can be used to get clear on the light you shine for the world.

Approach One: Using Your Shadows

The first approach is to use your shadows as a way to work backwards and get clear on the light that you are. Our shadows are often easier for us to see, as we tend to criticize and judge ourselves much more quickly than we accept and acknowledge our light.

In order to use your shadows to get at your light, you will need to resist your desire to *fix* them. Every light casts its own unique shadow. The human condition is that we develop our shadows to stay safe, then judge ourselves for the impact of these shadows. From our judgment, we then try to eliminate, fix, or lobotomize them, hoping that if we could just eliminate this way of showing up in the world, everything would be great.

In order to use your shadows to get at your light, you will need to resist your desire to fix them.

We can see our shadows in two places: Projected outwards, as our judgments of other people, and projected inwards, as our judgments of ourselves.

Since your shadows are a function of the light you are, you cannot excise this part of yourself without losing the light that causes it. This is the reason people create sweeping changes in their lives, fully addressing the impact of a particular shadow in their life, only to find that some other aspect of their fullest expression is now missing.

Instead of fixing your shadow, you will need to be willing to simply sit with it. To do so, sit and answer the following questions:

1. What are the aspects of my behaviour that I judge myself most harshly for?
2. What do I wish I didn't do, or would change about myself if I was able?

3. What are the aspects of other people's behaviour that drive me nuts?

4. What would I fix in other people or change if I was able to?

5. What ways of being do I judge other people most harshly for?

Upon answering these five questions, you should have a good list of qualities, behaviours, and patterns that you wish weren't there in yourself or that you judge others for. Examples might be:

> 1. *I judge myself for being lazy, flaky, arrogant, and condescending.*
> 2. *I wish I didn't pull out of projects once I'd committed. I wish I listened better to people.*
> 3. *I hate it when people play dumb.*
> 4. *I would stop people being phony and inauthentic.*
> 5. *I judge people when they're droning on or belabouring a point.*

You can then merge these answers into a single list of qualities, behaviours, and patterns of being. An example might be:

> *Lazy, flaky, arrogant, condescending, pull out of things once committed, don't listen well, play dumb, phony, inauthentic, droning on, belabouring a point.*

One of the ways we avoid simply sitting with our shadows is that we try to make excuses, explanations, or justifications for them, like, "Well, I hate that I ______, but it's actually okay because..." or "Well, it drives me nuts that Roger does _____, but it's not really his fault because ..."

Everything that comes after the behaviour you've listed ("I hate that I ______" or "it drives me nuts that Roger does _______") is unnecessary and gets in the way of you simply owning your shadow.

Another way we can get in the way of sitting with our shadows is by refusing to acknowledge that we have judgment. This can sound like, "Oh, I don't judge myself—I just don't think that's healthy," or "I don't judge other people. I really think people are fine exactly as they are."

That's all fine and good, but the nature of a human is to judge, and in the thousands of people I have worked with, I have found that the people most insistent that they do not judge are often the most judgmental of all. Our insistence that we aren't judgmental provides the perfect blind spot for our ego to hide in.

Be willing to own that you have judgment—even if you simply start by owning that you have judgment about being judgmental.

Once you've answered these questions and have the list of qualities formed from your judgments (like the one shown in the example above), look through the list of shadows at the start of Section Two, and see which ones best match up with the list you've created. Which keywords jump out at you? Then, you can trace these shadows back to the light they reflect.

It may be hard to trust the quality of being that your shadow traces back to. If you judge yourself (or others) for being "flaky," it can be hard to accept that this reflects the being of Commitment that you *are*. Reading the section on that particular quality of being can be helpful in seeing how and why you arrived at this shadow, and how it really reflects the underlying way of being.

Approach Two: Using Other People

Rather than using your shadows to distinguish your light, you can also have other people reflect it to you. Remember that other people get the benefit of being in the room when you aren't and seeing the impact when you enter it. People will not typically have thought about the words to distinguish your particular qualities of being, which is perfect—this is something that is best distinguished in the moment.

To get at your essential nature this way, the best way I've found is to ask them this simple question, in person or on the phone:

What qualities do I bring into the room?

This question *must* be asked in person or on the phone. It can't be asked over e-mail, text message, or any other medium that removes the intimacy and immediacy of the moment. When you ask people in person or on the phone, they have the gift of being present with you and have an opportunity to answer the question from their heart before their head gets a hold of it and ruins everything.

When you ask this question in a different medium, it strips out all your warmth and being, as well as theirs, not to mention the fact that they will overthink it and get into their heads.

People tend to get nervous about a question like this, as they are worried they won't give you the right answer or aren't sure how to be with the intimacy that it invites. If you are willing to simply be quiet with them, allow them to stay in their process, and wait for their answer, eventually they will give you one.

Write down what people say, and then go on and ask more people. The more people you can ask the better; this will provide a broader perspective and provide opportunities to see where there is overlap.

Every person you ask will be viewing you (and the world) through the set of qualities they embody in themselves. If you ask someone who possesses the quality of Connection this question, they will be more likely to see this quality in yourself. As a result, asking multiple people will give you the best, most well-rounded reflection.

Once you have a bunch of answers, you can bring this back to the qualities listed in Section Two and read through to see what qualities you see reflected.

Each of the qualities of being listed in Section Two has a set of synonyms written out in its section—a series of descriptors that may

QUICK TIPS

- Ask the question in person or over the phone
- Be quiet, allow them to stay in their process, and simply wait for their answer.
- Write down what people say
- The more people you ask, the better.

be used to describe it. For example, Brilliance is often reflected using words like, "big picture thinker," "strategic," and "mentally agile." Wisdom is often reflected using words like, "deep thinker," "contemplative," and "asks the deeper question."

If you're unsure which quality is being reflected to you, read through the various qualities in Section Two, and see which jumps out more for you. For example, you may find that a lot of what people say you bring into the room sounds like both Brilliance *and* Wisdom. If this is the case, read through the chapters for each of these qualities of being and determine which resonates most for you.

Putting It All Together

To finish up, you want to settle on three to five qualities of being. This will give you a nice lens through which to see your breakthroughs, your shadows, and places where there might be an opportunity to express more of a particular quality of being.

Just like these two approaches can be used to get clear on your own light, they can also be used to determine what qualities are embodied by your team members, clients, and those you lead.

We typically judge our team members for the way their shadows occur. If one of your leads is showing up as mousey, quiet, and insignificant, you could apply the first approach to trace these aspects of their shadow back to the light they are. (Showing up quiet and insignificant sounds a lot like the shadow aspects for the quality of Presence/Radiance.)

If you're finding yourself confronted by someone, you can always pause and ask yourself, "What qualities does this person bring into the room?"

As you practise each of these approaches, you will get better at distinguishing the qualities of being that underlie both people's actions, and the shadows that show up on the surface. Like a sommelier, practising on your own will only ever get you so far—working with your own masterful coach or leader, trained in this same art, will ensure you grow far faster, and help you avoid the pitfalls that will inevitably be caused by your own blind spots.

HOW TO USE THIS BOOK

THIS SECTION DETAILS some ways you can use *Who Do You Think You Are?* to improve, develop and transform your leadership, your coaching, and your life.

Get Clear on Who The Person In Front of You Is

How you relate to someone will largely be determinative of your ability to develop them and successfully create partnership and growth with them. If you're relating to someone as flaky, rather than the Commitment they are underneath their fear, you will be challenged to support them in embodying that quality in their leadership. Instead, you will likely try to apply one of the obvious (but ineffective) fixes to them, hoping that if you just force them to honor their commitments, or give up on trying to make them do anything, somehow that will create the breakthrough you are hoping for. (It won't.)

By starting with the shadow-based way someone is showing up and tracing it from their shadow to their particular light, you can get to who this person truly is. From there, you can relate to them differently. What is it that would have led someone with the quality of Commitment to show up as flaky? Simply acknowledging that the way this person is showing up is incongruent with who you know and trust them to be can create a remarkable difference. We all want to be seen for who we truly are—*especially* when our fear has us showing up in a way that's opposite that truth.

If you can connect to someone's deeper truth and recognize that the shadow you are currently dealing with reflects that truth, it becomes easier to recognize it as their fear showing up, not their real self, and to love them in the face of that fear.

Seeing someone's light is a muscle, and it's a muscle that most of us have little to no practise in using.

Practise Seeing Their Gifts

Seeing someone's light is a muscle, and it's a muscle that most of us have little to no practise in using. At first, you will have a hard time seeing anything other than the shadows of the people that are annoying you. Rather than being able to see past their obnoxious habits to the gift that they are, you will get stuck on what is driving you nuts.

As an example, looking for the Commitment that someone embodies, in the face of their fear-based flakiness, may at times feel fake or like you're making it up.

At first, you will be. You haven't yet developed the muscle to truly see someone, and so you will have to practise trust. Trusting that what lies beneath the surface is really there. Trusting this framework and trusting that if you acknowledge someone for the gifts they possess, it will resonate.

It's scary work acknowledging someone for who they truly are. We get concerned that we'll get it wrong, or we won't acknowledge the part of themselves they want us to see. Practise trusting yourself and letting go of the need to get this right. If you are willing to practise in the face of your own fears, you will discover that people are delighted when you acknowledge these under-seen parts of who they are, and, over time, you will become better and better at simply seeing the light that each human being brings into the world.

Own Your *Own* Light

One of the things people often remark after distinguishing their own particular set of qualities is an immense sense of freedom. Finally, they feel like they have permission to express and own the way they've felt all their lives. Of course, that doesn't necessarily mean that the world around you will agree with what you are now expressing, but we have to start somewhere if we want to create change, and the best place to begin is always within.

By seeing yourself in any particular quality of being, you can take ownership of who you are and why you may show up in particular ways. Especially the ways that you are likely to have a good deal of judgment around. (For example, people of Presence and Radiance will often feel a huge relief that it's okay that they have an innate desire for people to *notice* them.)

By learning to own your gifts, as well as the needs that accompany them, you can start to get *responsible* for those needs, ensuring that you ask for and get them met directly. This is a shift from the indirect approaches we take to getting our needs met when we've been trained that those needs are *wrong*. Practise owning and asking for what you want and need and notice how it shifts your experience of yourself and your power. Powerful leaders get responsible for and ask to have their needs met—this includes asking for things like acknowledgment, reminders that they're awesome, being told they are loved, requesting food, sleep, rest, and anything else you can think of.

Get Present and Responsible for Your Impact

People often want to lobotomize or obliterate their shadows, or, conversely, glamorize them. Upon discovering that someone is Brilliant, they may be repulsed to discover that arrogance is part of their shadow, and either try to hide that fact or trample on people's feelings while saying, "That's just part of who I am".

This is missing the point entirely. It is not an opportunity to relate to yourself as a fixed entity, and then resign yourself to staying the same. It's an opportunity to recognize that there will be particular gifts and particular shadows that you tend to cast, and then to be *responsible* for the impact of those shadows.

If arrogance is a common shadow of yours and you can come to terms with this, then you can grow to accept that you will, at times, hurt people's feelings, despite your intentions. Instead of being defensive or justifying why you came off as arrogant when someone reflects it to you, the opportunity available is to accept this is predictably in your nature and to apologize for the impact. To really get that it's okay and that you can still be sorry for getting slime on someone.

From this place, we can all live a better life. We can let go of the blame and defensiveness we feel and still apologize for causing someone else's hurt, regardless of whether or not we intended it.

Put differently, our common shadows are really an indication of the ways that we will predictably hurt someone (including ourselves). If we can learn to love ourselves through that hurt *and* accept that we have still hurt someone, it frees us up to get responsible for our lives and our impact and play a bigger game with the knowledge that we can clean up any messes we make.

HOW WHO YOU THINK YOU ARE SHOWS UP IN RELATIONSHIPS

YOUR PARTICULAR WAYS of being will interact with your romantic partners in a variety of ways based on who you are. However, there is a predictable pattern that everyone acts out as a result of being unaware of the deeper cause of relationship breakdowns.

The Default

The default approach to (romantic) relationships tends to be meeting someone we find ourselves drawn to, getting to know them more, finding them attractive (not only physically, but also in personality and their particular qualities of being), and then deepening our intimacy with them. This whole process is aided biologically by the production of chemicals and hormones.

As time passes, the chemical support starts to wear off, and we find out that this person also brings along a whole host of other personality traits too—the stuff we don't really care for.

About two years in, we're left spinning around in the question of "Is this person the right one?" There's nothing wrong with any of this, but it is fairly undistinguished, and what we can't distinguish, we can't do much about.

How You Create Your Relationships

You'll naturally be drawn to people that exhibit many of the same qualities of being that you do. We automatically look for ourselves in the world, and so if you embody the being of Generosity, you're going to be drawn towards other people that share this same characteristic.

These people will not only affirm who you are (they'll admire the Generosity in you, just like they admire it in themselves)—you will affirm the same in them. This is an exquisite experience. It's like being truly seen by someone, which is ultimately the deepest form of validation and one of the most basic human cravings.

Two other things will also happen. First, the chemical infatuation at the start of a relationship will lower your (very human) defences. You will let down your guard and drop the need to play out the tendencies of your shadows. Second, you will naturally have chosen someone whose shadow aspect either aligns with your own or represents the other end of the side of the shadow.

You'll naturally be drawn to people that exhibit many of the same qualities of being that you do.

Let's use Generosity as an example, with its two shadow aspects of Martyring Doormat and Selfish Zealot.

In situations where you might normally respond from a need to stay safe with your new partner, you may instead be willing to let down the defences and trust them (this choice is always available, but at the start of a relationship our body is producing chemicals that make this easier). If you possess the quality of Generosity, instead of showing up as your shadow, you will simply bring Generosity to your partner. They will revel in who you truly are as your deepest self and respond in kind. It's a beautiful dance that unfolds.

Additionally, when you see their shadow playing out, you will admire them for the similarity to your own shadow, or alternatively, envy their ability to bring a way of being that seems so fundamentally different to your own (but is actually just the other side of the same coin).

In situations where you tend to show up as a doormat, sacrificing your needs for everyone else's, your partner may be willing to put their needs unflinchingly above everyone else's. You're amazed at their courage and willingness to be seen as selfish in service of getting their own needs met and wish you could do the same for yourself.

This example demonstrates why we often have the experience that "opposites attract" in relationships. At our core, we possess the same underlying qualities of being, and that is what draws us together. However, closer to the surface, we tend to act out the opposite sides of the shadow for any particular quality. This, for example, explains why people unwilling to take up space for themselves often end up in relationships with people they complain are "narcissistic." These are simply the two opposite aspects of the shadow of Presence/Radiance. Of *course,* they would wind up together.

At other times, your partner may mirror the same side of their shadow as you do, validating the strategies you've learned to stay safe and liked.

Because we judge ourselves for our own shadows, it is inevitable that, over time, and as our chemical infatuation wears off, you will begin to judge your partner for their shadows—they are, after all, simply a reflection of yourself.

It's at this point that people usually start to ask themselves the question "Is this the *right* person?"

Creating the Relationship You Want

The secret to relationship success doesn't come from finding the "right person." It comes from trusting that you are choosing the perfect partner for where you are at, in any moment, and that all that really matters is you both, collectively, agree that you are going to stop asking that question, and instead choose to relate to each other as the right person. Once you've made this decision, your relationship can become fertile ground for seeing your own *stuff* reflected back to you and an opportunity for real growth.

Predictably, people tend to end their relationship and go seeking someone else they are drawn to. Most often, we end up starting a new relationship with someone who embodies the opposite shadow aspects to those of our previous partner. After all, the underlying qualities of being we are drawn to are so compelling. We think (unconsciously) that if we can just find someone whose shadow shows up differently, *then* we'll have gotten this relationship thing solved. Alternatively, we may seek someone out with more of that same shadow but with just a few tweaks and modifications.

The upshot of all of this is that the thing you seek in someone else (their innate goodness, free of any shadow) is what you are unwilling to express in yourself. Shifting that unwillingness is a function of taking on your own work, as well as learning to accept your humanity. We will always have shadows as long as we have an ego, and we will always have an ego as long as we are alive.

Discovering your power in a relationship comes from realizing that you are choosing people because of their essential nature and that no amount of trying to tweak for their shadow is going to get you the *right* relationship.

Instead, the opportunity is to practise seeing your partner's greatness—their light—when their shadow is speaking loudly. Reconnect to the way of being that lies beneath this and do your best to relate to them from this place. When you are toying with the idea of finding someone better (and it's always fine to make that decision, by the way), you may consider that you will inevitably and irresistibly be drawn to the same kind of person out there in the world, and the only real decision to be made is "Am I going to take on my work here and now, with this person, or am I going to find someone else to take that work on with?"

TRYING OUT A DIFFERENT APPROACH

CAROL SAT DOWN and took a breath. Everything she'd been trying hadn't been working. She was frustrated with Brent and Doris, and underneath that frustration, she was disappointed with herself. At times, when she softened and could feel beneath her own tough exterior, Carol realized she was afraid she wasn't up to the task of leading this team and this company. Carol's fear only drove her desire to make a difference further. It had Carol get fervent and overbearing to overcome the failure she was committed to *not* being.

Carol had been working with the *Who Do You Think You Are?* model and getting supported by her coach Jonathan in implementing this approach to leading and relating to people.

Carol decided to take another swing with Brent. She remembered Jonathan sharing a concept in *Who Do You Think You Are?*, rooted in the idea that when people are confronted—an inevitable part of creating the unknown—they will predictably show up from their shadows.

Carol took a breath and thought about Brent. As of late, Brent had been alternating between flakiness and tyrannical rigidity. Before going any further, Carol looked up these ways of being in her reference guide and noticed that both flakiness and rigidity were aspects of the shadow of Commitment.

"That's odd," thought Carol. "I wouldn't have thought flakiness would be a sign of someone who is Commitment."

"That's odd," thought Carol. "I wouldn't have thought flakiness would be a sign of someone who is Commitment."

Carol continued reading, noting how those with the trait of Commitment can learn early on that there are consequences to being committed. Brent may have learned that when he commits too soon, or too late, he either misses out on opportunities or gets himself stuck in opportunities that he can no longer seem to extricate himself from.

Carol thought about that and then pulled out her notes from the last meeting, showing the responsibilities she and her senior staff members were taking on. Carol remembered this meeting well; she had been simultaneously frustrated and relieved with Brent. Her relief had come from the fact that Brent was owning so many different moving parts for their upcoming release. Compared to herself and Doris, Brent had twice as many responsibilities. Carol had been frustrated by Brent's unwillingness to set down deadlines and to make any kind of commitment to completing these tasks. When Brent *did* make deadlines, he was unreliable to keep to them, often responding with apologies and excuses.

Carol thought about this, setting aside Brent so she could solely consider the quality of Commitment for a while. What would Commitment do while it was afraid—when it was feeling like it was inadequate or not enough?

"Hmmm," thought Carol to herself. "Commitment would probably say YES, committing to more. If you're not enough, then you better double down."

Carol continued to read through the section on Commitment's obvious (but ineffective) fixes, seeing that part of how the pattern played out is that those leaning heavily into overcommitment then end up finding themselves overworked, overburdened, and dropping balls, which then reinforces the fear that they are not enough, and correspondingly, the need to continue over-committing.

Carol thought in silence for a while.

"Wow. So, Brent isn't flaky. He's the opposite of that—he's Commitment. And he's scared. From his fear, he *creates* flaky. Now he's avoiding making commitments, because he's afraid he can't keep up with the ones he's already made."

This insight struck Carol like a thunderbolt. She slapped her forehead. "And *of course,* he can't keep up with the commitments he's already made—from the part of his fear that had him overcommit in the first place, he's basically created the reality of his fear."

Carol sat in thought for a while. She was seeing Brent in an entirely different light. At the start of her day, she'd been considering that it might be time to replace Brent with someone that was "more dedicated" and "willing to do what it takes to make things happen." But Carol was realizing that that was *exactly* who Brent was—that was what was getting them into trouble in the first place. The problem wasn't that he lacked those qualities. It was that he had them in spades and was trying to use them over top of his fear to resolve it.

Carol sent Brent a text message. "Hey, got time for a quick chat?"

Rather than respond, Brent knocked on her door five minutes later.

Now that Carol was present to Brent's light, she could see his Commitment even in his willingness to show up at her door without hesitation. Carol felt a moment of gratitude for who Brent was. Along with that gratitude, Carol noticed how burdened Brent felt. It was clear he was taking on too much.

"Hey, Carol. What can I do for you?" Brent asked.

"Hey, Brent. I was hoping we could talk about the things you're currently taking on and the last meeting we had."

Brent immediately got apologetic. "I know, I know, Carol. I need to come up with deadlines. I've added that to my calendar and I'm going to have you deadlines for everything by the end of the day tomorrow, I'm just..." Brent trailed off for a moment, then visibly steeled himself. "I'll have them for you by end of the day tomorrow."

With her shift in perspective, Carol saw a whole new side of Brent. She was in awe of his ability to recommit in the face of being clearly overburdened and overtaxed. Brent felt like he was buried under a mountain of obligations, and from his Commitment, he was willing to say yes to try and keep moving things forward.

Carol was clear that this way of being of Brent's—this tendency to double down on his Commitment—wasn't working. But seeing this tendency as simply the way Commitment looks when it is afraid, gave Carol a lot more space and compassion for where Brent was at than she would have if she had just written him off as flaky.

Carol paused and took a deep breath before responding.

"Thanks for that, Brent. But let's put that aside for now. I wanted to check in. How are things going for you?"

Brent responded quickly, "Oh, they're good, I just need to get those deadlines to you, and push a few things off my plate, and then I'll be back to where I need to be."

"Hmmm," thought Carol. "That just doesn't sound like the whole story to me." Carol decided to slow down and just sit with Brent a little longer.

When Carol didn't say anything, Brent kept talking.

"I mean..." Brent sighed. "I have a lot on my plate. It's hard, you know? I wish I could get this stuff done faster. I know you and the rest of the team need deadlines. I'm feeling like I don't have time for that, but I know that's not acceptable. I know I need to just knuckle down and do it. I'm thinking maybe if I stay late tomorrow night, that will help."

Carol interjected softly, "That sounds really hard. It sounds like you have way too much on your plate?"

Brent paused, caught by how gently Carol had spoken. Tears welled briefly in the sides of his eyes before he hastily blinked them back.

"Well, honestly, I feel like I've said yes to way too much. I'm not sure how to make it all fit together, and simultaneously I feel like I'm letting the team down by not getting it all done. I don't really know what to do. I know you and everyone want me to get better at saying deadlines, and I've been trying to do that, but it only seems to make the problem worse. I think I just need to work more hours and maybe get better structure?"

Carol took a breath. Well, *this* felt new.

"Brent, I've got to tell you; this all makes a lot of sense. I've been getting some support in my leadership, and today I realized I've been relating to you as flaky. I'm really sorry about that, and I want to do what I need to do to clean it up. But before we go there, I want to share that I realized earlier today that who you actually are *is* Commitment. If you're afraid of not being enough, or not getting enough done, *of course* you would commit more. And, *of course* committing more would just worsen the problem, because now you have way too much on your plate, are going to drop some balls, and then you're going to feel even more inadequate, afraid, or whatever."

Brent took a deep breath. He nodded his head to what Carol was saying, but otherwise stayed silent.

Carol continued, struck by what now seemed so clear. "Brent, this is all making way too much sense to me. And not in like a bad way, but in an '*Of course* what we're trying to do to resolve this isn't working' kind of way. We're just perpetuating the problem. I don't know what the solution is yet, but I want to work on this with you. I feel like there's something available for both of us. Would you be game to partner with me on this?"

"***Of course*** *what we're trying to do to resolve this isn't working.*"

Brent blinked again, the relief and gratitude in his face showing up as his eyes moistened.

Brent answered softly, "Yes, please. I would like that."

SECTION TWO

Twenty-Five Qualities of Being

QUICK REFERENCE GUIDE

QUALITY OF BEING	SHADOW ASPECTS + THEIR OBVIOUS (BUT INEFFECTIVE) FIXES	
	Over-Expressing Shadow Aspect *Obvious (But Ineffective) Fix*	Under-Expressing Shadow Aspect *Obvious (But Ineffective) Fix*
ADVENTURE page 74	**Treacherous, Careless and Irresponsible** *Get Real and Knuckle Down*	**Controlling and Controlled** *Make the Dramatic Leap*
BRILLIANCE page 86	**Condescending and Skeptical** *Sell Your Ferrari and Become a Monk*	**Dense and Manipulative** *Trade in the Dunce Cap for a Mortarboard and Gown*
CHAMPION page 98	**Zealous Taskmaster** *Stop Caring So Much – People are Gonna be People*	**Pessimistic Cheerleader** *Rally the Troops – Guys, We Can Do Better!*
COMMITMENT page 108	**Enslaved Tyrant** *Chain Yourself to Being Unchained*	**Flaky Hummingbird** *Suffer Your Way to Transformation*
CONNECTION page 120	**Superficial and Exhausted** *Withdraw From the Exhaustion*	**Shy and Isolated** *Force Yourself To the Party*
CREATION page 132	**Unmanned Firehose** *Lock Yourself Down With Structure*	**Narrow-Minded Drone** *Become a Bull in a China Shop*
CURIOSITY page 144	**Fence-sitter** *Throw Curiosity Out the Window – It's Time To Make Things Happen*	**Rigidly Following Rules** *Slow Down, Let's Just Chill Out Here*
EASE page 156	**Vague and Non-Committal** *The Dude Gets Real, and Life Gets Heavy*	**Overly Significant** *Let Go of Commitment and Chill Out*
GENEROSITY page 168	**Martyring Doormat** *It's Time to Get What's Yours*	**Selfish Zealot** *Stop Keeping Track...*
GRACE page 178	**Haughty Spectator** *You Can't Beat 'Em, So Join 'Em*	**Profane and Plebeian** *Rise Above It All*
INTEGRITY page 188	**Tyrannical Dictator** *You Only Live Once, So Start Living*	**Oblivious Hypocrite** *Get Right and Live Straight*
JOY page 200	**Obnoxious Child** *Get Serious and Put Away the Toys*	**Pit of Despair** *Just Have Fun – Nothing Matters Anyway*
LEADER page 212	**Leader of Followers** *Let Other People Lead*	**Follower of Leaders** *Step Up – It's My Time*

QUICK REFERENCE GUIDE

QUALITY OF BEING	SHADOW ASPECTS + THEIR OBVIOUS (BUT INEFFECTIVE) FIXES	
	Over-Expressing Shadow Aspect *Obvious (But Ineffective) Fix*	**Under-Expressing Shadow Aspect** *Obvious (But Ineffective) Fix*
LOVE page 224	**Cloying and Suffocating** *Just Stop Caring So Much*	**Cruel and Heartless** *Become a Being of Pure Love*
MAGIC page 234	**Escapist** *Hang Up the Wizard Robes*	**Jaded and Mundane** *Paint Outside the Lines*
PASSION page 244	**Compulsive and Obsessive** *Throttle the Compulsion*	**Apathetic and Bored** *Get Swept Away in the Passion*
PEACE page 256	**Rigid Buddha** *Begin the Season of Yes!*	**Frenetic Problem-Solver** *Embody the Irrefutable No*
PERMISSION page 268	**Sloppy, Swampy and Messy** *Button Things Up and Get Real*	**Censored and Censoring** *Put an End to the Apologies*
POWER page 280	**Irresponsible Monster** *Cage the Monster*	**Tamed Lion** *Unleash the Beast*
PRESENCE/RADIANCE page 290	**Obnoxious Diva** *Give Other People All of the Space*	**Elephant Behind a Blade of Grass** *Take Up All the Space You Need*
PURPOSE page 300	**Purposeful Fascist** *Turn Off the Purpose and Pour Another Glass of Wine*	**Listless Freedom** *Roll Up Your Shirtsleeves and Get Shit Done*
SPIRIT/DIVINITY page 312	**Spiritually Bypassing** *Abandon God and Walk with the Mortals*	**Faithless Cynic** *Ladle on the Piety*
UNITY/ONENESS page 322	**Indecisive and Frozen** *Stop Soft-Pedalling and Take Action*	**Righteous Crusader** *Give Up the Fight and Hold It All Sacred*
WISDOM page 334	**Self-satisfied and Oblivious** *Play the Jester and Join the Party*	**Foolish and Ignorant** *Grow Up and Get Wise*
WIT page 344	**Obnoxious Clown** *Kill the Clown and Get Serious*	**Humour-Free Zone** *Get to Playing—None of This Matters Anyhow*

TWENTY-FIVE QUALITIES OF BEING

At this point, you're finished Section One, and have a grasp of the underlying model we're working with, how it all gets put together, and some of the impact of how it plays out in our lives.

You're now onto Section Two, where twenty-five qualities of being are described and distinguished in detail. Remember, this section is not intended to be read from start to finish (though you are welcome to do so if you feel inclined.)

Rather, this section is intended to be read as a reference guide. Once you've gotten clear on the quality (and its shadow aspects) that you're working with in yourself or in others, use the index to find its chapter in this section and read through it.

This book captures twenty-five common qualities of being, or ways of being, that I have noticed in my work. The good news is that the capacity for human expression is infinite, and there will always be new ways of being. Just because I used the word "Wit" and describe that particular quality doesn't mean that you couldn't differentiate it from qualities like, "Humour," "Mirth" and "Play."

When you begin learning to ride a bike, it helps to remove some of your options to let you focus on a single aspect of the skill. Training wheels take away the variable of balance to let you practise steering and pedalling. Glider bikes take away the need to pedal and let you put your attention on learning to balance.

Your ability to distinguish someone's truest self from their fear will, at first, be a weak muscle.

Like someone who has never ridden a bike, your ability to distinguish someone's truest self from their fear will, at first, be a weak muscle. We aren't trained in this work, and we relate to people as the entirety of how they are showing up rather than distinguishing someone's light from their fear. Consequently, by breaking out twenty-five specific ways of being, we are giving you some ways to practise and some places to look.

As you develop your ability to distinguish and see the natural leader and light that exists in everyone, you will begin to see more than these twenty-five ways of being. When that starts to happen, you can begin creating your own versions of the ways of being included in this section.

But first, learn to operate within the distinctions provided by this book. Spend about a year distinguishing and working with people using the twenty-five qualities listed in this section, so that you can develop your muscle rigorously and with intention. This is like going to the gym and doing warm-up sets with very light weights. Everyone wants to skip over the warm-up and put their attention on lifting heavy weights—but in doing so, we tend to sacrifice our form and integrity. Give yourself time to become masterful in this work.

HOW EACH OF THE QUALITIES OF BEING IS LAID OUT

Each of the individual qualities is laid out this way:

Common Descriptors

This section consists of a set of words, adjectives, phrases, and synonyms that are often used to describe the particular quality. People will not necessarily use a word like, "Brilliance" to describe someone with this quality. They may use words like, "whip-smart," "fast thinker," and phrases like, "deep strategic level of thought." This section is designed to help you hone in on the particular trait in question.

The Quality

We come on to this planet with our own beautiful, essential nature—the unique combination of qualities of being that we possess, and the "Gift" that each one brings us.

People typically struggle with this part, insisting it's overly optimistic or lacking in critical judgment. This is fine but misses the point. We cover the shadow aspects of your gift further down. Your gift is exactly that: a gift.

The Gift

We come on to this planet with our own beautiful, essential nature—the unique combination of qualities of being that we possess, and the "Gift" that each one brings us.

People typically struggle with this part, insisting it's overly optimistic or lacking in critical judgment. This is fine but misses the point. We cover the shadow aspects of your gift further down. Your gift is exactly that: A gift.

People typically struggle with this part, insisting it's overly optimistic or lacking in critical judgment. This is fine but misses the point. We cover the shadow aspects of your gift further down. Your gift is exactly that: a gift.

People also distance themselves from truly owning their gifts because we are trained that owning one's strengths is arrogant or sets you up to be torn down. These reasons to dim your light might work for you as an individual but won't work as a leader. Remember: How the leader is being is how the team is being. Leaders who repeatedly dim their light create teams that do the same.

What is Predictable

This section represents what is predictable for someone who possesses this particular quality. This is a function of the challenges and burdens you face with a given quality, the shadow that gets created to overcome these challenges, the way people react to your quality and accompanying shadow, and the common approaches you will take to overcome the impact of your shadow (described in detail in the "Obvious (But Ineffective) Fixes" section below).

What is predictable is typically a function of trying to take on your own work without the support of a coach, counsellor, masterful leader, or someone else who can support you in seeing your blind spots.

People don't usually end up going down the predictable path because they're lazy, stupid, or just don't put in the effort. In fact, you can be diligent, committed, and avidly engrossed in reading self-development books, and this will only further the likelihood of arriving at the life that is predictable. All that hard work will be filtered through the lens of your blind spots, which ensures you find yourself at the predictable result.

Remember: Every gift is a curse, and every curse is a gift. Even though the gift may sound awesome when you read it, it brings its own unique flavour of heartbreak, devastation, sorrow, etc.

What is Possible

This section speaks to what becomes possible when someone with this quality takes on their work with the support of a trusted coach or mentor. Some of this potential is always reflected in wherever you currently find yourself in life.

What is possible is not what is predictable.

What is *possible* is *not* what is predictable. Despite your best intentions and the certainty of your commitment, the nature of blind spots is to lead you towards the predictable. *Embodying your possibility requires support from people outside your own head.*

Achieving your possibility is usually a function of doing the uncomfortable and unpleasant work of opening and unfolding yourself, in the face of a natural resistance to doing so. Embodying this potential is counterintuitive and challenging because your ego is every bit as brilliant as you are and will co-opt everything you learn to serve its own nefarious purposes.

Common Experience Coming of Age

Every quality of being has a unique coming of age experience; you will probably resonate with a number of the experiences described. They don't represent a universal truth, and there will be nuances to your particular experience. Nevertheless, each quality tends to have a particular pattern to how the world will respond to it, creating a specific formative experience.

For example, people with a great deal of Presence or Radiance will tend to get comments like, "You're too much," and "Stop showing off," when growing up. This pattern doesn't suggest that you were doing something wrong; it's simply a part of your path.

Consequences of Owning Your Gifts

When you really own your gifts instead of hiding, overemphasizing, or apologizing for them, the world around you will predictably have a reaction. Some of the common reactions are described in this section.

Shadow Aspects

Every light casts its own unique shadow. The ways we learn to adapt, compensate for, and mitigate the stories we are taught and learn about being too much, or not enough, show up as our shadow. Here, we list two aspects to the quality's shadow, one representing the under-expression of the gift and the other the over-expression.

Our shadows are not *bad*—they simply are. They're a part of us, just like our gifts. Our shadows support us in surviving and thriving, and simultaneously limit us from achieving what is next. People often find themselves in careers where the expression of their shadows is valued.

People tend to express both aspects of the shadow, with one side being more of their *lean*. Part of the way the shadow keeps you trapped is by having you bounce back and forth between its two aspects. Taking on the Obvious (But Ineffective) Fixes to the shadow (see below) will occur to you like you're creating a breakthrough, but in actuality will simply move you to the other shadow aspect.

Often, we express one shadow aspect in certain areas of our lives, and the other in different areas—in this way, creating an odd kind of compensatory balance between the two. For example, if someone is expressing the two shadow aspects of Generosity, they may be a complete doormat at work, but selfish and zealous about their personal time and space at home. In this way, they can justify the two against each other: "Yes, I may be acting selfishly here, but I deserve to because I give and give and give at work."

If you find yourself identifying with one aspect of a shadow, great! Don't stop there though. See if you can catch yourself in the expression of the other. Where do you create the compensatory balance?

Over-Expressing

The over-expressing aspect of the shadow is a product of experiencing situations where you may not feel seen, recognized or acknowledged for your gift, or learned to rely on your gift to resolve a particularly troubling experience or circumstance.

If you were trained that the natural expression of your Brilliance wasn't enough (perhaps the A you got was good, but what about that A+?), then you will predictably respond by over-expressing your intellect. You will over-emphasize and exaggerate its expression, leading to predictable, patterned ways of being around anything that resembles that original training.

The over-expressing aspect of the shadow is ultimately a response to the situations where you were trained, learned, or concluded that who and what you are innately is *not enough*. Consequently, you compensated by turning the volume way *up* on your particular gift.

Under-Expressing

The under-expressing aspect of the shadow is a product of learning that your gifts are unsafe, dangerous, or undesirable. If you were trained by the world around you that the natural expression of your Love and acceptance leads to betrayal and heartbreak, you will predictably respond by pulling that love away. You will stifle and withdraw its expression, leading to predictable, patterned ways of being around anything that resembles the original training.

The under-expressing aspect of the shadow is ultimately a response to the situations where you were trained, learned, or concluded that who and what you are is *too much*. Consequently, you compensated by turning the volume way *down* on your particular gift.

Obvious (But Ineffective) Fixes

The Obvious (But Ineffective) Fixes are the solutions that we tend to reach for when confronted with the bankruptcy of our shadows. Our shadows serve us in the short-term and enable us to survive (and to a lesser extent, achieve a degree of thriving), but they are also limited in their application and approaches. While they served to get us *here*, they now hold us in place. Over time, they lead to burnout and a predictable life, as described earlier.

Each shadow aspect has an obvious fix that will *feel good* when undertaken, providing you with a sense of change and relief. "Finally, I'm taking a new approach to this old problem!" Obvious fixes are also *intuitive,* in that they make sense to us when we're on the ground and lack perspective or altitude (which is how we live most of our lives). In the pages below you'll find descriptions for how these fixes usually lead us back to the other aspect of the shadow, keeping us caught in a pendulum swing in which nothing ever really changes.

The obvious but ineffective fixes for our shadows are like saltwater for our soul. They provide a short-term experience of what we're craving while in the long-term push us further away from what we want.

Imagine yourself on a life raft in the middle of the ocean with no water. As your thirst builds up, drinking ocean water feels increasingly like a good choice. Eventually, you'll take a sip of that water, and when you do, your mouth suddenly feels cool, your lips and tongue less dry, and you can speak a little more clearly—for a time. The obvious but ineffective fixes for our shadows are like saltwater for our soul. They provide a short-term experience of what we're craving while in the long-term push us further away from what we want.

Finally, the obvious fixes are how your ego perpetuates its work. They are the approaches that feel like progress when you take them on while simultaneously protecting you from work that would actually set you free. This is the ego's sweet spot: Giving you the illusion of transformation while actually keeping it at arm's length.

Creating the Breakthrough

This section speaks to the typical path that people with a particular gift take en route to their breakthrough. The breakthrough path is challenging to walk on your own; *obvious fixes* will regularly look like the breakthrough you seek. Your real breakthrough path isn't a fix for who you are, or who you're not, and it doesn't lead you away from potential pain. Rather, it leads you *through* pain towards the possibility of creating what you really want.

Leading and Working with People of ______

In this section, I talk about ways to develop leadership for yourself and for people who possess this particular quality.

Each quality brings with it its own unique shadow, and each aspect of the shadow is a pitfall for a potential leader to get caught up in. This section breaks down why each shadow aspect is challenging, and how to maneuver with and support someone to grow beyond their limitations.

What most often separates transformative leadership (developing more leaders) from good-enough leadership (developing more followers) is that, in the latter case, the leader in question is no longer taking on their own work, having concluded that they've overcome their ego and can now simply dispense wisdom and leadership.

You will notice how often this section speaks to your own work as a leader. Wherever you and your team members share particular qualities or have shadows with overlapping tendencies, you are at risk of unconsciously colluding with your team member's ego and its need to remain safe and resist real change.

Do not forego your own work. Your work is never finished because you will always have an edge. Do not fool yourself into believing you are immune from the machinations of your ego. Magnificent leaders seek out, hire, and work with magnificent leaders and coaches, because that is what ensures they continue their own growth.

Practises

Practises represent opportunities to create something beyond the obvious fixes. Practises are not homework. Homework is something we complete. A practise is something ongoing. When we practise something, we take it on daily, weekly, or with some measure of frequency, and continue on an ongoing basis.

The practises listed in this section are intended to provide you with ways to support someone (or yourself) to move into the edges their shadows are designed to protect. As a result, they may feel a little edgy, and there may be resistance to taking them on. This resistance is a healthy thing—if there was no resistance, there would be little new to be gained from the practise.

OVER-EXPRESSING SHADOW ASPECT
Treacherous, Careless and Irresponsible

OBVIOUS (BUT INEFFECTIVE) FIX
Get Real and Knuckle Down

Adventure

UNDER-EXPRESSING SHADOW ASPECT
Controlling and Controlled

OBVIOUS (BUT INEFFECTIVE) FIX
Make the Dramatic Leap

COMMON SHADOW ASPECTS:

- Treacherous, Careless and Irresponsible
- Controlling and Controlled

COMMON DESCRIPTORS

Daring, Courageous, Thrilling, Unhindered, Explorer, Independence, Openness, Uninhibited, Spontaneity, Traveller, Impulsive

The Quality

Your Gift

You bring not only the sense but the experience of Adventure to every space you enter. People come to know you as a force for the unpredictable and the spontaneous, building up stories about, for example, that time they spent with you when they unexpectedly woke up one morning on a fishing boat in Nova Scotia. Your innate love for Adventure leads you to many different walks of life, and you can thrive in almost any environment (except for those that are unchanging and mundane).

Being around you brings out the innate joy of the unknown and discovery in people. Much of our lives are spent in fear of what might show up if we let go of control and predictability in our daily lives. Your very being is an invitation to release the safety of the known and lean into what is different and unique.

You may be drawn to multilingualism, a nomadic lifestyle, fascination with international cuisine, or many other reflections of Adventure. The truth is that there isn't any *one* thing that denotes the Adventure you are—it's the way you show up everywhere.

You bring a degree of fearlessness that enables you and others to lean over the edge, spread your arms, and discover you can fly (though not

Being around you brings out the innate joy of the unknown and discovery in people.

without the occasional bump and fall along the way—but that's what makes for good stories).

You may be an incredible storyteller, able to regale people with the adventures and journeys you've been on and sharing excitedly about what's next. Sitting around the campfire or in a bar with you is a treat—there's never a dull moment.

You may be drawn to and especially suited to entrepreneurialism. Your willingness to take risks and love of Adventure makes launching new enterprises especially compelling. When you choose careers inside a company, you will be drawn to jobs that afford travel, exploration, and an opportunity to feel into the unknown.

What is Predictable

Over time and without adequate scaffolding to support your innate Adventure, this aspect of yourself can become a risk you have to manage. As time wears on and the stakes of life become greater (better jobs, more money, raising a family, etc.), you begin to see Adventure as an undesirable habit and feel compelled to lock it down.

This leaves you experiencing life like a caged animal. You swing between the states of being locked up, bored and safe on one hand and breaking free with reckless, wild abandon on the other—followed by intense regret and a recommitment to lock the cage even tighter from now on.

Your relationships may fall into this trap. You may choose a partner who is magnificent at establishing routine, structure, and control in their life. Their structure feels soothing at first, a healthy way to balance the reckless (over-expressed) side of your Adventure's shadow.

Over time, your partner's structure will begin to feel suffocating and smothering—very much like your attempts to cage Adventure in yourself. This quality in your partner creates a dynamic where you're projecting an internal conflict onto them. You get frustrated and blame them for the lack of Adventure in your life—even though that's precisely why you chose them. At that point, your partner becomes a scapegoat for a situation you created, and you feel an overwhelming need to escape.

COMMON SHADOW ASPECTS:

- Treacherous, Careless and Irresponsible
- Controlling and Controlled

As you age and mature, you may find that even creating relationships becomes a challenge. Your love of Adventure brings you into many different people's orbits but propels you to leave them just as quickly. Brief romantic encounters may become your norm, as opposed to a sustained, consistent relationship that grows with you. These romantic interludes are moments of bliss—but they're fleeting.

When your sense of Adventure becomes too much or the stakes of your life become too high, you opt out of expressing Adventure altogether and build systems, rules, and relationships around yourself that establish control and keep you safe. Life becomes more and more boring for you—but you appreciate the safety, even as you long for adventure and live it vicariously through others, including the *you* that you remember from your youth.

Your unresolved internal contradictions create messes in your life and relationships that you have no desire to resolve. This just ramps up your need to escape into a new Adventure. Over time, Adventure stops feeling like freedom and joy and starts to feel more like a "fix."

What is Possible

You embody the possibility of ever-present Adventure, regardless of our circumstances. Your gift during your time on this mortal coil is to show the world that life isn't as risky as our biology would have us believe and to help us see that we are so much more adaptive than we're willing to trust. As you do the work to own and fully express (responsibly) the Adventure that you are, you teach the rest of us to let go of at least some of the control and restrictions we place around our lives. You are here to teach us how to be free, beginning with the freedom you discover in yourself.

As you learn to trust the Adventure within, you unfold into the truth that you cannot experience freedom on a beach until you can experience freedom in an office. Your journey and the possibility you represent for the world lies in discovering that Adventure is available to us in every single aspect of life—not just those moments hanging off a train in India on your way to some mysterious destination.

Part of your work involves bringing a degree of sobriety to your thirst for Adventure and making it less compulsive.

Part of your work involves bringing a degree of sobriety to your thirst for Adventure and making it less compulsive. A willingness to stay rooted and let Adventure emerge naturally—as opposed to rushing off and seeking the next thrill—opens space for Adventure to be brought to you and co-created, as opposed to only being generated by yourself.

Your journey helps us heal our collective wounds about having taken too many risks and made too many mistakes. It helps free us from over-controlling ourselves to avoid getting into trouble.

As you become more willing to stay grounded for periods of time, you begin the work of taking responsibility for your impact and start cleaning up the messes you've left in your wake. Trusting yourself—in times of Adventure and times without (obvious) Adventure—allows you to address those tough personal issues your shadows would prefer that you avoid. You become the possibility of growing roots as well as wings and model this to those around you.

Common Experience Coming of Age

Your natural love of Adventure probably made you difficult to contain, frustrating your parents, caregivers, and teachers, who say they just want to keep you safe. You may have been told you were disobedient and struggled with efforts to control you in the form of guilt, shame, lectures, structure, and rules. Those who are Adventure may have been labelled with attention deficit or other disorders and even medicated to address this aspect of who they are.

COMMON SHADOW ASPECTS:

- Treacherous, Careless and Irresponsible
- Controlling and Controlled

Consequences of Owning Your Gifts

Owning your Adventure can lead you into unpredictable and, at times, dangerous situations. While you may thrive in these situations, you may also lean out too far and put yourself into hotspots. When other people must come to your rescue, you may end up labelled as risky to be around and as someone who creates messes they don't clean up. Before others can fully trust you, you may need to learn to trust yourself, be responsible for your impact (not wrong for it, mind you—just responsible), and clean up what's yours.

Shadow Aspects

Over-Expressing: *Treacherous, Careless, and Irresponsible*

Tired and exasperated with the control that the world seeks to impose upon you, you don't just throw caution to the wind—you drop-kick it into outer space. You have an allergic reaction to any kind of control or structure and take on ever-increasing risks, wantonly putting yourself and those around you in danger.

Growing up, the world framed you as a dangerous risk-taker, and you internalized that story.

Because you tend to run off to the next Adventure, you rarely have the opportunity to truly *get* your impact and take responsibility for it. You may become an unwilling listener when people want you to sit with them and understand how you've shown up.

As you battle your own and others' efforts to control you, you have a growing problem with structure of any kind. You spend less and less time in one place before feeling "the itch" to move on.

Love of Adventure becomes a cover for your fears about intimacy, giving you an easy out when things get a little too real. You may be skilled at forming relationships quickly and have a lot of fun with people but never achieve the depth you crave.

Obvious (But Ineffective) Fix: Get Real and Knuckle Down

Desiring some of the aspects of life that require a willingness to grow roots, you try to create more and more control in and around your life, holding yourself steady and settled.

Because the Adventure you're attempting to control is who you truly are, at best this is like plugging a pressure cooker and hoping the pressure magically goes away. Like most approaches rooted in "fixing" our shadows, this provides you temporary respite, but it's only a matter of time before you can white-knuckle no longer. Your contained Adventure explodes and blows your structures of control to smithereens.

When the dust has settled, you have little ability to be responsible for your impact—instead, you make yourself wrong for it. All of this ultimately reinforces your disempowering story: You're reckless, careless, and need to impose more control on yourself. The cycle continues.

Under-Expressing: *Controlling and Controlled*

Growing up, the world framed you as a dangerous risk-taker, and you internalized that story, creating a strong need to control yourself and avoid risk. You see yourself as what you were called growing up (reckless, careless, maybe even a playboy/debutante), especially by people who themselves have a disempowered relationship to their own Adventure.

You close off avenues for the expression of Adventure and lead a small, contained life in which you are bored, boring, safe, and predictable.

You may find yourself proposing grand schemes and adventures, but quickly finding reasons why they're too risky and dangerous to pursue. This desire to be free, immediately followed up by the energetic act of locking yourself back in prison, can leave you feeling a little schizophrenic at times.

You may feel clear on what your heart wants but just can't seem to take action to make that happen. This leads to a great deal of heartbreak over journeys you never take and adventures you can imagine but feel unable to bring to life.

Ironically, this tendency to imagine Adventure, then shut it down quickly, just reinforces an internal narrative that you are a dreamer and a risky bet who can't be relied on to see something all the way through.

Obvious (But Ineffective Fix): Make the Dramatic Leap

Fed up with your boring, controlled experience in the places where you have asserted control, you attempt wild and grand gestures designed to break out of this prison.

This leap may take the form of a sabbatical or as short-term bursts of adventure. When you do free yourself, there's likely so much of you built up that the impact is massive and dramatic. You don't express a

COMMON SHADOW ASPECTS:

- Treacherous, Careless and Irresponsible
- Controlling and Controlled

little bit of your Adventure—you pack a lifetime's worth of adventure into a few days.

Over time, your ability to be with your own Adventure has atrophied. Consequently, the journeys you do undertake are rewarding but leave you exhausted or possibly overwhelmed—just like if you went to the gym on January 1st and tried to cram a year's worth of workouts into one day.

You conclude that this was a great break but is not the game for you. You're glad for your simple, mundane life and are now more justified than ever in continuing to lock the door to your cage.

Creating the Breakthrough

Your shadow aspects reflect the innate risk that comes with your gift. Those who seek Adventure will inevitably encounter peril—there is no reward without risk. Your fears and shadow will work overtime to convince you that failure is catastrophic, something you won't be able to recover from, and that you have a binary choice: To eliminate risk and potential failure entirely or to take risks and live out a string of consecutive failures.

There's often a breakthrough available in sitting and noticing that you are the source of Adventure, as opposed to changing your circumstances to ***create*** *Adventure.*

Your breakthrough often lies in swinging for the fences. Not in the sense of taking every risk or transforming every circumstance in your life to create nonstop Adventure but in a willingness to take risks in the here and now. Creating and *being* Adventure, day to day, moment by moment. Put yourself at risk and experience the thrill that is your birthright—*carpe diem*. At the same time, bring forth a willingness to stay with people, be present to your impact, and clean up any mess you have created.

Finally, there's often a breakthrough available for Adventure in sitting and noticing that you ARE the source of Adventure, as opposed to changing your circumstances to *create* Adventure. When Adventure becomes available no matter what your circumstances, the innate freedom you represent stops being an escape and becomes an experience of peace, joy, excitement, and exploration.

COMMON SHADOW ASPECTS:

- Treacherous, Careless and Irresponsible
- Controlling and Controlled

Leading and Working with People of Adventure

Members of your teams that operate with a sense of Adventure will tend to be masterful at exploring the unknown—especially when the stakes for them personally are relatively low. In other words, they will roll the dice and take big risks when it's not their money or reputation on the line but freeze up in the face of meaningful risk. This is a little bit like playing a VR game that allows you to scale a mountain top without safety gear, as opposed to physically climbing that mountain. The former may provide some excitement but isn't really an expression of Adventure.

This can be seductive to a leader because their Adventure-type team members *appear* to be pushing things forwards in a positive direction, but beneath the surface they are probably feeling more and more dissatisfied. Eventually, this form of Adventure "held in check" will have consequences—team members suddenly departing, for example, and taking valuable clients with them or otherwise acting out in ways that satisfy their itch to put real skin in the game.

Team members with the quality of Adventure benefit from coaching that encourages them to step up, put their reputation on the line, and run the risk of making real mistakes. As a leader, this requires giving them space to make those mistakes and not piling your own fears atop theirs.

There is no mess too big to clean up.

When mistakes are made by people of Adventure, their leader's job is to slow them down, have them take a sober look at what happened, and be responsible for cleaning up the mess so they can then take whatever step is next. In this way, you, as their leader, become a healing source for Adventure, helping these team members learn that their willingness to risk is a gift, and there is no mess too big to clean up.

Practises

Pay attention to your boredom, wanderlust, and desire to escape.

Is that itchy feeling in your feet an indicator that you're trying to escape your fears rather than confront them? What, specifically, would escaping allow you to avoid?

There may be nothing wrong with your tendency to weigh anchor and sail away, provided it's chosen rather than automatic. If your impulse is that you simply *have to* leave a situation—as opposed to feeling drawn towards Adventure—slow down and feel into what's in front of you right now.

Create a balance between routine and discovery in your life.

Create places in your life where you can express and live out your innate sense of Adventure. If your life feels constrained and controlled, begin with low gradient approaches. Experiment by cooking entirely different meals one night a week, trying out different restaurants or going for long drives without a map and getting lost. Find ways to express one percent more Adventure in your life and work your way up from there.

COMMON SHADOW ASPECTS:

- Treacherous, Careless and Irresponsible
- Controlling and Controlled

Practise cleaning up and departing gracefully.

If your track record has been to leave in a puff of smoke, new possibility becomes available when you slow down and survey your impact. What do you need to put in order before leaving? Whose voices need to be heard?

Take on long-term projects.

Much like Passion, long-term projects can be of great benefit to you. By providing some degree of structure for you to operate within, long-term projects allow you to build greater positive impact than what would be available in letting yourself to be blown about by the wind.

Imagine you can create an experience of Adventure no matter what you're doing. What would you want to create over the next year? What difference would you like to make in the world, and how would you like to make it?

What, specifically, would escaping allow you to avoid?

Create commitments and play the game of having it all.

Instead of simply doubling your profits this year, aim towards doubling your profits *and* traveling to five countries while you're doing so.

Because you tend to swing towards the extremes of all Adventure or no Adventure (imprisoned and constricted), your breakthroughs often lie in transcending this binary choice. You can create projects from a no-Adventure perspective and force yourself to finish them, but at the expense of expressing who you are. How might this project be created so that you achieved both these aims? Find support (from someone other than yourself) to create projects from a *both-and* perspective.

OVER-EXPRESSING SHADOW ASPECT
Condescending and Skeptical

OBVIOUS (BUT INEFFECTIVE) FIX
Sell Your Ferrari and Become a Monk

Brilliance

UNDER-EXPRESSING SHADOW ASPECT
Dense and Manipulative

OBVIOUS (BUT INEFFECTIVE) FIX
Trade in the Dunce Cap for a Mortarboard and Gown

COMMON DESCRIPTORS

Smart, Intelligent, Genius, Masterful, Sharp, Erudite, Strategic, Brains, Gifted, Deep Thinker, Nerdy, Cerebral, Rational, Analytical, Academic

Brilliance

COMMON SHADOW ASPECTS:

- Condescending and Skeptical
- Dense and Manipulative

The Quality

Your Gift

You embody the trait of Brilliance. This isn't necessarily a matter of scoring high on tests that aim to measure intellect. While you often *will* succeed in those areas, IQ and other tests only test a particular manifestation of Brilliance. Your Brilliance shows up in everything you do, simply by virtue of who you are. The way you play soccer and think about the game is brilliant. The way you dress yourself in the morning is brilliant—which may include the system you created that lets you not have to think about how you dress yourself.

Putting you on a team or project means that the approach and solutions will be better thought out and more brilliant in conception and implementation. Part of your gift lies in drawing out the Brilliance in others. People around you are called to bring their own Brilliance forward, elevating the level of thought and introspection that goes into a given issue.

Tactics, strategy, and other mental exercises come easily, and you likely feel surprised at how others struggle when the answer seems so obvious to you. Brilliance makes mental problems a snap; by the time you reached adolescence you probably developed mental heuristics that make solving problems easier.

"Wow, that guy is brilliant... and I'm not."

Abstract concepts come easily to Brilliance; you probably zoom in and out of problems with relative ease, providing altitude when that's what is required and diving into nitty-gritty details when that's what is needed.

When people bring problems to you (or you're confronted with a problem yourself), you reliably help them see the problem in an entirely new light, shifting the frame through which they had been seeing things to reveal potential new solutions or revealing that in fact there is no problem at all.

What is Predictable

Despite reliably creating great results, you may slowly but surely alienate people, leaving them with the experience of: "Wow, that person is brilliant... and I'm not."

Your Brilliance becomes a curse. You feel frustrated that you never seem to be truly recognized and respected for how smart you are and are surrounded by people who are, frankly, morons.

We all fear being what we are not. Phrased differently, our core fears often relate to potentially being seen as the opposite of our gifts. People with the gift of Brilliance tend to fear being or looking stupid, ignorant, or clueless. Driven by a need to manage this fear, your Brilliance becomes something that needs to be jealously guarded.

When your Brilliance is threatened, you latch onto proving that you're right. When that path isn't available, you may lean into proving how others are wrong. This leaves you reassured that you aren't stupid but at the expense of others feeling small, diminished, and resentful.

Brilliance can create an experience of loneliness. Your ability to abstract yourself from a given situation and find safety as an observer becomes a default when faced with difficult emotions and experiences.

Of all the ways of being, Brilliance is probably the most likely to create a life that looks phenomenal on the outside but feels empty and dull on the inside. When everything fits into a neat, tidy equation, all the variables have been accounted for, and life has been solved, what then?

Taken to the extreme, the shadow of Brilliance leads to opulent boredom and seeing the world in shades of gray. Didn't the world used to be more colorful?

Because of fears about being stupid and ignorant, Brilliance often holds a lot of judgment when it perceives itself or others showing up this way. Predictably, your muscle for *being* with these qualities atrophies over your lifespan, creating quick impatience and frustration—for yourself and others—at the stupidity of the world at large.

Brilliance

COMMON SHADOW ASPECTS:

- Condescending and Skeptical
- Dense and Manipulative

What is Possible

What is possible is that the Brilliance you are liberates the Brilliance in the people around you. Rather than seeing the Brilliance in others as a challenge or affront, you relish the opportunity to see your Brilliance *and* your ignorance simultaneously. You lead teams that create impossible results, and leave everyone you meet with an experience of "Wow, I'm so much more brilliant than I realized!"

Didn't the world used to be more colorful?

You grant permission to those around you to express their Brilliance because you're willing to let them see you having fears. A brilliant person who only expresses their Brilliance will wow and awe those around them. A brilliant person who expresses their Brilliance—but also admits when they've made a mistake and feel like a doofus—can

set the world free, enabling people to express themselves without fear of looking stupid.

When you embrace your fear of looking dumb, the Brilliance in others ceases to challenge you, and you realize there are no dummies. Instead, you're surrounded by Brilliance and delighted at what others bring to the table in their unique ways.

You lead teams that create impossible results, and leave everyone you meet with an experience of "Wow, I'm so much more brilliant than I realized!"

Freeing yourself from knee-jerk judgment about stupidity unfolds and expands your capacity for leadership. You may be surprised at your patience with people as they learn, and become a champion for people's growth and development—without the aggressive attachment to doing everything "right" you once had. Instead of needing people to get it right, you allow them to get it wrong first, so they can learn on their own instead of being told what to do.

Those with Brilliance tend to be exquisite teachers, in part because of their unique ability to abstract comprehension at many different levels and their facility with metaphor. When those with Brilliance are unafraid of how they may be perceived, they become highly sought out for their ability to teach, mentor, and lead others. Best of all, people in your presence find themselves learning for themselves rather than simply parroting back what you have said.

Common Experience Coming of Age

Pressure may have turned your Brilliance from an innate pleasure into an impossible burden

Growing up, you nay have experienced high expectations from your teachers, peers, and family. That pressure may have turned your Brilliance from an innate pleasure into an impossible burden, leaving you with only two apparent options: Doing whatever it takes to live up to your potential or diminishing the expectations placed on you.

You may have worried—as you created what seemed like obvious shortcuts and heuristics—that others would think you were being unfair and cutting corners. When people around you struggled to figure something out, and you just seemed to know the answer, you may have wondered, "Am I cheating here?"

COMMON SHADOW ASPECTS:

- Condescending and Skeptical
- Dense and Manipulative

Consequences of Owning Your Gifts

Ownership of your Brilliance can lead others to feel dumb in your presence and label you as a nerd, loser, or worse. Societally, showing up as a "smart person" may cause others to label you as arrogant and to look for opportunities to prove that you're not *really* as smart as you think you are.

Shadow Aspects

Over-Expressing: *Condescending and Skeptical*

Your internalized expectations and horror of making mistakes are projected outwards as well as in. You're the terrifying leader of brilliant teams. You get results, but your inability to accept even the possibility of making mistakes means you do so joylessly and without the natural playfulness that adds richness to life.

"Am I cheating here?"

Cynicism and skepticism become bulwarks of safety for you, ensuring you are never taken advantage of or left in a situation where you "should have known better." Skeptical of anything outside what you already know, your world and experience of life are narrow and highly controlled.

You give people around you the distinct impression that there is little if any room for mistakes, especially those that could have been foreseen.

This leads you into careers that demand high levels of pre-emptive planning and perfection (law, medicine, accounting, etc.), but your experience as you excel in these pursuits feels sterile and removed.

You may find yourself judging and simultaneously envying those who experience joy and bliss in their lives. Living by the maxim that there's "no free lunch," you can never truly enjoy a free lunch. You're certain there's a hidden cost somewhere, and you're obsessed with finding it.

You see the world through a calculating and efficient lens, which is great for your career but leads to boredom and a desire for something more exciting. This leaves you open to substance abuse and other addictions, as you desperately seek to release and experience the magic of life.

Obvious (But Ineffective Fix): Sell Your Ferrari and Become a Monk

As you grow weary of the world you have created, you conclude that your dissatisfaction is a function of your circumstances and environment, and you make a dramatic change. Whether that's a four-hour workweek, selling the Ferrari, or switching careers, the reprieve is temporary. It's just a matter of time before your old patterns and habits begin to transform the new world around you.

Any reprieve is only temporary. Alas, wherever you go, there you are.

You begin to feel bored and lacking in impact. You may be sitting on the beach, but you're thinking about e-mails and the next project. Alternatively, you may lean into substance abuse or whatever your favourite vice might be to stave off dissatisfaction and restlessness. As things start to get out of hand, you find yourself wondering if maybe the problem is that you have nothing to work on. Yes, you decide, it's time for a new project.

Alas, wherever you go, there you are. Changing your circumstances won't shift the relative safety that you feel when things are reduced to algorithms and analysis. Your self-defence mechanism settles back in, and after each attempted change, you feel a little more resignation—life is disappointing, but that's just the way it is.

Brilliance

COMMON SHADOW ASPECTS:

- Condescending and Skeptical
- Dense and Manipulative

Under-Expressing: *Dense and Manipulative*

You play dumb to reduce the burden of high expectations and get yourself into situations where you're told, "You should know better." In fact, you do know better, but it fits your coping strategies to *not* foresee consequences. Playing stupid causes people to give up on you. You relish the freedom this provides but feel boredom and resentment towards people for not seeing you for who you truly are.

When your leadership demands answers from you, you may have learned to "go limp," waiting for someone else to tell you what to do. This approach serves you in two ways: First, it lets you off the hook for generating your own path forward; and second, when things go awry, you don't get blamed.

These tactics create more space in your life for fun and delight, but you're left frustrated that your Brilliance isn't recognized and painfully aware that others are making most decisions for you. Your unwillingness to expend mental effort, and your failure of courage when there's a risk of making a wrong decision, leave you resentful of those who do take these chances. They're doing what you could be doing—and might be doing better—if you were willing to step up.

You may resort to manipulating others as a way of proving to yourself that you're smarter than they are.

You may show up as an arm-chair critic, skilled at pointing out what's wrong with a given performance or body of work but unwilling to create anything original on your own.

When you grow tired of having your Brilliance go unrecognized, you may resort to manipulating others as a way of proving to yourself that you're smarter than they are. You feel a perverse form of pleasure at your ability to push people's buttons and create reactions.

Obvious (But Ineffective) Fix: Trade in the Dunce Cap for a Mortarboard and Gown

Tired of feeling unseen for your Brilliance, you vow to stride into the intellectual arena and start taking on challenges. You study, read, and possibly launch into a career or pursuit, choosing the path you always thought you would be good at. It's time to create the life that you've always known you were here to live.

While you likely succeed in your new path, both aspects of your shadow remain rooted in a fear of looking stupid. You've changed the circumstances of your life, but the underlying fear is still there. Now that you're going after something that matters, your need to do everything right is increased a hundredfold.

Let go of needing to know the answer before stepping courageously into the unknown.

You become overly serious, driven to get things right every time, and slowly but surely lose sight of the simplicity and ease you once felt. You excel in the new direction, but you're still preoccupied with not looking stupid rather than living in ways that unabashedly express your Brilliance.

Creating the Breakthrough

Your shadow is designed to protect you from the risk of blundering and looking or feeling stupid. By contrast, your breakthrough path rarely leads in a direction you know ahead of time.

Your breakthroughs require a willingness to venture forwards from a place of being completely lost (rather than knowing the answer before you venture forth or waiting until you have figured out the answer). The heart of your Brilliance—your true compass—will become available when you let go of needing to know the answer before stepping courageously into the unknown.

Your breakthroughs won't be created by fabricating or forcing situations where you look silly, dumb, or foolish—as this is just one more layer of control. Instead, the opportunity is to show up as you are and allow for the entire range of possibilities to manifest.

From this perspective, you free up your Brilliance from the task of ensuring that you never feel X—X being whatever experience you're resistant to, whether it's screwing up, looking stupid, or something else. This allows your Brilliance to express its innate creativity in ways that lead you into joy, wonder and fulfilment.

COMMON SHADOW ASPECTS:

- Condescending and Skeptical
- Dense and Manipulative

Leading and Working with People of Brilliance

Members of your team with the gift of Brilliance will naturally tend towards roles that provide avenues for the expression of their intellect. Complicated data work, nuanced interactions between systems, and creating order from chaos are all an excellent fit for Brilliance. You will also find a high degree of Brilliance in places where (sometimes risky) arbitrage can secure an advantage, such as trading stocks and commodities.

Those with Brilliance may show up with traits like rudeness, anti-social behaviour, or even sociopathy, especially as their shadow aspects become more entrenched. Their gift doesn't automatically make them cold and heartless, but they sometimes find that easier than venturing into the messy unknown of intimacy and relationships. The calculated logic of reducing human beings to rational entities with measurable inputs and outputs just feels safer and more efficient.

You'll find it essential to support such team members by building and maintaining real relationships with them and by encouraging such relationships with their peers. This matters as much if not more than incentivizing results.

Because those with Brilliance can see a truth that others are not yet able to conceive, they sometimes have trouble bringing others along with them. Confronted with the natural skepticism this causes, they may try to bully other team members towards their vision. In developing their leadership, you need to cultivate their willingness to slow down and discover patience and kindness, enabling them not only to see a future beyond the current paradigm but to lead people towards that future.

Developing compassion when people show up as less than perfect expands your humanity, opens your heart, and allows you to see that even bloopers can be an example of Brilliance in action.

When working with brilliant team members, it's important to be willing to acknowledge when you've been left in the dust and have no idea where they've gone with the conversation. Help them understand they need to help everyone across the finish line, and that doing so will grow their ability to enroll others in a compelling vision.

Practises

Sit with the experience of feeling or being seen as less than brilliant. See if you can bring love and compassion to yourself in these moments.

The most important practise for Brilliance is developing a willingness to be seen as less than brilliant, even foolish on occasion, and to sometimes miss the mark. Doing so requires a willingness to feel or be seen this way, without qualifying or justifying the experience. This is all about your ability to sit with feelings of inadequacy and to love yourself anyway—meaning complete and total acceptance in the midst of those feelings.

Hold others with love and compassion.

What you practise with other people will benefit you internally, and what you practise internally will benefit your relationships with others. Developing compassion when people show up as less than perfect expands your humanity, opens your heart, and allows you to see that even bloopers can be an example of Brilliance in action.

Notice when you fall back on logic and reasoning to prove you're right.

Practises in intimacy can serve Brilliance greatly. In a given conversation, try setting aside the conclusions you come to and find a way to fully get over there with the other person. Allow what they're saying to occur for you as an absolute truth. The more you can release the notion that you are "right," the more capacity you have to be close to the people you care about.

When you find yourself growing frustrated with other people for not following you, recognize this as your edge of comfort rather than a deficiency with the person in front of you.

Brilliant people can often be intellectually lazy. Rather than taking the time to explain their thinking and walking through the steps required to reach the answer, they rely on just "knowing" something. Practise looking for the people who need more of an explanation. Work with them to figure out what they need to get to your conclusion—or to a different conclusion entirely.

COMMON SHADOW ASPECTS:

- Condescending and Skeptical
- Dense and Manipulative

Brilliant people can often be intellectually lazy

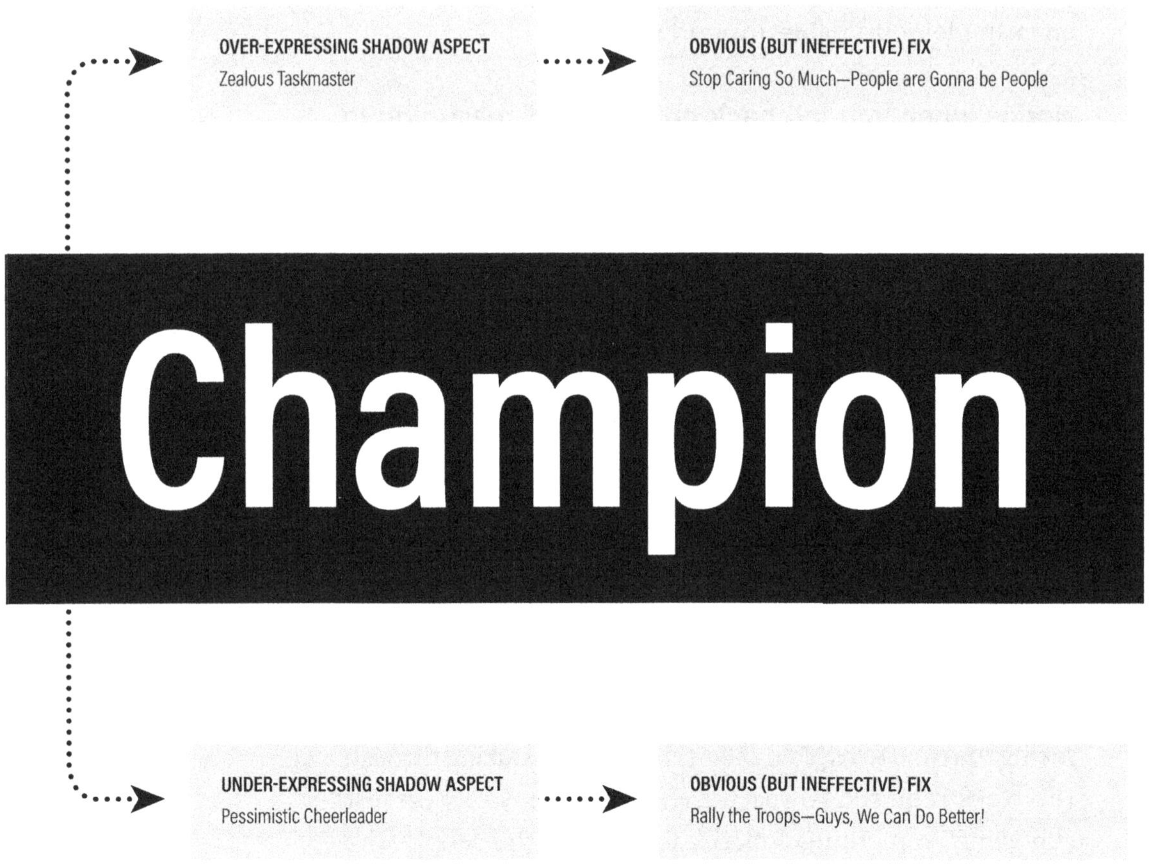

OVER-EXPRESSING SHADOW ASPECT
Zealous Taskmaster

OBVIOUS (BUT INEFFECTIVE) FIX
Stop Caring So Much—People are Gonna be People

Champion

UNDER-EXPRESSING SHADOW ASPECT
Pessimistic Cheerleader

OBVIOUS (BUT INEFFECTIVE) FIX
Rally the Troops—Guys, We Can Do Better!

COMMON DESCRIPTORS

Advocate, In My Corner, Defender, Warrior, Promoter, Protection, Has My Back, Cheerleader, Devoted, Concerned for Others, Believe In People

Champion

COMMON SHADOW ASPECTS:

- Zealous Taskmaster
- Pessimistic Cheerleader

The Quality

Your Gift

You are an innate Champion for all people, ideas, ideals, and humanity at large. In your presence, people find themselves buoyed in their ideas, inspired to take on more than they would on their own, and present to a greater possibility than they would have conceived of left to their own devices.

Having you on a team imbues your teammates with an automatic sense that they can achieve what they set out to do. When you join a project, each hardship along the way feels less significant, and overcoming pitfalls becomes part of the journey rather than something wrong with the path.

Part of the gift you provide people, simply by being with them, is a reminder of how much they can accomplish. Often, this is when you're at your most powerful. Not telling people to remember their potential, but simply being yourself and naturally seeing and believing in what people are capable of. In this way, your gift is not something you actively create or push into the world through your actions. It's something you innately cause to happen, simply by the way you are and the way you relate to the world around you.

The human tendency is often to aim towards "good enough" or what we "think we can get." We determine what is reasonable for us to want

and set our sights accordingly. Your presence invites people to play beyond these limiting boundaries.

Part of the gift you provide people, simply by being with them, is a reminder of how much they can accomplish.

What is Predictable

Predictably, the world around you will let you down. It's almost inevitable, because you naturally see people and the world at their best and become attached to that vision.

Humans are flawed biological creatures, equal parts spirit and humanity. When they act out of fear, make compromises, and take the easy way out, you experience it as a personal affront. Why would they settle for anything less than their very best?

You have the same experience of yourself, never living up to the infinite possibility you know you are capable of. You will find yourself pushing out to the two shadow poles of your gift—that of continually diminishing your expectations or becoming obsessively perfectionistic.

Over time, you will predictably harden and experience mounting frustration and bitterness with yourself and the world around you. You become ruthless and unforgiving, eventually giving up on humanity and resigning yourself to lowered expectations or pushing those around you (and yourself) to strive, strive, and strive.

What is Possible

Everyone you meet is left with an experience of how powerful and capable they are.

The possibility you represent is that everyone you meet is left with an experience of how powerful and capable they are—not despite their weaknesses, foibles, and mistakes, but in partnership with them.

Your shadow aspects often serve to avoid reliving a specific experience in your past that was frightening or disappointing. Your work is often about a willingness to be with your experience in the moment, no matter how scary or unsatisfying it may feel when things don't work out the way they *could*.

Champion

COMMON SHADOW ASPECTS:

- Zealous Taskmaster
- Pessimistic Cheerleader

You'll notice that both aspects of your shadow (see below) are strategies to compensate for the letdown of watching others (or yourself) fail to achieve their potential. You step into your possibility when you hold space for people's potential while simultaneously loving them when they choose something different.

When you do the work to stop compensating and mitigating for disappointment, and instead stay open to everything you feel in those moments, you are ready to present the world with your highest gift: Teaching us all how much we can create in the world if we aim high and forgive our shortcomings.

Common Experience Coming of Age

Your tendency to see what others are capable of and get behind them enthusiastically leads to disappointment and heartbreak when their fear gets the better of them. Your attachment to people pursuing a particular course of action may cause you to feel resentment and bitterness towards them.

You become ruthless and unforgiving

You may have found it easier to turn people away than to live with this disappointment. Alternatively, you surrounded yourself with high performers (fellow perfectionists) who were less likely to fail you.

Group projects may have been incredibly frustrating—a wealth of opportunities to get excited about a given outcome, each followed by dissatisfaction with the result.

Consequences of Owning Your Gifts

Your vision of perfection will cause people to feel inadequate around you (how could they ever live up?). They respond by overpromising or even bragging as a way to prove they can meet your expectations—or by making themselves small to avoid your expectations entirely.

Shadow Aspects

As life goes on, you are continually met with the disappointment and heartbreak that's innate to getting your hopes up with humans.

Over-Expressing: *Zealous Taskmaster*

As life goes on, you are continually met with the disappointment and heartbreak that's innate to getting your hopes up with humans. Something clearly needs to be fixed in the people around you, so you develop a strategy that becomes ever more militant about people manifesting the possibilities you see in them.

As you become more attached to people living up to their potential, free choice slips away. Put differently, someone's potential stops being "potential" and becomes an imperative. Your gift eventually feels like punishment—something people would rather avoid. This can be confusing: Why wouldn't someone want you in their corner?

You crack the whip mercilessly on yourself and those around you. You and your team may generate results, but the experience of doing so becomes a heartless grind.

Obvious (But Ineffective) Fix: Stop Caring So Much—People are Gonna be People

Man, people just seem to suck. You're tired of being their Champion only to have them show up in a half-assed way. People don't seem to appreciate your devotion to them becoming high achievers. Maybe you should just stop caring.

This course of action leaves you less attached to their outcomes and feels like a breakthrough at first. You've left behind a cocktail of excitement and burden to feel peace and ease. You still notice people's inherent potential but get better at dismissing it as illusion.

Over time, life starts to feel pretty dull. You've become, in effect, the wet blanket at the party, persuading people not to get too excited here because what if things don't work out? (And being the wet blanket is just about as fun as it sounds.)

Champion

COMMON SHADOW ASPECTS:

- Zealous Taskmaster
- Pessimistic Cheerleader

Under-Expressing: *Pessimistic Cheerleader*

You already know the inescapable truth: No one is really going to achieve their highest goals and dreams and getting excited for them is a recipe for letdown. Rather than facing that letdown for what it is, you adopt a strategy of keeping your expectations low, actively diminishing the possibility that you and others represent. If you don't expect much from people, it's hard to be disappointed.

"Let's cheer for this team—even though we know they're going to lose."

And yet—because you haven't *actually* let go of the potential you see in yourself and others, you end up as a bizarre version of a cheerleader. You encourage people to be their very best while steeling yourself against getting your hopes up. Yeah, let's cheer for this team—even though we know they're going to lose. Over time, this behaviour feels ever more desperate and emptier, to both yourself and others.

Ultimately, diminishing someone's potential is not who you truly are, and so you try to find your way back to positivity and cheering them on for what you know they are capable of, all the while maintaining the safety of your skepticism and cynicism.

And so, the cycle repeats...

Obvious (But Ineffective) Fix: Rally the Troops—Guys, We Can Do Better!

To escape this pessimistic apathy, you create a big stretch goal and pour your heart into achieving it. You've had enough of holding yourself in check and expecting mediocrity. Deep down you're convinced that you and others are capable of so much more. Let's make this happen!

QUICK TIPS

- Practise grace and love in the face of our (and your own) humanity.
- Remember that what you bring to the rest of the world, you bring to yourself tenfold.

You feel increasing attachment, again, to nailing your goal one hundred percent. You're making things happen, and you give a damn—that's awesome! But you've been through this cycle before, and you just wish there was a way to give a damn that didn't come at such a cost to your peace and ease.

Once again, disappointment looms, and you're frantic to avoid it. Both aspects of your shadow are working overtime to prevent you from experiencing the very thing that would set you free: Remaining present to disappointment and accepting that it sometimes happens.

Creating the Breakthrough

As human beings, we are infinite in our potential and finite in our capacity to express that potential. For Champions, heartbreak exists in that gap. Rather than crafting strategies to avoid that heartbreak and disappointment—either by bullying people to overachieve or diminishing their potential before the game even begins—your breakthrough lies in learning to *be* with the heartbreak that is the human condition. Allowing people to disappoint you without taking it personally and allowing yourself to fall short of your own potential are the wings that will give you lift.

Do invest yourself in the dreams and potential of those around you. Let yourself be heartbroken when life, at least some of the time, doesn't turn out the way you think it should. Find your way back to love and repeat, feeling it all the way. This is the path that sets you free.

Leading and Working with People of Champion

The Champion-types on your team will be natural... well, champions, for what your team might achieve and for the achievement of each member. Early on, this will be exciting and thrilling for everyone. Over time, as people fail to live up to the high expectations placed on them, your Champion teammates become increasingly militaristic about achieving total success, and the gift starts to become toxic.

The most powerful way you can support the Champions on your team is to help them recognize and be with their flaws, cushioning this message with healthy doses of understanding and humanity. They are likely to be incredibly hard on themselves, and while you may be tempted to pile your disappointment atop what they already feel to ensure they don't make the same mistakes again—this is the worst thing you can do. Your job is to bring them love and acceptance and to remind them that their job is not to do things perfectly and never fail—but to do their best and expand their abilities in so doing.

Keep an eye out for people on your teams who show up as cynical. They may be Champions showing up as the under-expressing aspect of their shadow. It can be incredibly potent to acknowledge someone whose Champion nature has long been suppressed, and to call that truth forward. When such people realize the expanded role they have to play and what that will demand of them, they often become a catalyst for breakthroughs in their teams.

It's important for Champion team members to be aware of and enrolled in the leadership role they have to play. They can cause everyone and everything on the team to soar or to sink. Are they willing to take on their essential role as leaders who make sure this team shows up, or would they rather hang out in the cynicism that comes all too easily?

Champion

COMMON SHADOW ASPECTS:

- Zealous Taskmaster
- Pessimistic Cheerleader

Stay open – In the midst of everything life brings.

Practises

Notice the places in your life where you act out the two poles of your shadow.

Where do you hold people as their highest and greatest, but with a tyrannical level of attachment, and where have you given up on people's potential?

Notice your relationship to heartbreak and disappointment, and practise remaining present to those experiences.

When do you find yourself working especially hard to keep disappointment out of your life, whether it's disappointment in yourself or others? At those moments, practise just being with what you feel, rather than trying to reject or distract yourself from it. Practise grace and love in the face of our (and your own) humanity.

Relaxing some of the high standards you've set for yourself is how you begin to develop greater trust in the capacity of others. Remember that what you bring to the rest of the world, you bring to yourself tenfold. Practising here, with yourself, will make it easier to practise with the rest of the world.

This may feel counterintuitive, especially at first. Practise simply being with the shortcomings and failings of the world around you rather than fastening yourself to them as unacceptable failures. Your deepest form of practise is to hold fast to your vision of people's highest potential while recognizing, without judgment, that they will sometimes get scared, trip, or falter.

Practise completion and forgiveness.
Practise forgiving yourself and others for our humanity, especially when we fall short of our highest potential. By getting complete each time you or someone else falls short, you'll build the capacity to stay open in the midst of everything life brings rather than pre-emptively closing to protect your heart.

Champion

COMMON SHADOW ASPECTS:

- Zealous Taskmaster
- Pessimistic Cheerleader

ASK YOURSELF...

- Where do you hold people as their highest and greatest, but with a tyrannical level of attachment?
- Where have you given up on people's potential?

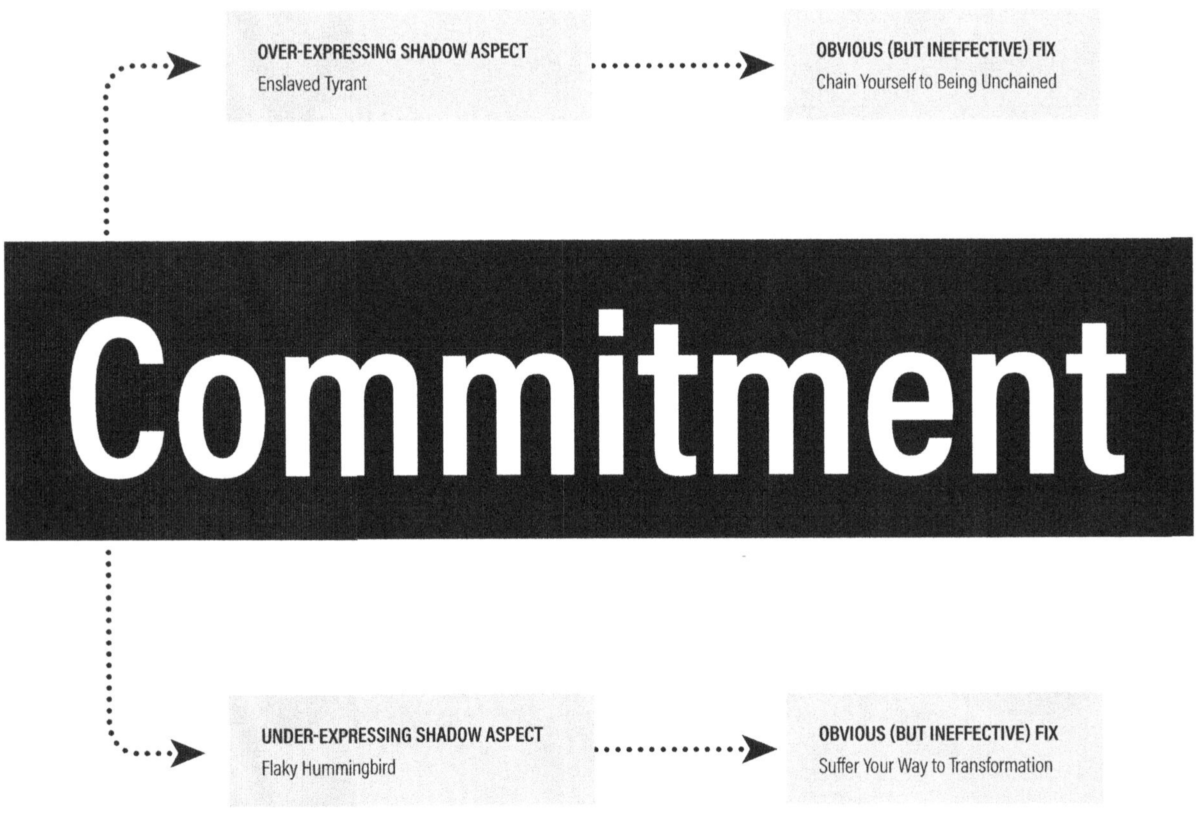

Commitment

OVER-EXPRESSING SHADOW ASPECT
Enslaved Tyrant

OBVIOUS (BUT INEFFECTIVE) FIX
Chain Yourself to Being Unchained

UNDER-EXPRESSING SHADOW ASPECT
Flaky Hummingbird

OBVIOUS (BUT INEFFECTIVE) FIX
Suffer Your Way to Transformation

COMMON DESCRIPTORS

Devotion, Responsible, Dedicated, Loyal, Faithful, Unstoppable, Persistent, Perseverance, Tenacious, Doggedness, Unfaltering, Unwavering, All In

Commitment

COMMON SHADOW ASPECTS:

- Enslaved Tyrant
- Flaky Hummingbird

The Quality

Your Gift

When you join a team, its projects, goals, and dreams are imbued with a greater degree of Commitment. Your ability to focus, rally, and recommit through all obstacles is a godsend when things get tough or the way forwards is unclear. You rarely need to worry about achieving your goals—once you've said you'll create something, you're pretty reliable about getting it done.

Your presence on a team inspires people to go all the way to the finish line and beyond. People are less likely to quit in your presence and more determined to stay the course. You're the person we want at our side when making declarations and commitments, whether that's strategizing a work project or planning a trip.

You may find yourself drawn to and able to excel in sports that demand a high level of commitment, both physically and mentally—marathons, Ironman and Tough Mudder competitions, and other extreme challenges. Others marvel at your persistent training regimens; you don't understand how they could do anything less.

When people fail to create the transformation they desire in their lives or leadership, lack of commitment is often why. You begin this part of the game with one foot ahead of the rest. Once you lean into something, you go as far as you can, no matter the cost. This can lead to problems if your goal or vision isn't well thought out before you commit to it. Nonetheless, your capacity to push through breakdown to breakthrough, compared to most leaders, is remarkable.

Your willingness to go beyond where most people stop means you're excellent at supporting others to do the same. You're a catalyst for achieving the impossible.

You're the person we want at our side when making declarations and commitments, whether that's strategizing a work project or planning a trip.

What is Predictable

At some point, the strength of your Commitment becomes an albatross around your neck. Once you commit to something, you're locked in, rigid and unwilling to pivot from that singular purpose. You resist adjusting your strategy, even in the face of new information.

If staying on your path means smashing your head into a brick wall until it gives, that's what you'll do. Sometimes this is exactly what's required. Other times, you overlook creative breakthroughs that require a different approach.

Because you, in particular, know the cost of seeing something through (and because you probably overlooked easier alternatives), you may resist making commitments in the first place or look for ways to back out of them, causing some to experience you as flaky, the opposite of your gift.

Frustrated by your apparent reluctance to commit, you may throw your hands up in the air, and shout, "Fuck it, let's do this!" in hopes of leaping beyond the blockage. But this may trap you into ill-considered commitments that you regret and try to get out of, only worsening the problem. Eventually, you begin to alternate between seeing yourself as unreliable and Commitment-phobic at one extreme and locked in and miserable at the other.

This isn't to suggest that you will fail in your life. You'll probably achieve some degree of success by doggedly hanging in on projects to the bitter end. You just won't enjoy it that much.

What is Possible

You possess the possibility of changing the way we show up around our promises. Teaching us how to honor our Commitment, you push forwards doggedly when appropriate while staying alert and open to course corrections. You are the gift of achieving the impossible—not despite the shifts that may occur along the way, but in partnership with them. In so doing, you discover that suffering, at least some of the time, is optional.

Rather than being a slave to rules like, "Once you commit, you never quit" (or whatever your flavour happens to be), you recognize those moments when you want to quit represent some of your greatest opportunities. Those moments become your compass, pointing you towards opportunities to examine your *relationship to* a commitment rather than the commitment itself.

By doing the work to shift your relationship to Commitment itself, you become a model for what is possible when we take both quitting *and* suffering off the table. From here, Commitment becomes a crucible for transformation. As a leader, you're able to invite and inspire people to say yes to their possibilities, and to stay the course when they most want to quit—after all, that's when the breakthrough becomes available.

When those with Commitment take on their work, they tend to be exquisite teachers, coaches and leaders, willing to stay with someone long after the person has quit on themselves. In this way you support breakthroughs where others cannot.

Commitment

COMMON SHADOW ASPECTS:

- Enslaved Tyrant
- Flaky Hummingbird

You become a model for what is possible when we take both quitting and suffering off the table.

Common Experience Coming of Age

Your childhood may not have looked or sounded like that of your friends or peers, by virtue of your absolute devotion to a given pursuit. While your friends were experimenting with dating, sports and hobbies, you may have already chosen an area of mastery. In recounting your childhood, you may find that most of your stories revolve around this particular pursuit.

It's not that suffering is a requirement of Commitment—simply that that is how you have created it.

Consequences of Owning Your Gifts

When you lean into the Commitment that comes naturally to you, you may find some people taking advantage of this. You may end up doing most of the work on team projects and stay up late working because you said you would get something done, even when others have stopped caring and abandoned the project.

Shadow Aspects

Over-Expressing: *Enslaved Tyrant*

You power through any obstacle that gets in the way and are reliable to get the job done, no matter the costs. However, your grimly dogged approach makes those victories feel Pyrrhic to you and your team. You judge others for their unwillingness to remain committed while simultaneously envying their freedom and ability to walk away.

Suffering is the hallmark of this particular shadow aspect. It's not that suffering is a requirement of Commitment—simply that that is how you have created it. You have the capacity to white-knuckle your way through anything that life might put in front of you, and while that capacity to "survive" something has left you resilient, it also means there's a great deal of suffering you impose on yourself, simply by virtue of being unwilling or unable to surrender when there is another possibility available.

You feel overwhelmed by how hard everything is but find it difficult to rest and reboot your energy and enthusiasm. Commitment becomes something to avoid if you can.

You're making great things happen—you just wish it didn't feel quite so heavy.

Commitment

COMMON SHADOW ASPECTS:

- Enslaved Tyrant
- Flaky Hummingbird

Obvious (But Ineffective) Fix: Chain Yourself to Being Unchained

At some point(s), you take a look around and notice all the commitments you've made that aren't serving you. You wonder how you got this way, and the conclusion you reach is that you say yes to far too many things (there is ample evidence to prove this).

In a burst of freedom, you throw off your chains, dumping commitments and letting people know you're out. It feels edgy but incredibly freeing as well. Your spare time opens back up, and you experience a spaciousness you haven't felt for a while. You have a new determination to be vigilant and selective about what you say yes to. Preserving your spaciousness and freedom becomes your highest commitment; inadvertently, you end up imprisoned by your need to avoid imprisonment.

...you feel like a bird chained to a cinder block.

You may create good things in the world, but more meaningful degrees of impact and experience are beyond your reach—at least until you re-invent your relationship to Commitment entirely and become willing to embrace it in service of something greater than your reactive need for freedom.

Under-Expressing: *Flaky Hummingbird*

Knowing the experience that commitments bring (in particular, the potential for suffering), you find reasons to avoid them entirely or commit to many small things rather than to a few larger ones that matter. You're left feeling like you have no time and find yourself saying no to things you would love to do and saying yes to things you care about less.

Like a hummingbird, you jump back and forth between the myriad promises you've made. You don't ever really have to be with the challenges, hardships, and frustrations that may come from truly committing to one big thing, but it's there, nonetheless, caused by the multitude of small things you've given your yes to.

Because you can't really keep all these smaller commitments and don't feel like doing so anyhow, you jump back out with the same impulsiveness, leaving people (and yourself) to wonder what's going on, and when, if ever, you can be relied on.

Obvious (But Ineffective) Fix: Suffer Your Way to Transformation

You notice that you tend to jump in and out of Commitment and are sick of feeling flaky and unreliable. This isn't who you are! Triumphantly, you decide it's time to end this pattern and stick to every promise.

You may dive into a relationship, job, investment, or other commitment and refuse to quit no matter how bad things get. THIS time you're going to honor your Commitment no matter what. Life might feel like a grind. You miss the freedom and ease you used to feel, but things are beginning to happen that were previously impossible.

It's just that you feel like a bird chained to a cinder block. An undercurrent of suffering and self-deprivation runs through everything. You brush it off by telling yourself, "It's okay. I'm choosing this. I feel better having committed." Occasionally, though, you find yourself wondering how it would feel to commit yourself wholly to something great without the experience of suffering.

Creating the Breakthrough

Your breakthrough lies in seeing and releasing your binary approach to Commitment. This is often less a function of what you do and more of who you *are* in action. As always, the way out is through. To create the breakthrough, you must step off the pendulum swing created by the obvious fixes—either avoiding commitment entirely or grinding yourself through it.

Practise leaning into Commitment and noticing what happens when you do. How do you show up inside of Commitment? What is predictable about the way commitments go for you? Practise creating more fluidity while still honoring your commitments.

Identify the places where a commitment feels onerous and ask yourself what kind of conversations would let you honor the spirit and intention of that commitment but shift or release what's weighing you down.

People may initially push back when you begin shifting the nature of your existing commitments. No surprise there—you've trained them to reflect your rigidity. Be willing to partner with them through this process. As you stay this new course, demonstrating a willingness to dance with them inside the larger spirit of a Commitment, they too will slowly shift.

COMMON SHADOW ASPECTS:

- Enslaved Tyrant
- Flaky Hummingbird

Leading and Working with People of Commitment

The members of your team who possess Commitment are incredibly reliable at whatever task you put before them. They rarely complain and will get the job done, no matter what it takes. As a leader, this gives you a seductively reassuring sense of safety, especially when everyone else seems to be falling apart. What you don't see is the individual cost to your team members' relationships, morale and health when they focus on getting the job done no matter what.

The result? Those rock-solid team members drop a resignation letter on your desk the day after the project wraps. As a leader, you need to see them more deeply. Make a point of checking in with them along the way, not only on the progress and quality of their work but on their quality of *being*. Does their presence feel light and joyful or heavy and burdened?

Many leaders brush off this kind of burnout, saying, "Well, that's just the way they are." But that misses the point of this book entirely; the "way they are" is predictable for their particular quality of being. Your opportunity as a leader is to stay in close conversation with these team members and to model for them how to honor the spirit of Commitment while remaining fluid and open to new possibilities. Don't settle for your team members' suffering.

Remember that leadership and breakthroughs sometimes leap far beyond the realm of the manageable.

The flip side of your team members with Commitment are those who say yes to too many things, doubling down on their commitments because they feel they have no option. Paradoxically, this leads to them looking uncommitted and flaky—when in fact, they're just over-committed. Trying to motivate them to lean in even further is a management trap to avoid; it will just reinforce their belief and yours that they're unreliable.

Instead, make a point of knowing what they have committed to and work with them to find a healthy, achievable list. At the same time, remember that leadership and breakthroughs sometimes leap far beyond the realm of the manageable. If a team member with Commitment seems to be overprotecting themselves from saying yes, check this out with them. There may be a transformational breakthrough available for them in taking on more than they currently know how to achieve and getting supported to have things go differently than the usual path of suffering and overwhelm.

Practises

Audit your commitments.

A good place to start is by creating an audit of the commitments you have currently entered. Sit down and write out a complete list. If it's easier, break this down into areas of your life, say, finances, family, career, friends, and self.

Sit with the list, and be present to the impact on you of these commitments. If you find the list overwhelming and feel like running away (or you notice yourself avoiding making a list altogether), this is precisely the experience you need to stay with.

Get clear on what would need to change.

Look at each commitment on your list and identify whether you feel empowered or disempowered by it. Disempowered doesn't mean you necessarily need to drop that commitment; it's just the feeling state you have around it.

For each disempowered commitment, ask yourself what would need to shift to change your experience. Is it time to renegotiate this commitment? To change how you hold it? Or is it time to end the commitment entirely?

Be careful about this last option, which can become an easy way out. Remember that breakthroughs are more often achieved by shifting who you *are* with your commitments than by abandoning them.

COMMON SHADOW ASPECTS:

- Enslaved Tyrant
- Flaky Hummingbird

Identify how you relate to the commitments you choose to keep—what's your underlying story?
What is the story you tell yourself about each commitment you choose to keep? If you're staying in your marriage by telling yourself, "I'm doing it because it's the right thing to do, and because I'm scared to leave," that isn't really empowering, and isn't likely to feel light and joyful over time.

Once you identify the story, you can take on shifting the relationship. What story can you generate and live from that would create a lighter experience of this commitment?

Identify how Commitment, in general, goes for you.
Sit down and draw out the cycle that most of your commitments move through. What's your experience at the very beginning? After you've been working towards it a while? If it starts to sour, what do you think and feel about it? How do you end your commitments?

Simply noticing and being aware of this habitual behaviour makes it possible for you to change it.

QUICK TIPS

- Have things go differently than the usual path of suffering and overwhelm.
- Audit your commitments.

Commitment

COMMON SHADOW ASPECTS:

- Enslaved Tyrant
- Flaky Hummingbird

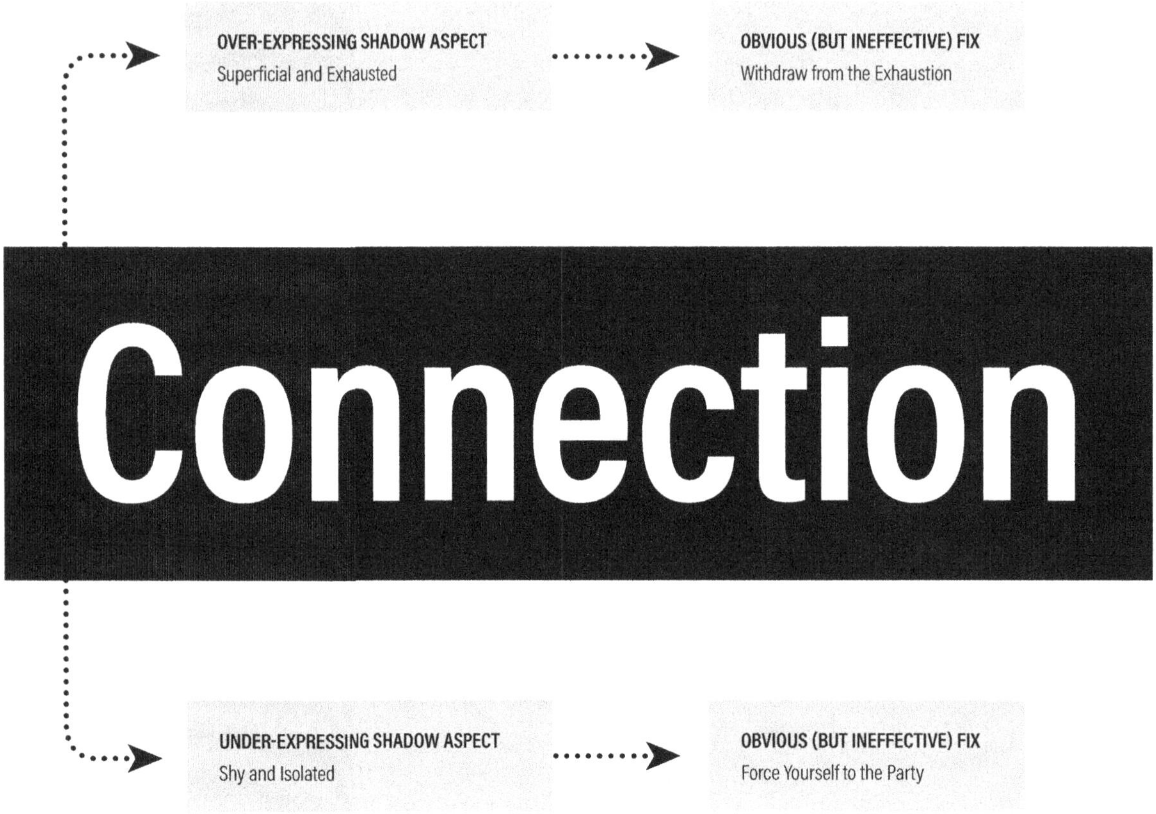

OVER-EXPRESSING SHADOW ASPECT
Superficial and Exhausted

OBVIOUS (BUT INEFFECTIVE) FIX
Withdraw from the Exhaustion

Connection

UNDER-EXPRESSING SHADOW ASPECT
Shy and Isolated

OBVIOUS (BUT INEFFECTIVE) FIX
Force Yourself to the Party

COMMON DESCRIPTORS

Relationship, Relatable, Deeper Conversation, Curious About Other People, Extroverted, Familiarity, Feel Comfortable Talking With You, Good Listener

Connection

COMMON SHADOW ASPECTS:

- Superficial and Exhausted
- Shy and Isolated

The Quality

Your Gift

You embody Connection. When you enter a room people immediately know themselves and each other better, and you become the life of the party. People are always glad to have you show up at their event—things just seem to happen when you're around. You ARE social lubricant.

You generate conversation easily, so people feel excitement and relief when you show up. If the conversation was a little quiet or awkward until now, no problem—you've arrived, and things will pick up from here. You have a gift for drawing people out, regardless of whether they identify as extroverts or introverts. Those on the quieter, shyer side may at first be suspicious of you, but it's just a matter of time before they feel grateful for your Connection. You make it okay for people to be in the space.

You can hold the attention of and entertain large groups of people, and moments later go deep into a one-on-one conversation with someone you've just met. You find traditional small talk a challenge at times because you're fascinated by people and love to dive in with them. But as you hone your gifts, all levels of conversation, from the surface to the deeply intimate, become part of your domain of mastery.

In your presence, people feel like they matter and make a difference. Your capacity to remember people's names and interests makes them

As you hone your gifts, all levels of conversation, from the surface to the deeply intimate, become part of your domain of mastery.

feel relevant and important. You leave people feeling seen and lit up, which has a ripple effect, such that they show up in all their interactions with more ease and authenticity.

Relationships come easy to you, and you probably have a plethora of relationships growing and progressing at any given moment. Friends may come and go, but the constant throughout is your capacity to relish the time you spend with people.

What is Predictable

Your innate Connection makes the experience of disconnection especially painful for you. When you see other people feeling disconnected, this becomes a cause you rush to take on. Parties and social functions can become nightmares when you're constantly working the room to ensure that everyone else is having a good time, at the expense of your own experience and well-being.

People who are Connection often find themselves surrounded by people, never truly alone, but feeling lonely amid the crowd. You may find yourself entertaining everyone in the group but feeling empty as you do so, wondering why none of them truly know who you are.

Conversely, some people of Connection find themselves spending great amounts of time alone. Rather than be with the vulnerability that's inherent to the deepest levels of Connection, they immerse themselves in hobbies, entertainment and addictions that allow them to find contentment in isolation.

The shadow aspects of Connection may present on one hand as a continual stream of charming chatter without real Connection, and on the other as outright isolation. If you have this gift, you may be frustrated by binary distinctions like introvert versus extrovert. You probably exhibit both these tendencies, which are reflections of your underlying gift.

If you lean towards the charming but superficial aspect of your shadow, you're surrounded by acquaintances but have few deep, authentic relationships. In essence, relationships have become *fungible* for you—each one is the same as the next.

You appreciate some traits about whoever you're currently in relationship with, but it's simply a matter of time before this relationship falls apart and you create a new one. This leaves you craving the depth and intimacy that is your birthright.

COMMON SHADOW ASPECTS:

- Superficial and Exhausted
- Shy and Isolated

What is Possible

Your possibility lies in helping everyone around you connect more deeply with themselves and the world. When you let go of the belief that other people's experience of you means something about you, you will be able to connect with them regardless of how they show up in the moment.

Because Connection creates new relationships so easily, it can create fertile ground to avoid ever facing up to your impact. When you create a mess with someone and they get upset, it can be easier to "cut the relationship and run" rather than to stay and hear what's showing up for them. When you do the work to stay deeply connected, despite the pain and heartbreak that may show up, you discover your ability not only to create new relationships but to deepen them.

You find traditional small talk a challenge at times.

The possibility of your Connection is not only a high quantity of relationships but also a high *quality*. Those with Connection create breadth and depth in their ability to relate to others, sharing effortlessly (even when it requires effort) and generously hanging out when discomfort comes up.

You may be frustrated by binary distinctions like introvert versus extrovert.

One of the joys of Connection fully expressed is becoming a super-node of connection and possibility for everyone you know. Your capacity to hold many relationships with depth, and your genuine interest in and love of what people are up to and expressing in their lives, makes you a master networker.

While you may hate the concept of networking, you represent the possibility of doing it effortlessly. Your innate caring about what people are up to makes it effortless to connect those that would best be served by knowing each other. People are continually touched by the generosity with which you put people together.

Common Experience Coming of Age

Your ability to connect with people naturally and deeply feels overwhelming or painful when they pull away. To avoid this, you may have learned to keep things superficial, providing all the doing of Connection without any of the being underneath it as a way to stay safe and ensure you're liked.

It's also possible that you found your natural ability to connect with others led you to the awkward point of not wanting to stay in relationship after getting to know them. Consequently, you may have turned your Connection inward, avoiding relationships altogether.

Consequences of Owning Your Gifts

Connecting with everyone imposes a burden. People expect you to be the life of the party and rely on you to make things happen. Connecting with people whom no one else is able (or willing) to can make you their "only friend," imposing expectations you may not have anticipated.

Shadow Aspects

Over-Expressing: *Superficial and Exhausted*

The experience of disconnection with someone is painful and frightening, and you make it mean something about you. To compensate, you go into social overdrive, becoming superficial and a bullshitter. You talk and talk and talk without really saying anything. People leave a conversation with you feeling entertained but with no idea who you are.

Relationships begin to feel hard and exhausting, and you feel resentful of how much energy they demand. Someone pulling up a chair to sit beside you, unless it's a close friend, means you have to start up the party machine again until they've moved on. You find yourself needing downtime, doing things like having a date night just with yourself. Ironically, the thought of going to a party where you know everyone becomes more intimidating than going to a party where you know no one. In the latter case, you won't have to make it your sacred duty to ensure everyone is getting along and no one feels left out.

In your weariness, you lose track of what you know on a deeper level: That real Connection is never exhausting. Rather, it fills your cup and leaves you nourished because it's simply you acting in alignment with who you are.

Obvious (But Ineffective) Fix: Withdraw from the Exhaustion

Parties and social functions may have become increasingly draining for you—effectively situations where you are forced to be "on" and make sure everyone is having a good time. You stick to your clique at parties and events, reducing your overwhelm and exhaustion (at least for a time) but leaving others feeling left out and like they don't belong.

Relationships are fluid, however, and people inevitably move in and out of your chosen groups. When someone new enters, it's back to

COMMON SHADOW ASPECTS:

- Superficial and Exhausted
- Shy and Isolated

People leave a conversation with you feeling entertained but with no idea who you are.

the same drawing board, so you put increasing emphasis on cherishing your downtime.

Despite the surface peace and ease you feel when you're alone, a growing sense of loneliness tinges your life.

Under-Expressing: *Shy and Isolated*

Connection becomes a burden, something to fear, and you find it easier to separate and avoid. You become aloof, slowly but surely distancing yourself from those around you. Connection makes you feel something like an autistic child overwhelmed with too much stimulation. As you pull further inward, your capacity to be with Connection atrophies, creating a downward spiral.

...until you can sit and be with people in the awkwardness of disconnection—and the discomfort that comes up sometimes with intimacy—you won't really be creating Connection.

You self-identify as shy, introverted, or withdrawn, leaving you resigned that this is simply the way you are. You construct a life around this truth. Your self-assessment has become a self-fulfilling prophecy.

You find a degree of relief and peace in isolation, but you're left with an underlying yearning to be in relationship and intimacy with people. The strategy will work to protect you from your fear, but it can never completely quell the voice of your desire.

Because your desire for Connection is fundamentally a part of who you are, you latch onto a very small number of relationships in which you've managed to create depth and safety. You convince yourself that intimacy can only exist for you in these few relationships, and you become increasingly dependent on them. You may be demanding, attached, and clingy in the few relationships that give you a real taste of the fullest expression of yourself.

Obvious (But Ineffective) Fix: Force Yourself to the Party

Over time, your growing loneliness forces you to go back out and meet people, doing whatever it takes to create Connection. At first, this feels revelational. You discover (or remember) that you're quite good at connecting with people and that they seem to like what you have to offer. You still feel discomfort at the thought of attending social functions, but at least you're spending time in the presence of other human beings.

And yet the reality is that you're engaged in the *performance* of Connection—placing your emphasis on being agreeable, likable, and charming—rather than experiencing real connection, so this too feels lonely and empty.

Your underlying challenge is a function of the fact that until you can sit and be with people in the awkwardness of disconnection—and the discomfort that comes up sometimes with intimacy—you aren't really creating Connection. Rather, you're creating an artificial state of "not being disconnected." These are two radically different things. Eventually, you find yourself tempted to return to your solitude. Yes, it was lonely and too damn quiet, but at least it was less work.

Creating the Breakthrough

Your shadows are ultimately there to protect you from your fears about connecting too deeply or with the wrong people in the wrong circumstances. While this strategy worked for you in the past, it's now an old pattern that prevents you from creating the Connection and intimacy you *are*.

Your shadows also serve to protect you from the existential pain of disconnection. Everyone finds disconnection somewhat difficult; for you it sears your soul. Your breakthrough often lies in simply connecting

COMMON SHADOW ASPECTS:

- Superficial and Exhausted
- Shy and Isolated

with people exactly as you are. Unsure what to say in a conversation? Connect *as* and *from* that challenging place. Frustrated and uncertain about how to connect with someone without hurting them? Share that struggle with them and connect from there. Sit with them and *be* in the awkwardness. Like breathing into an uncomfortable stretch in yoga, a willingness on your part to stay with the discomfort of disconnection will allow you to discover intimacy and Connection on a level you never dreamed was possible.

Leading and Working with People of Connection

Members of your teams with the gift of Connection will naturally find themselves in roles that involve a lot of interaction with other humans. Common roles for these people include project management, business analyst, networking-type roles (think of company rainmakers, going to social events to drive up more business), and sales.

While your Connection-type people will excel in these positions, it is important to remind yourself that they may be relying on their shadows to succeed, which will lead them towards burnout. This may not present the way you expect it to. They're the life of the party, clearly having a great time—how could they not be happy? The next day an e-mail lands in your inbox informing you they're moving on. (For them, this beats having to share the ugly truth that they're burnt out and sitting in the awkwardness that would create.)

You may also have team members who are, given the under-expressing shadow aspect of Connection, operating in roles that minimize their interaction with people.

While these shadow-driven team members may excel in the work they do, remember that in these roles they are honing their shadows and resisting their fear. This is not wrong per se, but if and when they desire to step further into leadership (or you wish to cultivate this in them), they will have to be willing to step out from that safety.

While personality assessments and typing quizzes can be helpful, it is important to be careful about binary distinctions like introversion versus extroversion. Those members of your team that are Connection will tend to relate to one side or the other as "the way they are" and build evidence for the shadow aspect that is strongest for them. Helping your team members see that their introversion and extroversion are functions of the same underlying gift can be revelatory.

To support and develop the leadership of those with Connection, you will need to model it—to cultivate your willingness to sit in disconnection, discomfort and awkwardness. Getting to true Connection means you must go deeper than the glibness and chatter that comes easily to these team members. Connect with them regularly, and don't be swayed by the charm. Ensure authentic Connection: How are they doing? How do they feel to you?

Connection

COMMON SHADOW ASPECTS:

- Superficial and Exhausted
- Shy and Isolated

COMMON ROLES FOR PEOPLE OF CONNECTION

- People with the gift of Connection will naturally find themselves in roles that involve a lot of interaction with other humans.
- For example: project management, business analyst, networking-type roles, and sales.
- Given the under-expressing shadow aspect of Connection, they may operate in roles that minimize their interaction with people.

Practises

Sit and be with the experience of disconnection that is a function of human intimacy.

Growing up, we experience plenty of these moments—your first oral presentation at school, your first time asking someone to dance, your first kiss. Over time, we learn to pave over the discomfort they cause us. Notice how you use charm and a glib tongue almost automatically to pave over awkward moments, and practise letting that go.

Practise nurturing and growing relationships.

Regardless of the shadow aspect you most identify with, you thrive on Connection, and it is your lifeblood. You may have convinced yourself that you don't need people that much, but this is a setup and buying into your fear.

Consider that the melody of a conversation exists in the pauses, and practise allowing space in all your communication.

Most people who are Connection have at least three to four deep relationships that they cherish and that offer places where they can sit in awkwardness. Practise growing relationships outside of this core group.

Practise increasing your Connection in small ways.

Make eye contact with everyone you pass in the street. When someone meets your eyes, say, "Hello," and see how it goes. Practise asking people for their names when they serve you. When you see someone that you remember, say hello and give them the gift of being remembered. We often avoid doing this for fear that they won't remember us and will feel awkward. This is not your issue to manage. Go ahead and give people the gift—and see what it creates for you.

Find or create groups for the hobbies you enjoy as a way of allowing more Connection in your life.
If you enjoy knitting, join a knitting group. If you like languages, go and join a language class. If fine wine and spirits are your thing, go to tasting events. Practise striking up conversations (or again, simply sharing a smile) with the people next to you.

Allow more silence in conversation.
People who are Connection often find themselves filling every gap in a conversation with more conversation. Consider that the melody of a conversation exists in the pauses, and practise allowing space in all your communication. If needed, count to five before opening your mouth and saying what's next. Let yourself sit in the spaciousness of Connection rather than desperately filling it up. Trust that Connection is always present and available to you.

COMMON SHADOW ASPECTS:

- Superficial and Exhausted
- Shy and Isolated

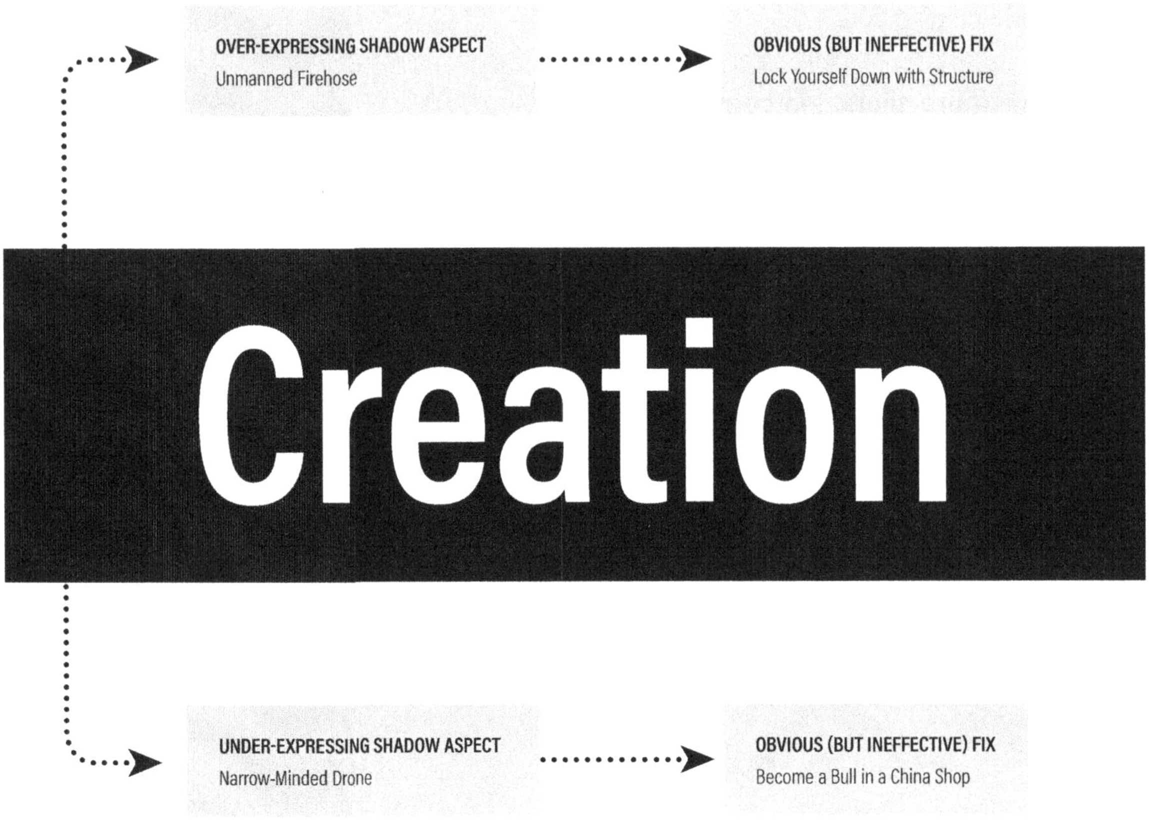

OVER-EXPRESSING SHADOW ASPECT
Unmanned Firehose

OBVIOUS (BUT INEFFECTIVE) FIX
Lock Yourself Down with Structure

Creation

UNDER-EXPRESSING SHADOW ASPECT
Narrow-Minded Drone

OBVIOUS (BUT INEFFECTIVE) FIX
Become a Bull in a China Shop

COMMON DESCRIPTORS

Catalyst, Make Things Happen, Stimulating, Starter, Action-Oriented, Ideas Person, Producer, Builder, Bring Things into Existence, Inventive, Designer

Creation

COMMON SHADOW ASPECTS:

- Unmanned Firehose
- Narrow-Minded Drone

The Quality

Your Gift

You are the gift of Creation. When you join a space, that space becomes more creative around you. You are a catalyst for growth, constantly creating anew and inspiring people around you to do the same.

Your personal experience is a wellspring of ideas. You feel plugged directly into Source, bombarded with new ideas, approaches, and ventures to pursue.

You are particularly adept at blue-sky thinking and love pursuing large-scale ideas and opening up the world to new possibilities. Implementation? Well, that's less interesting. The moment you have to choose one idea and push it forward, it becomes a hindrance to your innate Creation.

You are magnificent at starting things, drawing people to you, and inspiring the possibility of what might be created. You see creative possibilities in everyone's ideas, inspiring them to pursue what they previously considered a vague possibility. They feel alive to the possibility of what they might bring into existence.

You might find yourself drawn to careers in movie and TV production, authorship, large-scale project design, construction, and anything

You are magnificent at starting things, drawing people to you, and inspiring the possibility of what might be created.

else that provides the opportunity to build something. You're a gift to any project and any brainstorm. As soon as you enter the arena, ideas emerge from people around you and begin taking shape.

What is Predictable

Predictably, your nonstop creativity will become a burden. You have a billion ideas but a finite amount of time in which to execute them. People tell you to choose and focus on just a few ideas, but you struggle with this. How can you discard any of these beautiful concepts? Especially since your most recent idea is always the most exciting of them all?

Predictably, instead of doing the work to expand your capacity to be with everything that comes to you, you try to control and manage the flood or are simply overwhelmed by it. This leads to the shadow aspects you may find yourself oscillating between.

On one hand, you resign yourself to being an ideas person with little talent for implementation, management, or completion. People love your creative energy but are not willing to trust you beyond that point. When your shadow is fully empowered, you assemble project teams that allow you to thrive in the early stages of fleshing out your ideas, then pass things off to those who are better at day-to-day management. This works great in the places where you can create teams that support you this way but leaves you flailing everywhere else. You may find yourself with a million projects on the go, and nothing ever seems to get finished.

On the other hand, you may conclude that the geyser-like quality of your Creation is too much, and over-compensate in the other direction, shutting down your innate creativity and choosing reliability and consistency instead. You sacrifice Creation—all the colors you're capable of seeing and pulling into existence—and create a managed life.

This feels boring and narrow, and you don't experience the pleasure of exercising your true talent. But at least stuff gets done and you can be relied on.

As with most shadows, you bounce back and forth between these two aspects, attempting to create balance but never quite landing in a place where you're truly open and embody your gift. You may spend years of your life in one shadow aspect before jumping to the other, or you may run one aspect in some areas of your life and the other in different areas. Life feels like a binary choice between keeping a tight lid on yourself or being an explosive mess.

Creation

COMMON SHADOW ASPECTS:

- Unmanned Firehose
- Narrow-Minded Drone

What is Possible

You are the possibility of marrying boundless creativity with structure and rigor. When you do the work of creating the right kinds of boundaries and structure—such that they don't impede you but set you free—you teach the rest of the world how to harness its creative potential.

Those with the magic of Creation often experience an either-or relationship between explosive Creation on one hand and highly restrictive structure on the other. You deepen your leadership by tackling this either-or relationship head-on, creating a new and productive relationship to structure. You learn (and teach others) to draw inside the lines before drawing outside of them, to master the scales before improvising, and to learn existing dance steps before dancing freestyle.

Learn the rules like a pro, so you can break them like an artist.

You embody the adage (commonly misattributed to Picasso): *Learn the rules like a pro, so you can break them like an artist.* You develop the capacity to harness not only the breadth of your Creation but its depth.

You also become an incredible teacher, able to support others as they learn to integrate structure with creativity. You turn drones into artists and wildlings into masters.

In your presence, people experience the gift of openhearted, loving Creation, married with consistency and rigor. You create order out of chaos and infuse order with spontaneity.

Common Experience Coming of Age

You show up like a firehose with no one directing it, smashing around, spraying ideas (which the world needs) everywhere, but with little direction or purpose.

You may often have experienced people relating to you as too much, scattered, and lacking commitment. Your ability to bring projects magically to life—in their early phases at least—may be dismissed in a world where getting things done is what matters most.

People may have been overwhelmed by the sheer enormity of ideas you generate, teaching you to clam up and keep some of this creative energy to yourself. Parents and teachers, in a desire to help you finish things, may quell your innate creativity, turning your focus instead to rote projects and mindless completion of tasks.

Consequences of Owning Your Gifts

Owning your Creation can make you disruptive. The rest of the world may be fixated on the task at hand while you see an infinite number of other possibilities. Some people dismiss you simply because they can't keep up with the pace at which your brain creates.

Shadow Aspects

Over-Expressing: *Unmanned Firehose*

The world around you tried to make you conform to its rules and regulations. In response, you reject structure entirely. No one's going to contain you—that would be antithetical to who you are! Consequently, you struggle to empower structure in your life. You show up like a firehose with no one directing it, smashing around, spraying ideas (which the world needs) everywhere, but with little direction or purpose.

You feel almost manic in moments of high creation, sometimes scrawling out pages upon pages of thoughts. Because you're allergic to constraint, your ability to bring something from idea into reality happens in short, explosive bursts. With little ability to scaffold and focus your creativity, you *have to* build things fast, meaning they sometimes turn out to be a little rickety.

You may have found yourself in relationship with partners (romantic, business, or otherwise) who embody the other side of your gift's shadow, providing useful structure and allowing you to achieve a semblance of balance. Without the ability to generate structure from within, however, you will eventually find yourself chafing at your partner's efforts to control and tamp down your wellspring of creativity.

You create some beautiful things in the world, but the experience is all on and then all off (much like what is represented by the polarity in your shadow aspects). You create late into the night for days on end, then find yourself exhausted and under-nourished. The flip side of this cycle is bouts of lethargy and an inability to make yourself do anything.

The firehose is either on at full force, wildly creative but also smashing around, or it lies limp, absent of the vitality that should be coursing through it.

COMMON SHADOW ASPECTS:

- Unmanned Firehose
- Narrow-Minded Drone

Obvious (But Ineffective) Fix: Lock Yourself Down with Structure

Because you lack calibration in your relationship to structure (and to your Creation), you tend to be all or nothing. Experiencing the impact of this tendency, you vow to focus resolutely on the thing in front of you, straitjacketing your creativity and restricting your freedom to choose in the moment. At first, this change feels refreshing and powerful—you're finally moving directly towards a goal. You're creating, implementing, and, best of all, concluding projects. This hasn't happened in years, and so it must have been the right choice, right?

You've empowered structure at the expense of your gifts rather than in partnership with them.

Except—you've empowered structure at the expense of your gifts rather than in partnership with them. It's only a matter of time before you yearn for the full expression of your gift. This path goes one of two ways: You either clamp down harder, fearful of giving up what feels like progress, or you swing to the other extreme, returning to the wild freedom of reckless creativity.

Under-Expressing: *Narrow-Minded Drone*

Having learned that your Creation is dangerous and undisciplined, you box it in, resigning yourself to a life of structured predictability. You feel bored and hemmed in by your narrow scope, missing the experience of your full expression, but at least you don't create the reckless results you once did.

This feels like a relief, but, over time, you feel increasingly that you have so much more to express and give. The absence of imagination and scope in those you work with compounds this feeling, and before you know it, you crescendo in anger before collapsing back in on yourself and returning to default.

In this place of resigned default, it becomes easier to judge other people for their unwillingness to step into true Creation than it is to take this on in your own life. When others *do* exhibit creativity, you may envy them for it, forgetting that it's a reflection of your own, truest self.

Obvious (But Ineffective) Fix: Become a Bull in a China Shop

Fed up with the rigidity you've imposed on yourself, you cut loose and aim toward full-on Creation mode. The creativity that has been held in check for so long is suddenly released and you feel its manic pull. Rejecting all structure, you reclaim your freedom and creativity—while simultaneously watching your former purpose and direction vaporize.

For a while, like all obvious fixes, it feels great. Finally, you're able to express yourself truthfully and honestly and you feel free for the first time in ages. But, over time, that freedom becomes an illusion. The mania that accompanies your relationship to Creation ends up leading to it feeling like a burden. You're free while you're creating, sort of, but exhausted and drained at the end of your long spells of trying to get everything handled. Further, without any more structure, it's only a matter of time before you discover that things just don't seem to get done like they used to.

COMMON SHADOW ASPECTS:

- Unmanned Firehose
- Narrow-Minded Drone

Creating the Breakthrough

Your breakthrough generally begins by coming to terms with the fact that you have an infinite capacity to create but a finite capacity to manifest your creations. In coming to terms with this, you find powerful medicine in the adage that you can have anything you want, just not all at once.

The shadows of Creation are often geared towards avoiding the need to *choose*. By saying yes to one thing, you say no to so many others, which may be lost forever. But this is like fearing that if you don't put your attention on the next star that appears in the sky, you will run out of stars to look at. Your capacity for Creation is infinite—there is no running out.

Yes, you may forget the idea that just popped into your head, and it may be a good one, but there is an infinite number of good ideas behind that one. In accepting that you will not run out of ideas and that you need to choose and focus on a small handful at a time, you relax into your innate way of showing up in the world, creating an empowered relationship with structure and choice.

The energy of Creation is chaotic—wild, magical, seductive, powerful, and sometimes destructive. By integrating structure, you bring yourself into balance and harness the full, focused power of your creative nature.

Watch out for a tendency to adopt multiple forms of structure simultaneously—wanting to try *all of them, right now.* Instead, choose one, integrate it patiently, and let that be sufficient for now. You have a lifetime of good work in front of you and an infinite number of possibilities from which to choose. The real work for you is in the choosing.

Leading and Working with People of Creation

Members of your team who possess Creation will be an incredible source of ideas and brainstorms. You almost can't stop them once they get started. They will be drawn towards blue-sky thinking and initiating new projects. This is where they're most comfortable—launching a process, then moving on to the next when they formulate a new idea.

If you only cared about slotting people into the positions they're best suited for, you could put your Creation employees in roles that don't demand much in terms of implementation—ideas people, networking roles, etc. However, it's worth taking a moment here to remind yourself that good leaders develop leadership skills in everyone. Sooner or later, your team members with the quality of Creation will be ready to step up to a higher level of leadership, bringing their existing skills with them.

This means inviting them to develop a healthier relationship to structure and taking projects all the way to conclusion. These team members will resist and drag their feet because it's what they know to do. Rather than imposing structure yourself—which is tempting but may tilt them into resistance and feeling victimized—your job is to walk beside them, staying in connection as they learn to identify and overcome their shadows. What will support them in taking this project all the way through? What might they need to let go of to have this one initiative be their focus?

Creation

COMMON SHADOW ASPECTS:

- Unmanned Firehose
- Narrow-Minded Drone

One of the challenges with Creation is that something "better" is always coming along.

Practises

Take on choice as a daily practise.

So many breakthroughs for Creation can be created by developing the practise of choosing. Practise by deciding what you will eat for breakfast, lunch, and dinner at the start of the week, and then stick with it. Notice what your resistance looks like, and when your desire to jump to something new comes up. Make it a practise to honor the choice you've made.

Practise working with the muscle of commitment.

One of the challenges with Creation is that something "better" is always coming along. Recognize that it may not actually be better. It may just look that way because implementing your current project has become a little challenging. A bright and shiny new idea that you don't (at least for the moment) see any challenges with is more attractive, and, suddenly, you feel stifled by the current project.

Choose your projects carefully, anticipate that some challenges always emerge, and commit to taking them through to completion. Get support from people who can practise with you and talk to them when you notice a desire to bail out in favour of a new commitment.

Take on projects that drive up your shadow aspects.

Your experience of straitjacketing yourself is not something to be avoided—rather, it's the needle of your compass, pointing you towards greater possibility. Recognize that your shadow tendencies are not conducive to breakthrough. Rather, their appearance is how you know you're on the right path, and where your work as a leader lies.

Creation

COMMON SHADOW ASPECTS:

- Unmanned Firehose
- Narrow-Minded Drone

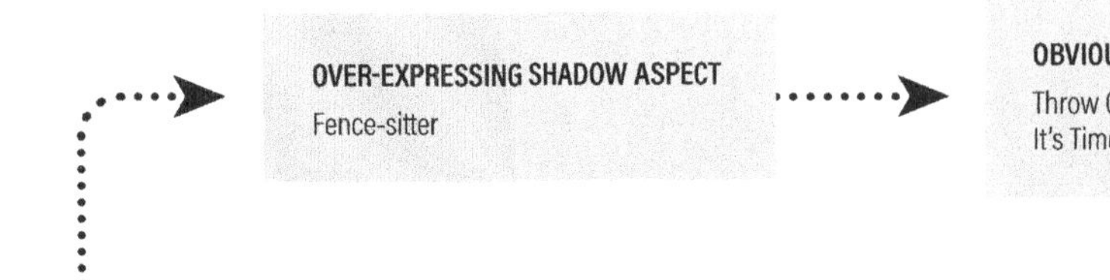

OVER-EXPRESSING SHADOW ASPECT
Fence-sitter

OBVIOUS (BUT INEFFECTIVE) FIX
Throw Curiosity Out the Window—
It's Time To Make Things Happen

Curiosity

UNDER-EXPRESSING SHADOW ASPECT
Rigidly Following Rules

OBVIOUS (BUT INEFFECTIVE) FIX
Slow Down; Let's Just Chill Out Here

COMMON DESCRIPTORS

Inquisitive, Interested, Fascinated, Intrigued, Inquiring, In Awe, Seeker, Childlike, Engaged, Entranced, Captivated, Deep-Diver, Want to Know How Things Work

The Quality

Curiosity

COMMON SHADOW ASPECTS:

- Fence-sitter
- Rigidly Following Rules

Your Gift

You are the gift of innate Curiosity. A sibling to those with the trait of Wonder, you are deeply fascinated by existence itself. No rabbit hole is without interest. You are inspired and amazed not just by the facts you uncover but by the journey of discovery itself.

People become more curious in your presence, and projects unfold with a greater degree of perspective and exploration. Curiosity provides a reprieve in the face of pressure, leading you off on tangents that might seem frivolous at first but in the end open up new avenues and resolutions that might otherwise have been stepped over.

Your gift expands permission. You ask questions with the same transparent lack of judgment that children do; you're curious for the sake of being curious. This makes you a desirable conversation partner, endlessly fascinated about everything the person in front of you is willing to share, leaving them with the feeling that they are intriguing and special. You also show up as humble, in a positive sense, because you understand better than most that the "obvious right answer" is sometimes just a small fraction of the picture.

What is Predictable

Fascinated by the simple joy of exploring the world at large, your parents, teachers, and guardians may have gotten fed up with you and insisted you act now.

Growing up, you likely received training that your innate Curiosity was problematic and cost you opportunities. As you would get fascinated in the simple joy of exploring the world at large, your parents, teachers, and guardians may have gotten fed up with you and insisted you act now, or simply taken the decision out of your hands.

As a result, your Curiosity predictably becomes a double-edged sword, cutting you both ways. At times, your decision-making becomes swift, rigid, and almost impulsive, attempting to cut your Curiosity off at the knees. This prevents you from getting lost in the details and ensures that life doesn't pass you by but at times leaves you feeling like you're making hasty decisions and losing out on the joy of exploration.

At other times, you feel fed up with the rigidity that the world seems to demand in order to move forward, and instead eschew decision-making in favour of exploring the full depths of your Curiosity. In these situations, you resist any decisiveness and instead spend hours and hours in the exploration of whatever is currently in front of you.

Because of these two poles of your shadow, you and your leadership predictably swing back and forth between impulsive, rigid expectations, and decision-making and long bouts of inactivity and unreliable deadlines.

What is Possible

The marshmallow tower is a test where groups of people are given a number of dried sticks of spaghetti, marshmallows, string, and tape and instructed to build the tallest tower.

On this test, children invariably build the highest tower because they are unaware of what they "should" do. Instead, they simply explore—take action, see what works, and grow from there.

This childlike freedom to explore and adapt as you go is the possibility you embody. You bring with you the opportunity for all of us to release our expectations of how things *should* unfold, and instead, trust where our natural curiosity will take us.

Part of your work is to trust both your natural Curiosity and that you don't know how things are supposed to unfold. By empowering deadlines, declarations, and commitments, you create a safe space in which you can explore with your natural childlike wonder, and then decide with what you've gained.

As you practise this, you will start to become attuned to the satiation of your Curiosity. You start to learn when you feel satisfied, and heed this feeling—rather than the insistent fear that you've taken too long or haven't taken long enough. From here, the next step simply becomes known and you are able to move forward—with freedom and ease.

Letting go of using Curiosity as a way to ensure you have the *right* answer frees you up to be delighted both by the process of exploration as well as making decisions and stepping into the unknown. Being in your presence, people rediscover their innate Curiosity, remembering what it was like to be a child. You are the thrill of childlike discovery.

COMMON SHADOW ASPECTS:

- Fence-sitter
- Rigidly Following Rules

Common Experience Coming of Age

Growing up, you were probably told to get your head out of the clouds and stop daydreaming. While you were lost in fascination with how a fly can land on the ceiling (upside down!), your teachers, parents, and peers saw you as distracted and oblivious. Discouraged, you began to see your natural Curiosity as a problem and disowned it in favour of being seen as dependable and getting the job done.

Or you may have found safety in being ever more Curious about the correct answer. In going deep, you were able to, at least early on, find the right answer and avoid punishment, ridicule, and shame for having the wrong one.

In leadership, there is only the answer you arrive at, and then what you choose to do from there.

Consequences of Owning Your Gifts

When you embrace your Curiosity, the world around you may get fed up with waiting and insist that you come up with the answer now. That you relish gathering all the data available before deciding is increasingly seen as a weakness. Everyone else is just ready to move on.

Shadow Aspects

Over-Expressing: *Fence-sitter*

Because getting an answer wrong made you feel foolish, you spend forever and then some looking for the right answer. It's more comfortable to hover in inquiry than to be decisive and make a choice.

The impact of the training you received growing up was that Curiosity was not something to be appreciated for itself, but rather became a means to an end—and that end was getting the *right* answer.

Alas, there is never truly a right answer. In truth, especially in leadership, there is only the answer you arrive at, and then what you choose to do from there. By seeking a right answer, your Curiosity becomes tainted. It stops being a simple expression of who you are and instead becomes a desperate search to avoid being wrong.

You lean ever more fully on this aspect of your being as a crutch. In doing so, you lose the gift of your innate Curiosity for its own sake—every decision requires more and more time, energy, and effort.

As time wears on, simpler decisions seem to take forever. You remember the freedom you used to feel and wonder when it was replaced with the heavy burden of making the right choice.

Obvious (But Ineffective) Fix: Throw Curiosity Out the Window—It's Time To Make Things Happen

Frustrated with an inability to make decisions, you decide to play big and swing for the fences, making decisions aggressively and without any deliberation. This fix plays out in a couple of ways.

In the first, you take these big swings when it's safe and unlikely to cause change. On the surface, this feels like you're doing something differently, but underneath, your being hasn't changed. You're still someone who avoids getting things wrong, you've simply changed how that's being expressed. Alternatively, you throw Curiosity (and caution) to the wind in areas where the impact is dramatic. The short-term impact is that you escape idle Curiosity and analysis paralysis.

This is exhilarating at first, but then the kind of results you fear blow up in your face—hastily-made and sometimes flat wrong decisions turn out badly. Over time, this just proves to you that ditching Curiosity is a dangerous approach, and so you go back to the devil you know. Sitting on the fence is a better way to go.

Curiosity

COMMON SHADOW ASPECTS:

- Fence-sitter
- Rigidly Following Rules

Under-Expressing: *Rigidly Following Rules*

In the spaces where you've been trained out of your Curiosity (because it slows things down), you rigidly follow the rules and go with the *correct* way to do things. This shadow aspect evolves out of the belief that your Curiosity cannot be trusted. If you give yourself full rein to explore the possibilities in front of you, you'll become lost and lose sight of what matters. Curiosity may be a nice thing to indulge in from time to time, but it won't solve the problem.

Consequently, there's rarely time or space to explore things with Curiosity. You shut that part of yourself down, regardless of what would best serve the moment. This leaves you feeling dead inside, trapped in a life that is dull and predictable. But at least you don't get lost down any rabbit holes—everything is laid out and has its path predetermined.

In the spaces where you've been trained out of your Curiosity (because it slows things down), you rigidly follow the rules and go with the correct way to do things.

You become masterful at analyzing and applying rules, and build a career out of doing so, but you sometimes feel wistful. Where did your Curiosity go, and why does life feel so flat without it?

Obvious (But Ineffective) Fix: Slow Down; Let's Just Chill Out Here

Foregoing exploration has led to a life that feels arbitrary, chosen quickly, and without much color to it. Your rigid decision-making has left you feeling dead inside, so you renounce rigidity and reintroduce color to your life, giving yourself time to be Curious about your decisions.

The environment around you—especially in the realm of your career—is actively hostile to this approach (because you've created it that way), and so you find places where it's safe to be deliberate and take your time. It feels good at first (you're doing something different!), but because you're making these changes only when it's safe, you create a half-measure of change at best.

The polarized nature of our shadows is a function of pitting two different experiences or types of results against each other. You trade in the ability to move forwards consistently for the freedom and ease that comes from innocent exploration.

You ponder and explore every angle of every decision that comes before you, finding joy in the journey of exploration, but in doing so, you forego the ability to move forwards with purpose and direction. Is there no happy medium? No bridge between endless exploration and rigid adherence to what must be done?

Creating the Breakthrough

Curiosity

COMMON SHADOW ASPECTS:

- Fence-sitter
- Rigidly Following Rules

Your shadows are often designed to create safety from the risk of your two fears: Being hemmed in (rigidity and linearity) and being diffuse and distracted. Being rigid and linear is the fear of losing the richness of your innate love of discovery and instead marching in lockstep along a particular path. Being diffuse and distracted is the fear of losing sight of the "real" world around you and getting endlessly caught up in the infinite realm of mind and thought.

Your breakthroughs often lie in a willingness to come to terms with the fact that you will always see more doors open than you can go through, regardless of which one you choose today—and to start making decisions and choices without forgetting that Curiosity is available at any moment you feel you need it.

There is no such thing as making the *right* decision—only a decision to be made, and then deciding what to do from there. By allowing yourself to narrow your options, you discover that life is fractal and abundant. (Consider the vast difference between knowing this fact intellectually and embodying it through your actions). It is almost impossible to truly shut yourself off from Choice. When you let go of needing to protect yourself from it, freedom abounds.

Trust the feeling that you've reached a conclusion.

Your biggest breakthroughs come when you're willing to give yourself the gift of spaciousness around a given decision, and to trust the feeling that you've reached a conclusion. Because of your training and shadow aspects, your default tendency is to rush through Curiosity, not trusting yourself (or even being able to tell) when you actually reach at a conclusion.

There is no such thing as making the right decision—only a decision to be made, and then deciding what to do from there.

Practise trusting your intuition. Let yourself feel what there is to feel and give yourself time and space to explore your options. Then listen for the voice, feeling, or intuitive hit that tells you "Hey, I've done enough exploring for now."

Leading and Working with People of Curiosity

First and most importantly, notice how your tendencies, beliefs, and contexts around timely decision-making show up for you in a leadership role. If you feel overwhelming urgency when it comes to making decisions, you'll probably push your Curiosity-type people into their rigid and linear aspect. This will appease your urgent need for quick decision-making but stymie their development as leaders.

On the flip side, if you struggle with making decisions, you'll be prone to encouraging the over-expressing aspect of Curiosity's shadow. Their tendency to overanalyze and get lost exploring every possible avenue will appease your need to avoid making the wrong decision. Make sure you are held by your coach or leader and stand for the breakthroughs available to these particular people on your team. Support them in making declarations, decisions, and commitments.

A declaration is a commitment to move something forwards by a certain date. A "what" by "when."

What will you have accomplished, and by *when* will you have accomplished it?

In calling forth declarations from your team members, support them to get beyond finding the "right" answer and support their putting a limit on how long to remain in Curiosity.

The natural way we falter when making a declaration is to say, "I can't give you a declaration until I've done more research." This is usually Curiosity's shadow aspect trying to avoid being hemmed in. A dialog that can move your team forwards might look something like this:

"When will you be ready to make a decision?"

"Well, I need to do more research before I can tell you that."

"I have a sense that might go on longer than is appropriate to the project. By when will you commit to making a decision?"

"Ugh! A week?"

"Great, I'll expect it by then. Thank you."

Your job does not end at this point in the conversation. You must now not only stand for your report to honor their declaration, but also for them to be in the practise of making decisions rather than making the *right* decisions. If you are in the subconscious tendency of blaming them when their decision didn't go the way you thought it should, you will naturally polarize them out further towards their shadows. Instead, celebrate that they made a choice and ask them what they can see from this side of the choice.

Curiosity

COMMON SHADOW ASPECTS:

- Fence-sitter
- Rigidly Following Rules

Practises

Make declarations and practise leaning into them.

The paradox is that commitment (which is ultimately what a declaration is) provides you with greater rather than reduced freedom. Challenge the myth that setting deadlines for yourself restricts your creativity and honor your own deadlines.

Making a declaration provides its own challenge for people of Curiosity, as you try to cram in more and more exploration to get the "right" amount done before it's too late. Instead, practise making your declaration, setting the deadline, then trusting your natural process of exploration. Be willing to trust that you've done enough. If you haven't, then great—you've learned something new for next time and will make a better declaration then.

The paradox is that commitment (which is ultimately what a declaration is) provides you with greater rather than reduced freedom.

Practise embodying your innate Curiosity before and after making decisions.

Get curious about the decision in front of you and then practise being curious about how it played out and what there might be to learn from it.

Remember that there is no such thing as the "right" choice. There is simply a choice to be made and then how you choose to *be* on the heels of that choice. Rather than getting stuck on making the right choice, practise being in the act of *choosing*, over and over again. Then, notice where it's led you, and choose what's next from there.

Notice where you get linear and rigid in your decision-making.

Where do you resist embodying your innate Curiosity? When you catch this, ask yourself what you are afraid of. What are you resisting? What are you worried will happen if you choose back into Curiosity at this moment? For bonus points, practise leaning more deeply into that fear.

COMMON SHADOW ASPECTS:

- Fence-sitter
- Rigidly Following Rules

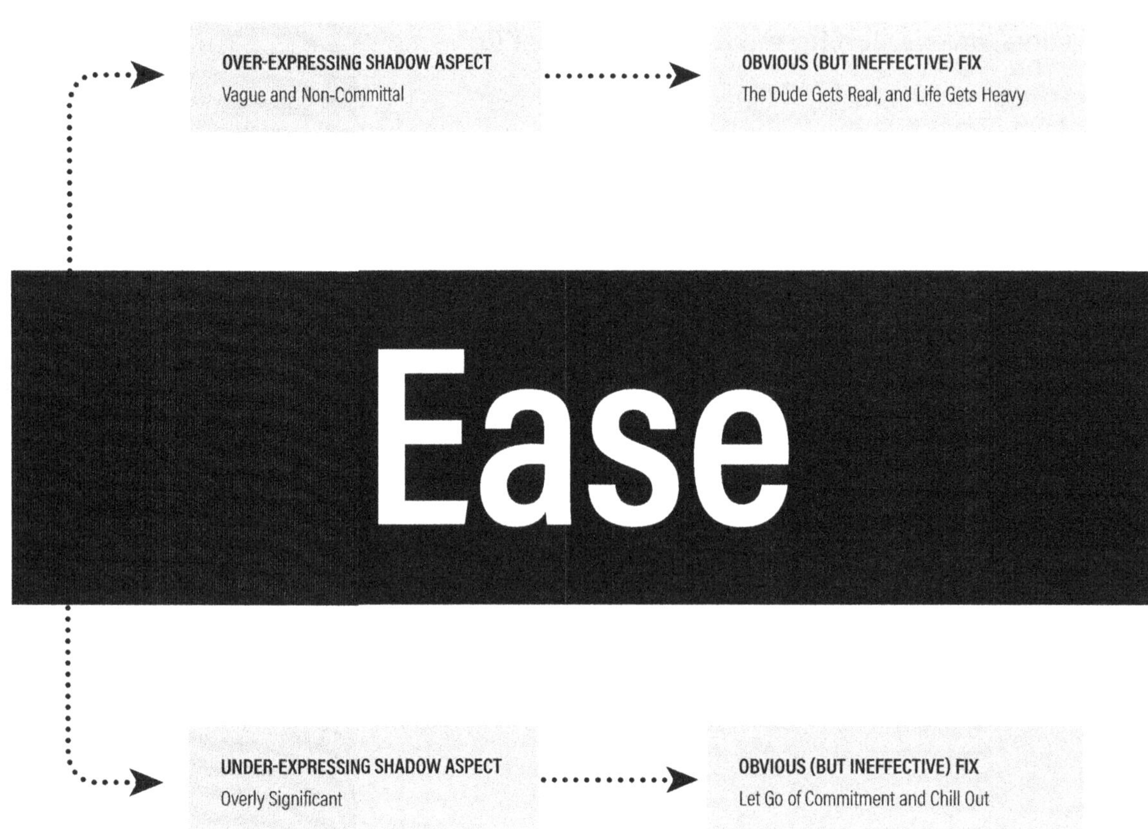
OVER-EXPRESSING SHADOW ASPECT
Vague and Non-Committal
OBVIOUS (BUT INEFFECTIVE) FIX
The Dude Gets Real, and Life Gets Heavy
Ease
UNDER-EXPRESSING SHADOW ASPECT
Overly Significant
OBVIOUS (BUT INEFFECTIVE) FIX
Let Go of Commitment and Chill Out

COMMON DESCRIPTORS

Effortless, Easy, Peaceful, Relaxed, Chill, Simple, No Worries, Informal, Lack of Pretence, Nonchalant, Casual, Laidback, Content, Comfortable

The Quality

Ease

COMMON SHADOW ASPECTS:

- Vague and Non-Committal
- Overly Significant

Your Gift

It all comes easily to you. You are the gift of life being effortless. In your presence, people wonder what they were so worried about. It just all kind of comes together, man. At times you confound others, leaving them wondering why you don't seem to share the struggles they do. When we spend time with you, we are reminded of the gift that is existence and can simply revel in the flow of life.

You embody the concept of flow. Trusting that whatever shows up is divinely inspired and all you have to do is "go with it," you navigate life like it's a dance. Whether it's a change in the weather, obstacles you hadn't foreseen, or emotions you weren't planning to stumble upon, you welcome all of life.

This quality of Ease is a true gift on projects, especially those with a lot riding on them (which usually means a lot of accompanying fear, at least for most people). Your ability to bring a lighter touch allows people to go after goals that really matter without the usual angst and struggle.

You align naturally with leaders who bring directive energy like Drive, Commitment, or Purpose, creating a beautiful partnership that marries determination with effortlessness and flow. Ultimately, your path is to create this same marriage of qualities within yourself.

In your presence, people wonder what they were so worried about.

Those with Ease may have an interesting relationship to their anger—the emotion which, paradoxically, makes them feel ill at ease. Part of their journey is to unfold into precisely those uneasy places, to be with that discomfort long enough to understand what lies beneath it.

What is Predictable

You may come to believe that Ease is not something innate to you but a product of your environment. You avoid people and situations that challenge your Ease and slowly but surely limit your opportunities to those with the lowest potential for disruption.

This becomes a game of actively limiting your circumstances to ensure that nothing intrudes on the flow you relish. Ease remains available but feels increasingly tentative, requiring a high degree of management and protection to maintain. You find yourself saying no over and over again.

In other places, you may get feedback that you're just too chill, lack seriousness, and dodge important decisions. In these areas, you relate to your Ease as a problem, and so you swing to the other extreme. You get serious and heavy, feeling the burden of every decision. Yes, there's a natural life flow *over there*, but right here and now we've got shit that needs to be done, and it is *significant*, dammit!

Life tends to vacillate between ease and flow on one hand and burden and significance on the other, depending on your circumstances. Neither end of the pendulum swing is a comfortable place to be.

What is Possible

When you eventually come to terms with the truth that your sense of Ease (or lack thereof) is ultimately generated from within, you realize that Ease is available in every moment, regardless of the circumstances.

You become the kind of leader who can take people into the most anxiety-producing situations and help them unfold into the divine serenity that is.

You recognize that when you feel overwhelm and burden, these are the milestones along your journey, showing up to provide you insight into new places you've been reluctant to explore, surrender and open.

Your work becomes a willingness to plunge into the dark, scary unknown, to be with the heavy significance that comes up, and to find ways to embody your innate Ease in these situations. This kind of work feels counter-intuitive at first. You're going against your natural grain, leaning into projects that generate *less* Ease rather than more. But as you do so, sitting with your overwhelm rather than trying to escape it, you begin to accept this as a normal response.

As you open a clearing for your own overwhelm and burden, you allow others to do the same. In this way, you become like yoga for the being—a simple, profound unfolding deeper into ourselves, regardless of the moment, the circumstances, or surroundings.

COMMON SHADOW ASPECTS:

- Vague and Non-Committal
- Overly Significant

Common Experience Coming of Age

Growing up, some people might have related to your natural state of Ease as a sign of indifference. They thought you were too cool for school and needed to "get serious, for once." You may have been labelled as "distracted," only to surprise people later with everything you retained.

Consequences of Owning Your Gifts

As you embody your innate Ease, some people enjoy you for who you are, but others criticize or are frustrated by how you never seem to struggle. They project their meaning onto your experience, deciding you're lackadaisical and lazy and just don't care about what happens.

Shadow Aspects

Over-Expressing: *Vague and Non-Committal*

When you eventually come to terms with the truth that your sense of Ease (or lack thereof) is ultimately generated from within, you realize that Ease is available in every moment.

Because getting too invested in something threatens your Ease, you become "The Dude," unflappable in your ironic detachment. You ease back on the couch, put your hands behind your head, and stop caring.

Creating an impact in the world sounds great but isn't worth the effort. It's your life and you get to choose how you live it, right? You abide, and it's all good.

This doesn't mean you don't have goals or desires. You may talk at length about your desire to create a company where everyone is paid fairly and social change is created, but you're more comfortable making this kind of vague sketch for the future than you are making a bold declaration of commitment. You shy away from saying that in two years your company will have revenues of three million and thirty employees.

You have your freedom, but you are largely irrelevant. Life is easy but insignificant. It's not a bad ride, but—is this all there is?

Obvious (But Ineffective) Fix: The Dude Gets Real, and Life Gets Heavy

You kick off the flip-flops, run a comb through your hair, and "get real." It's time to make shit happen! But as you pile on the decisions and commitments, everything becomes so heavy. You have completely lost the Ease that you once enjoyed and that felt so natural. And you notice that being heavy all the time wears on people. That heaviness cuts into the spontaneity and creativity that leads to breakthroughs.

You conclude it must be a lack of work-life balance. You're just overstressed. So, you throw your energy into meditation, which is helpful but chews up time. You try sound therapy and breath work. These are good too, but while they provide you moments of respite, you find yourself rushing to and from the appointments, feeling overwhelmed and overbooked. When Ease shows up, you've really had to work for it. And it's temporary, nothing like the effortlessness you remember so clearly.

You seek support from coaches, friends, and colleagues, who tell you to delegate better and stop forcing things. This tips you away from making declarations and commitments entirely, sending you to the other extreme of your shadow and sabotaging your ability to lead. You find yourself wondering if balance is even possible.

Ease

COMMON SHADOW ASPECTS:

- Vague and Non-Committal
- Overly Significant

With all of these attempted fixes, you're left continually paving over top of the underlying issue rather than really rooting it out and addressing it. The problem isn't your circumstances, or what you're doing; it's who you're being, as you show up to life.

Under-Expressing: *Overly Significant*

People have told you for so long to knuckle down and get serious that you take it to heart. You reject your natural Ease and tell yourself to man up because THE STRUGGLE IS REAL. You begin making bold declarations and commitments, which initially feels like a good thing—you've turned over a new leaf!

You kick off the flip-flops, run a comb through your hair, and "get real."

Unlike the other aspect of your shadow, you are willing to make promises, but each time you do, it lands on you like an incredible burden. You are reliable with your word and do what you say you will do, but each time you give your word, it represents another area of your life that you're already behind and must devote more of your precious resources toward.

You notice that every promise and commitment feels laden with obligation and heaviness. Your word is good, but you're falling behind, and every commitment demands more of your scarce resources. You're creating great things in the world, but at a cost you're increasingly reluctant to pay.

Obvious (But Ineffective) Fix: Let Go of Commitment and Chill Out

You've had enough of the burdensome life. It's just not who you are. It's time to just stop caring so much and let life be easy. You drop multiple projects, quit trying to force things, and stop worrying about everything so much.

Your freedom lies in the direction of the people, circumstances, and things that trigger your scarcity of Ease.

You hope that life will be amazing and wonderful and unfold beautifully—and decide that if life puts that in your path, that's what will happen. But if not, that's okay, too.

Because you're no longer willing to make commitments and push them forward, you lose the ability to stand for others to do the same. You go back to protecting the circumstantial experience of Ease that you remember. It's pleasant to no longer feel the stress and struggle that had become so painfully familiar, but you have a sense that the baby may have gone out with the bathwater. Oh, well. Maybe it's time for another White Russian.

Creating the Breakthrough

Your shadows tend to be actively engaged in either preserving ease at all costs or resigning yourself to the fact that Ease is unsafe and unobtainable. Instead, your freedom lies in the direction of the people, circumstances, and things that trigger your scarcity of Ease. Only in these places can you take on the work necessary to open up and embody the fact that you *are* Ease.

Put differently, for you to reclaim your innate Ease, you need to lean into the areas where you've learned to show up as stressed out and overburdened. Rather than avoiding the situations and circumstances that put you in a state of overwhelm and dis-ease, your path lies in realizing that *you* are the source of those symptoms. Only through a willingness to confront what triggers your overwhelm can you change the way you show up in the face of them.

You are capable of bringing Ease to any and every moment, regardless of the circumstances. When you notice Ease draining away, ask yourself, "What am I unwilling to be with right now?" and "What am I afraid of right now that has me showing up as something other than Ease?"

Leaning into the areas where Ease has always seemed to be unavailable and doing the work to rediscover your innate quality of being will change your life.

Ease

COMMON SHADOW ASPECTS:

- Vague and Non-Committal
- Overly Significant

Leading and Working with People of Ease

Members of your team with Ease will advocate for everyone's well-being and be the first to notice when things start getting overly significant. They will remind you and the rest of your team that there's enough time for everything, and we can get it all done.

If you as the leader have a bias towards hard work, intensity, and doing whatever it takes, you may clash with these members of your team. In these situations, it's especially important for you to be engaged in your own transformational work, supported by a coach or leader who can help you identify your blind spots. Absent this kind of support, you'll be unable to distinguish where your shadow ends and the shadows of those laid-back team members begin. Are they being overly protective of their Ease? Or are you pushing too hard from your own shadow, scared that things won't move forwards as quickly as they need to?

Team members with Ease may also show up as overburdened and almost breathless in their fear of being overburdened. Encourage them to slow down, breathe deeply, and simply be with whatever's showing up. There's no need to make them wrong. Remember that Ease may show up as frantic and overwhelmed when fear is on the table, and you don't need to add to their fears by making them wrong for what they're feeling.

When you feel overwhelm, rather than rushing to eliminate the cause, stay in the moment and get curious about what you're afraid of.

When operating from their shadow, Ease-type people may become unwilling to push forwards and volunteer much in terms of acting. You can support these people by inviting them to make declarations and express their opinions and stand behind what they declare. Help them slow down and breathe in the face of their overwhelm while continuing forward.

It is predictable that they will run into overwhelm when you stand for their leadership this way, and so you must remember that this is a predictable part of the pattern and the next stage of their leadership.

Remember that there is nothing wrong with the approach Ease's shadow takes of sitting back and letting life happens as it does—it's just in the way of their leadership. Stand for the leadership of those you lead and invite them to choose. If they are not interested in stepping into their leadership this way, then your job is to accept that and plan accordingly (possibly by shifting them to a different position, rearranging teams, etc.)

Practises

Audit the things in your life that lead you to feel overwhelmed and frantic.

These are typically the places where your fear has been aroused in some way. They are also the areas you will predictably look to cut away from your life in an attempt to rediscover Ease.

Get curious about what you're afraid of.

When you feel overwhelm, rather than rushing to eliminate the cause, stay in the moment and get curious about what you're afraid of. What is the specific fear that's coming up, and what's the worst-case scenario associated with that fear? How are you adding significance to, trying to manage, or compensating for that fear?

Lean into the overwhelm, significance and franticness.

Your overwhelm and franticness are your compasses. They arise when you take on something that really matters. What would be needed from you to feel Ease *without* changing your circumstances? This kind of inquiry will open the door for you to experience Ease continually and throughout life, regardless of what comes up.

Notice your resistance to making declarations about the future.

Notice the areas where you are unwilling to make declarations about the future. Where do you tend to avoid making commitments that you could be held to? Because fear and possibility show up in equal countermeasure, remember that

COMMON SHADOW ASPECTS:

- Vague and Non-Committal
- Overly Significant

your fear indicates the possibility of transformation available down these particular avenues.

Practise making declarations on a gradient.

If you're unwilling to commit to achieving big results a year from now, commit to something achievable within a month. If that's too frightening, practise with a week. There is no right declaration or commitment, but you'll know you're at your growth edge when your declaration triggers some degree of fear but doesn't become overwhelming or destroy your Ease entirely. Over time, you will be able to feel and radiate Ease while taking on bigger and bigger commitments.

Ease

COMMON SHADOW ASPECTS:

- Vague and Non-Committal
- Overly Significant

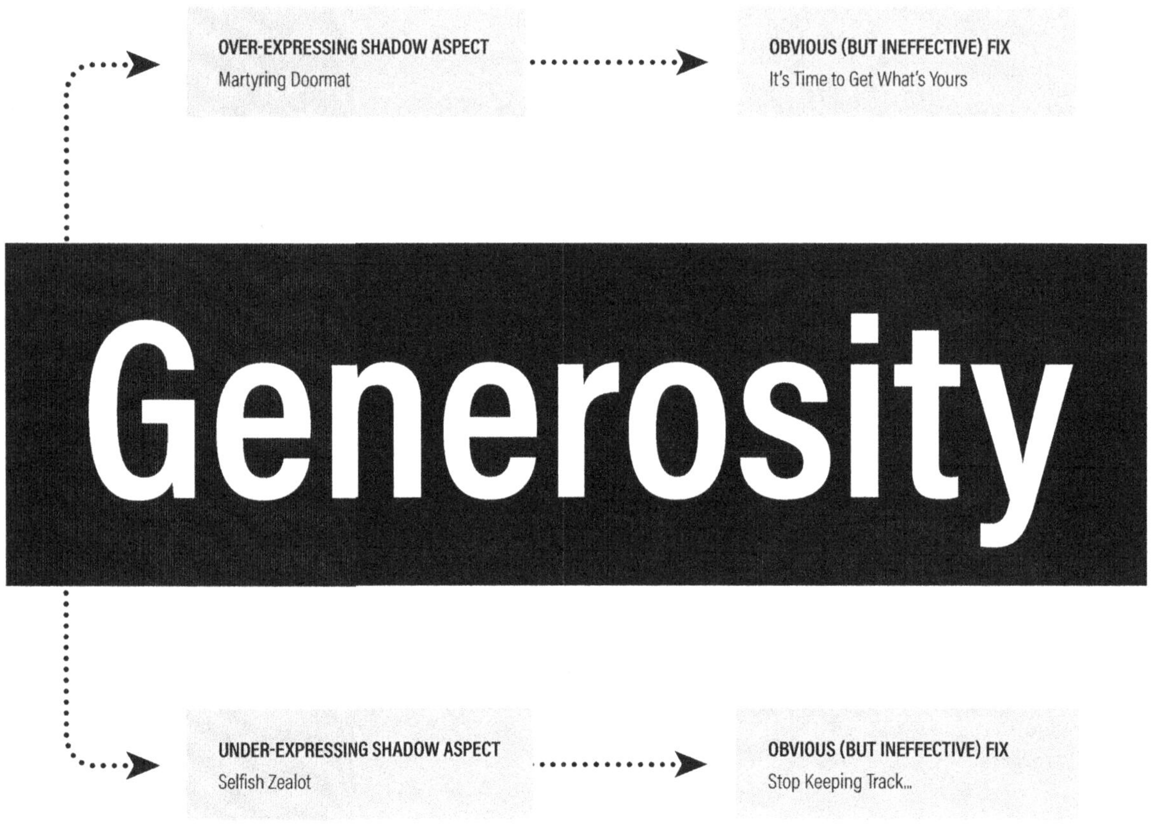

OVER-EXPRESSING SHADOW ASPECT
Martyring Doormat

OBVIOUS (BUT INEFFECTIVE) FIX
It's Time to Get What's Yours

Generosity

UNDER-EXPRESSING SHADOW ASPECT
Selfish Zealot

OBVIOUS (BUT INEFFECTIVE) FIX
Stop Keeping Track...

COMMON DESCRIPTORS

Magnanimous, Giving, Benevolent, Altruistic, Charitable, Bighearted, Abundance, Considerate, Decency, Philanthropic, Contribution

The Quality

Your Gift

You embody the trait of Generosity. It's not that the things you *do* are generous (even though they are), it's that everything about how you show up is a natural expression of Generosity. You would never think of arriving at a party or someone's house without bringing a gift. You would never receive a gift without thanking the person who sent it. This isn't about obeying the rules of etiquette or displaying "good manners." You may have been raised this way, but one or both of your parents probably also embodied Generosity and modelled its expression.

You are naturally drawn to causes to support those who have less and to stimulate welcome and warmth in those around you. Charity, volunteerism, and social work are in your wheelhouse. You may go into healthcare, fundraising, missionary work, or other vocations that provide regular opportunities to devote yourself to helping others.

You are a welcome addition to any event, ensuring that everyone gets an opportunity to take part and feel like they matter. Rarely if ever would you snatch the last piece of pizza, the toy that everyone wants, or the last seat available. You're naturally committed to making sure there's enough to go around. There's no need for racing to the bottom or clutching at what we decide we own. The spaces you join inevitably experience a greater degree of sharing, communal ownership, and shared purpose.

COMMON SHADOW ASPECTS:

- Martyring Doormat
- Selfish Zealot

You are a welcome addition to any event, ensuring that everyone gets an opportunity to take part and feel like they matter.

What is Predictable

Over time, your natural Generosity may start to wear thin as you notice that the world routinely fails to reciprocate. People are quick to thank you for your gift, because doing so is polite (and easy), but where are they when the chips are down? How come the same invitation doesn't come back your way when they're doing things? Why aren't they bringing you gifts when you invite them over?

Generosity becomes less a choice and more of an obligation, one that often feels unfair. Inevitably, a feeling of resentment seeps into your internal dialogue. People begin to sense that your kindness and consideration aren't just a beautiful gift but something of a quid pro quo. You're setting a standard they may not be want to or be able to match—it's just not who they are. Eventually, they either push back or pull away, leaving you in an almost toxic state of judgment.

At that point, you may go one of two ways. Despite the pain you feel at people's failure to reciprocate, you are *more* painfully aware of the immense suffering and inequality in the world. You just *have to* try harder to help, and so you do, turning your natural Generosity into an insatiable drive. People in need are a karmic debt imposed on your soul, and you throw yourself into paying off that debt as the only thing that matters.

At the other extreme, you end up tired and resentful from helping everyone without it being reciprocated. You turn your back on the demands of the world and look to your own interests. Ironically while who you are at your core is Generosity, this extreme creates the opposite impact—you, and others, are left feeling like you are selfish.

What is Possible

When you do the internal work to release your Generosity from being an obligation—allowing it to become present all the time—you also release your need for people to reciprocate in a particular way. Internally, you become able to see how they are already generous, regardless of whether it matches your expectations.

As a result, spending time with you unlocks something within each of us, leaving us with an internal desire to give just a little bit more of ourselves and our heart that we previously felt.

Conversations about selfishness fall away—you are no longer burdened by your giving, nor is anyone else around you. Generosity no longer drains you and instead becomes effortless. Giving gifts just feels good, and you do it for that reason, letting go of the need to keep score or get something in return.

You teach us the experience of living a life where Generosity is an end unto itself, and requires no repayment.

COMMON SHADOW ASPECTS:

- Martyring Doormat
- Selfish Zealot

Common Experience Coming of Age

Growing up, you were raw to the cruelty and unfairness around you. As a coping strategy, you developed a powerful bias towards fairness. You learn that it's easier to try and give to people in the hopes that they will reciprocate rather than asking for what you want.

Consequences of Owning Your Gifts

Your innate Generosity doesn't seem to inspire similar behaviour in others, at least not often enough. You give and give, setting a good example, and yet so many people just take and take without a second thought. When you finally ask to have your own needs met, some people call you demanding or selfish—your worst nightmare.

You teach us the experience of living a life where Generosity is an end unto itself.

Shadow Aspects

Over-Expressing: *Martyring Doormat*

Your horror of being seen as selfish leads you into Generosity overdrive. In order to avoid the fear of being seen as, experienced as, or actually *being* selfish, you give, give, and give away everything to everyone.

But this is a setup for you and those you give to. Your Generosity ends up having a hidden agenda—hidden from both yourself and others.

First, by giving to everyone else, there is no way in which your fear of being selfish can be realized. By ensuring that you always give more than you want to, you can effectively manage your allergy to the possibility of you being selfish. In this regard, you aren't actually being generous—you're just being "not selfish."

You learn that it's easier to try and give to people in the hopes that they will reciprocate rather than asking for what you want.

Second, because asking for what you desire gets wrapped up into your fears around being selfish, giving to other people becomes a way of getting your needs met without having to ask for them. If you're willing to give to people enough, hopefully, they will eventually give back to you.

Paradoxically, when people do attempt to give back they run into your lack of ease at being on the receiving end of Generosity. It either generates feelings of guilt, prompting you to take back the lead in a Generosity race, or it's like water in a desert—never enough. Either way, you cannot ask for what you desire cleanly.

Obvious (But Ineffective) Fix: It's Time to Get What's Yours

Tired of feeling used, you decide it's your turn to be selfish. You draw rigid boundaries around what you will give and not give and tell yourself you don't care what other people think.

Because you've reduced the spacious nature of Generosity to the mechanical act of giving, you no longer see that Generosity can be expressed in how we receive something, how we share with others, or how we allow others to share with us.

What's most problematic with this strategy is that it creates obstacles—judgment and boundaries—between you and simply sharing your desires with people and letting them react however they do. Everything needs to be justified and scored against the karmic account, which leads you, perversely, into being generous when you don't want to and withholding Generosity when you most want to let it flow.

Ultimately, you finally start getting some of your needs met, but at the cost of becoming what you most hate. You know there must be some kind of balance available, but it seems to perpetually elude you.

COMMON SHADOW ASPECTS:

- Martyring Doormat
- Selfish Zealot

Under-Expressing: *Selfish Zealot*

The world is unfair, pure and simple, and you resign yourself to the "truth" that no one will ever live up to your standards. Ruthlessly on guard against unfairness, you become increasingly insistent that people follow a complicated set of fairness rules, and you fixate on guarding your resources, time, and energy.

As long as you are being fair by your own rules, you can rest assured that you're not a selfish person. Those rules about what's fair and unfair become the guide for how you interact with and frequently judge others.

This shadow aspect, ironically, can express itself as quite selfish. Your complicated set of fairness rules make sense to you, but the rest of the world notices that you guard, snatch, and take for yourself in ways they don't understand.

Tracking your social interactions carefully, you act out in a way that seems selfish to others but justified to you, because of how things went four months ago when you last ran into this person. The rest of the world wonders why you shifted so far away from Generosity. In moments of clarity, you find yourself wondering the same thing.

Obvious (But Ineffective) Fix: Stop Keeping Track...

Exhausted by the burden of judging others (and yourself) for being selfish, you let go of fairness and try to simply dwell in Generosity. In the hopes that it will alleviate some of the guilt you feel you've been managing, you decide to stop keeping track and instead simply give to everyone.

Giving to other people becomes a way of getting your needs met without having to ask for them.

Because every deliberate shift like this is novel for a while, it feels like positive change and people may experience you differently. Unfortunately, this tilts you towards the doormat aspect of your shadow, which is unsustainable. You can only give freely for so long before you start to feel slighted and taken advantage of.

When you double down on this approach, your needs—rather than being expressed naturally—morph into gigantic blind spots. You believe that you've ruled out judgment and resentment, but people get a subtle feeling that your smile harbours something nasty underneath.

Creating the Breakthrough

Your protective mechanisms are designed to avoid the appearance of selfishness. The dance of Generosity's shadow aspects begins when you equate asking for what you want with being greedy or selfish. The breakthrough often begins by coming to terms with the fact that to want something and ask for it—cleanly, with no quid pro quo—is an expression of Generosity in and of itself. In acknowledging your desires and asking to have them met, you give people the gift of knowing more about who you are and of being able to meet your needs gracefully and easily.

For many Generosity-type people, the work begins with simply acknowledging their desires to themselves. Having repressed them for so long, you may have forgotten you have them. This strategy allowed you to act out your Generosity without feeling selfish, but it stands in the way of a breakthrough.

Practise listening for your own needs and desires, releasing any self-judgment that comes up, and, over time, begin asking to have those needs met. Release the significance you attach to people's responses ("They're selfish," "I'm selfish," "It was wrong for me to ask," etc.). At some point, you will probably get feedback that you're being selfish. Your temptation will be to collapse in apology or to fiercely justify your request. Instead, simply receive and be with this feedback. Come to terms with the reality that as a human being you have legitimate needs and a capacity for selfishness that will show up from time to time whether you like it or not.

COMMON SHADOW ASPECTS:

- Martyring Doormat
- Selfish Zealot

The more easily you own your needs and desires, the less significant a no response becomes and the less explosively you need to assert them. It's okay to be selfish—we all are. Therein lies your breakthrough.

Leading and Working with People of Generosity

Members of your team with the gift of Generosity will be quick to pick up work, pitch in, and work long hours. Their expression of Generosity is almost by definition a willingness to give beyond their short-term capacity. These team members may create an illusion of cooperation and teamwork, but problems are brewing beneath the surface. Because they can only give for so long without becoming resentful, it's important to identify and address this tendency early.

Tracking your social interactions carefully, you act out in a way that seems selfish to others but justified to you.

Your job as a leader is to spot this pattern before it becomes toxic—to see the shadow aspect at play beneath what looks like pure Generosity. Your team members may protest when you ask them to take better care of themselves, but your job is to help them identify their full potential. That means empowering them to feel good about asking their teammates—in a generous rather than judgmental tone—to step up.

Your team members that embody the trait of Generosity will tend to support and take on the work of others as a way of avoiding what might be confronting for themselves and provide their next breakthrough in leadership.

Anticipate resistance. By inviting your Generosity-type person to stop taking on the rest of the team's work, you may seem to be messing with success, especially if the team already feels besieged and busy. And yet as a leader, a willingness to create breakdowns (at least temporarily) is the only way to create breakthroughs—not only for your generous team member but for the rest of the team.

Holding on to the short-term payoff of Generosity's shadow is unsustainable at best and a recipe for resentment and friction in the medium-to-long-term.

Ask for what you want, and notice what shows up when you do.

Practises

Notice your needs and wants when they show up.

A lifetime belief that wanting things made you selfish probably led you to hide what you want from everyone—including yourself. Practise listening for your desires and giving them internal voice. Start small: What do you want for dinner? What do you wish your life partner would do for you tonight? When you look in your closet, what do you really wish you owned? Practise patiently until you get better. You're building an important muscle.

Express your desires out loud.

Once you can voice your desires internally, start voicing them out loud. Ask for what you want and notice what shows up when you do. What thoughts, feelings, and body sensations are triggered when you make a request of someone?

Release your attachment to how you're perceived

Just because you say you want something doesn't mean you'll get it (although it goes a long way!). Notice what meaning you create around the response. Are you making it wrong that you asked? Do you see yourself as an imposition or a burden on the person? Are they right that you were selfish just for asking?

Whatever meaning you attach, practise being at ease with your wants and needs. You're doing your job by expressing them. The rest of the world gets to respond however it wants to. They can say yes and feel burdened by it. They can fulfil your request and be delighted in doing so. They can snap, "Not a chance!" or respond any way they please. Your job is simple: To ask, without attachment, for what you want.

COMMON SHADOW ASPECTS:

- Martyring Doormat
- Selfish Zealot

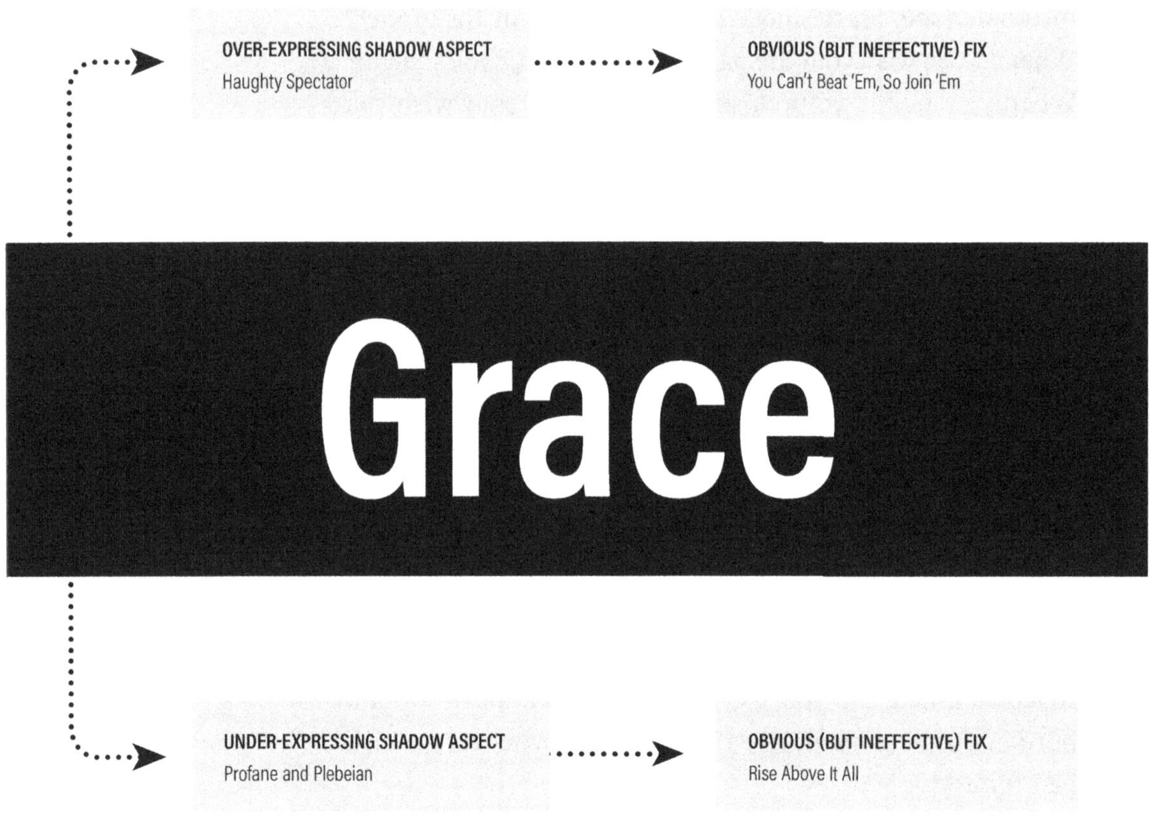

OVER-EXPRESSING SHADOW ASPECT
Haughty Spectator

OBVIOUS (BUT INEFFECTIVE) FIX
You Can't Beat 'Em, So Join 'Em

Grace

UNDER-EXPRESSING SHADOW ASPECT
Profane and Plebeian

OBVIOUS (BUT INEFFECTIVE) FIX
Rise Above It All

COMMON DESCRIPTORS

Elegance, Stylish, Poise, Finesse, Confidence, Courteous, Good Manners, Tactful, Diplomatic, Good Etiquette, Merciful, Smooth, Rise Above It

The Quality

Your Gift

Your gift is the ability to weather storms with absolute Grace. The way you carry yourself creates calm, peace, and dignity. When people are in your presence, they feel relaxed, knowing that on some level this will all work out.

You are the eye of the storm and have a remarkable capacity to be at ease with everything life throws your way. This doesn't mean you don't feel stress, anger, fear, or any other aspect of the emotional range. Rather, like a swan, you paddle invisibly below the water but glide gracefully upon it. In the face of complex challenges that might be approached in any number of ways, you have an uncanny knack for choosing the right way as if it had been obvious all along. You just seem to know how to be and what to do and take life for what it is.

We often equate Grace with nobility. Princess Diana and Nelson Mandela are beautiful examples of the quality of Grace. They hold a place in our hearts for understanding, acceptance, and tranquillity while the world rages around us.

Those with Grace often have a deep capacity for forgiveness, knowing that what shows up on the surface is not the entire picture. They see more deeply into what may have led this person to behave a certain way, and ask themselves, "How can I better hold them in this moment? How can I bring more Grace to what lies before me?"

COMMON SHADOW ASPECTS:

- Haughty Spectator
- Profane and Plebeian

You are the eye of the storm and have a remarkable capacity to be at ease with everything life throws your way.

What is Predictable

When we think of Grace, we often think of what lies on the surface and expect those with Grace to be dignified no matter what. If you possess the quality of Grace, one of your predictable paths is to be trained into this story as you grow up, believing Grace to be a function solely of how you appear to others.

You forget that true Grace might mean falling apart but doing so without awkwardness or self-consciousness. Instead, you maintain the appearance of Grace even if your underlying experience is anything but. This can lead to you coming across as haughty, indifferent, and removed from your surroundings. You avoid situations that might put your carefully cultivated Grace at risk, removing yourself from real life and deep connections with others.

Alternatively, you may decide you are simply unable to face everything life throws with Grace and give up on the possibility, showing up instead as frantic, profane, and with no awareness of the higher road that is naturally your birthright.

As time goes on, you may swing back and forth between the two, sometimes holding yourself above the awkward proletariats around you, other times becoming one of the most awkward and prone to upset of anyone. Or you show up as frantic and profane in certain areas of your life and untouchably serene in others. Both extremes leave you feeling out of balance.

What is Possible

Those with innate Grace may, ironically, have seen themselves at some point as clumsy, awkward, and completely lacking in Grace, particularly in certain situations and with certain kinds of people. Their real work begins when rather than avoiding what knocks them off balance, they shed the story that externalities are to blame. Instead, they walk courageously in all aspects of their lives including and especially those that drive them into one of Grace's shadow aspects.

The possibility of Grace fully expressed is the promise that we all hold one another with the best intentions, boundless mercy, and deep forgiveness. You carry within you the possibility of all human beings having more time, energy, and patience for themselves and the world around them.

This possibility becomes available to you when you stop avoiding situations that threaten your Grace. Leaning into such situations creates fertile ground for you to discover new places and ways to embody Grace under pressure.

COMMON SHADOW ASPECTS:

- Haughty Spectator
- Profane and Plebeian

As you do this work, you discover that Grace isn't something you need to protect but rather something accessible to you all the time. You find a deeper, more grounded version of trust in yourself and those around you. You no longer worry about making mistakes, trusting that you will embody Grace and find your way back to it no matter what happens.

Common Experience Coming of Age

A child with natural grace may be confronting for some adults, highlighting their perceived shortcomings and awkwardness. You may have been poked at or diminished by people and began to mistrust your beautiful gift. Other children may have also found you challenging to be with, unable to grasp what Grace is because they lack it themselves. You may have experienced your peers as quarrelsome, immature, and foolish, and they may have found you to be stuck up or snobby.

Consequences of Owning Your Gifts

When you show up fully, embodying elegance and dignity, the contrast with how others view themselves may leave them feeling particularly awkward and unlikable. This is especially true for others with the gift of Grace who haven't yet been able to embody their quality to the same extent. When you embody Grace rigidly, without an open and generous heart, it can leave people feeling resentful and left out in the cold.

You carry within you the possibility of all human beings having more time, energy, and patience for themselves and the world around them.

Shadow Aspects

Over-Expressing: *Haughty Spectator*

In situations where you are given the feedback that you are clumsy, oafish, aloof, or just plain not enough, you may have learned to double down on the Grace. The innate Grace you embody seems insufficient, and so you throw your effort into the appearance of your gift. No matter what's going on inside or around you, you project ease and poise.

Maintaining this facade isn't easy, and so you close down the parts of you that are vulnerable to becoming upset. This comes at the expense of your warmth, love, and ability to connect with people and the world around you but allows you to keep up the appearance of Grace.

As time goes on, you become ever more removed from reality and empathy. The trope of the dignified but steely-hearted matron is the embodiment of this shadow. You may experience yourself as graceful and dignified, but life feels cold and hard.

Obvious (But Ineffective) Fix: You Can't Beat 'Em, So Join 'Em

People respect you and hold you in high esteem, but life feels lonely and cold. You minimize those awkward human emotions to preserve your image, but as they pile up, you're left feeling inauthentic and further isolated. You want something beyond the veneer of a successful life.

Over time, you find yourself becoming angry at inappropriate moments, prone to bouts of sadness, and sometimes even cruelty. You long for a more joyful, expressive life.

Vowing to give up all pretence, you throw away Grace altogether. Fuck it! It's time to loosen up a little. You cut loose with everything in you that's awkward, petty, and selfish. Free of your former constraints, you act out in any way you feel like, whether that's making a fool of yourself at parties or having a tantrum at work. You may even give up your career as overly restricting. The people around you are stunned by the new you, which you tell yourself defiantly is a cost you're willing to bear.

And yet—you still feel inauthentic, just in a different way. This really isn't who you are, and you know it. People don't take you as seriously as they once did, and your new career isn't all that satisfying. Your earning prospects and impact on the world are diminished—but at least you're not feeling pent up anymore, right?

Grace

COMMON SHADOW ASPECTS:

- Haughty Spectator
- Profane and Plebeian

Under-Expressing: *Profane and Plebeian*

When the burden of being gracious becomes too much, the under-expressed aspect of Grace's shadow flares into being. You give up on Grace and balance, decide you're going to live large, and go for whatever you want with little sense of proportion.

You eschew Grace in service of living the good life, setting dignity and nobility and all that nonsense aside, instead, ploughing headfirst into all that life has to offer. You conclude that there is no room for both Grace *and* play or warmth or love, etc. Your natural Grace gets set aside and suppressed in service of a less restricted approach to life.

You give up on Grace and balance, decide you're going to live large, and go for whatever you want with little sense of proportion.

You ensure you get to have a good time and live life open-hearted, but this perpetually seems to be at odds with the dignity and Grace that is innately you. Even when you're living it up, it always feels like some part of you is missing.

Obvious (But Ineffective) Fix: Rise Above It All

While your life is filled with whimsy and freedom, you may start to find yourself frustrated with the lack of impact you are having in the world. You notice that people tend to take you for granted or look past you when it comes to your serious ideas. You decide that it's time for a shift—time to grow up and begin acting like an adult. You approach Grace not like it's something that has always been there but a new leaf that must be turned over.

You discover that Grace isn't something you need to protect but rather something accessible to you all the time.

You throw out the reminders of the past way of living and "get real" about life. You admire those who seem to have an ability to rise above it all and set about practising this same thing yourself. Because this change is happening on the surface rather than by creating the breakthroughs to bring your Grace forwards in the times when you are least comfortable doing so, it comes at the expense of letting the world have an impact on you.

You manage to create the experience of Grace for yourself by eliminating the things in your life that put it at risk, and by closing yourself off from feeling everything there is to feel. You become the picture of Grace, but only while your surroundings remain controlled, and you're closed to the fullness of the human experience. Your life feels less messy, but you've disengaged from the fun and joy available in each moment.

Creating the Breakthrough

The paradox for those with Grace lies in being able to embody and express the *being* of Grace while things fall apart around and within you. How can one bring Grace to a state of collapse?

Because this seems like an impossible conundrum, your default solution so far has been to avoid these situations—projecting an illusion of Grace at the cost of removing yourself from the world or choosing *into* those messy moments and abandoning Grace entirely.

Your breakthrough lies in embracing the people and circumstances that leave you feeling harried and awkward. Become willing to have egg on your face and be laughed at, and practise embodying both Grace, awkwardness, and embarrassment, all at once. Discover authentic Grace not by pretending or flailing, but by allowing yourself to be in on the joke and enjoying it as much as everyone else.

Those moments when you tried to maintain dignity and composure and instead fell flat on your ass serve as your greatest teachers. Put differently, learn how to fully embody Grace by accepting those moments when you're at your least graceful. People will be astonished and grateful at how you embody balance and ease—and are utterly lacking in self-consciousness— even in moments of great discomfiture. By doing so, you give them space to find ease in situations where they would normally be screamingly uncomfortable. If you can do it, they can too!

COMMON SHADOW ASPECTS:

- Haughty Spectator
- Profane and Plebeian

Leading and Working with People of Grace

Team members embodying the quality of Grace will tend to be a calming force on your teams. Difficult to rattle, they will serve as a bedrock of stability when your team is confronted with challenging obstacles. Their composure will be a godsend, helping everyone stay composed even in the worst of storms.

It is important to check in with these team members, however, to ensure they are making room for their humanity. If they maintain that graceful composure at the cost of repressing what's going on inside, it can lead to resentment, burnout, and exhaustion.

When you check in with them, go below the depth of being "fine." If they tell you they're feeling "great" or "good," recognize these as their judgments about what they are feeling. What is *actually* going on with them? If the team is in a challenging place, it would be weird for them not to have any experience of that.

Keep an eye out for team members whose strategy lies with the other aspect of Grace's shadow. When you see them not taking on a task because they feel too clumsy or awkward, help them understand (gently) that when they buy into a story of their clumsiness and inability to get things done, they're unconsciously escaping the burden of others' expectations and alleviating the fear of not being up to the task.

Your breakthrough lies in embracing the people and circumstances that leave you feeling harried and awkward.

Get present to these team members' underlying quality of Grace. Invite them to step into owning every part of who they are. Stand for their possibility, not their predictable path.

The temptation for these team members will often be like cleaning one's house before the housecleaners arrive. Rather than simply showing up as they are, they'll want to get a bunch of issues handled first. This sends them into a flurry of unnecessary work and leads to overwhelm. Support them in owning their Grace right now, not by having them go and do a bunch of work first but by leaning into the task that confronts them right now.

Starting with a deep breath is always a good way to find your way back to yourself.

Practises

Notice what you resist being with.
What are the circumstances, people, and situations you avoid because you know they drive your awkward *stuff* into the open? Slow down and pay attention to these moments of resistance and to how you lose Grace within them. Finding ways to say yes in those moments is a powerful impetus towards rediscovering a deeper embodiment of ease and Grace.

Notice the stories you tell yourself that take you out of Grace.

What are the internal narratives that tip you out of balance? Do you insist there just isn't time to find ease if such and such a problem comes up? Do you even have the capacity to slow down and take a breath, or do you get so wound up that you lose your capacity to imagine a different way?

Whatever those stories are, notice when you start telling them and when your Grace disappears. Ask yourself how Grace, fully embodied, would respond in these moments. Starting with a deep breath is always a good way to find your way back to yourself.

Notice where you show up silly or frivolous.

Notice the situations in which you ditch Grace for silliness, diversion, or a base response.

Your starting point here may be noticing this tendency in others and how you judge them for it. As this becomes clearer, notice how you too show up in these ways, and bring compassion to yourself for doing so. Can you find a way to own and love how you're showing up rather than judging or making yourself wrong? Can you identify what you're so afraid of in those moments that you abandon your natural Grace?

Bonus: As you do so, remember that you were trained into this behaviour by the world around you. Be at ease with what you fear, and rediscover in that moment the Grace that is your birthright.

COMMON SHADOW ASPECTS:

- Haughty Spectator
- Profane and Plebeian

OVER-EXPRESSING SHADOW ASPECT
Tyrannical Dictator

OBVIOUS (BUT INEFFECTIVE) FIX
You Only Live Once, So Start Living

Integrity

UNDER-EXPRESSING SHADOW ASPECT
Oblivious Hypocrite

OBVIOUS (BUT INEFFECTIVE) FIX
Get Right and Live Straight

COMMON DESCRIPTORS

Honest, Authentic, Say What You Mean, Truth, Virtue, Noble, Honorable, Do What You Say, Reliable, Solid, Sturdy, Principled, Trustworthy

The Quality

Your Gift

You create greater alignment in everything you do and everywhere you show up. At times this can be subtle like the way your muscles work more effectively when your spine is properly aligned. You make things operate more smoothly, powerfully, and honestly. You help people get clear on their truth by doing the challenging work of bringing your own truth to light.

You are often received by people as a clearing for the expression of truth and authenticity. There is depth to how you share your truth; when people are with you, they notice the same in themselves. It's not that you bear down on them or work hard to enforce this experience—this is simply the energy you bring.

You're an ongoing invitation for people to remember their values and create more alignment in their behaviour. You model the capacity to reveal what's out of alignment internally. This makes you trustworthy, and because of that trust, your teams tend to be efficient. Trust lubricates team dynamics—when it's present there's less friction, micromanagement, and doubling-back to check on people.

COMMON SHADOW ASPECTS:

- Tyrannical Dictator
- Oblivious Hypocrite

You make things operate more smoothly, powerfully, and honestly.

What is Predictable

Shaped by a world that seems to value blame over alignment and responsibility, your Integrity becomes rigid and a judgmental streak emerges. Feeling out of Integrity becomes an indicator that you're morally wrong rather than a useful readout on your internal state. Integrity morphs from a gift into a hardened set of rules and a stick to beat yourself up with.

Your relationship to your word becomes inflexible, stealing your sense of fun. When you say you'll do something, you march rigidly towards accomplishing it. Your ability to pivot, think on the fly, and be spontaneous has been replaced by an insistence on "doing the right thing, period." To ensure you're always in Integrity, you build a small, controlled life. Playing any kind of big game requires a willingness to give your word and at times fail to keep it, which is unacceptable.

Your rigidity creates impossible stresses within yourself, quick judgments of other people's behaviour and blind spots where you can't see that you're engaged in the same behaviour.

Because of these blind spots, you may predictably create a lot of breakdowns in relationship to your word—often glaringly obvious to everyone but yourself. You have righteous judgment of hypocrisy in others and an inability to own it in yourself.

As a leader, your teams notice and adopt the rigid way you hold your Integrity and tend to bring their Integrity breakdowns to light but with a great deal of self-judgment or try to hide those breakdowns until they're so big they can no longer be hidden. Team members also become prone to "gotcha" behaviour and blaming one another when things go wrong.

What is Possible

You are the possibility of us all changing our relationship to our Integrity. When you model forgiveness and compassion for yourself (and others), you create a space where others can do the same. As you let go of your knee-jerk judgmental response to falling out of integrity, you discover and share the space and compassion necessary to recognize these moments sooner, hold them more lightly, and make more generous moral judgments.

Imagine a world where the kind of people we see embroiled in huge scandals are willing and able to bring themselves back into Integrity far sooner. Your possibility is not a world where we are never out of Integrity. It is a world where we sometimes do fall out of Integrity—as living, breathing humans, this is inevitable—but can acknowledge it and bring ourselves back with ease, dignity, and compassion.

By acknowledging, recognizing, and cleaning up the messes you make, the world around becomes more capable of doing the same. Those with the greatest access to Integrity are nearly always those most present to where they go out of Integrity. When you let go of the significance you've created around Integrity, you help all of us see that what matters is not keeping our word but honoring it.

Integrity

COMMON SHADOW ASPECTS:

- Tyrannical Dictator
- Oblivious Hypocrite

Common Experience Coming of Age

Growing up, you struggled with hypocrisy. When you saw it in your teachers, parents, and peers and called them out for it, you found yourself in trouble.

If you were raised by parents who also embodied Integrity, you may have learned early to judge being in and out of Integrity as a black and white issue. When you're in Integrity, you're a good person, and when you're out of Integrity, you're bad.

You may have decided to create exceptions for your own rules (having seen the adults around you break their own rules) or have cut people out completely for what you saw as moral dishonesty.

Consequences of Owning Your Gifts

Owning your Integrity can lead to being called judgmental, holier than thou, and a tattletale. People don't much care for being called out as "wrong" or hypocritical. The ferocity with which you punish yourself for failures leads them to feel intimidated and nervous around you. Seeing how ruthless you are with your own mistakes, they worry that you'll treat them similarly.

Shadow Aspects

Over-Expressing: *Tyrannical Dictator*

Both of Integrity's shadow aspects develop by turning Integrity into normative judgment. To ensure you never become "bad," your shadow ruthlessly patrols your internal and external states. From this place, you are highly judgmental of yourself and others for any perceived breakdowns in Integrity.

To ensure you never become "bad," your shadow ruthlessly patrols your internal and external states.

When other people are out of Integrity, you have no ability to be with them. You blame and judge them for their shortcomings. You may let things slide for a while, but judgment grows internally until it explodes and you lash out. You are hard on people, and they feel it.

Because you inevitably fall out of Integrity as well, and because this is such a high crime in your eyes, this aspect of your shadow ends up hidden below the level of consciousness. Your Integrity breakdowns become blind spots.

Obvious (But Ineffective) Fix: You Only Live Once, So Start Living

Over time, the rigidity of your tyrannical shadow becomes exhausting. You notice that all the judgment and resentment that you generate towards other people doesn't change them a bit. It doesn't seem to improve your relationships or create the Integrity you want for the world.

Fed up with the effort and emotional strain, you give up, adopting a "Whatever, I don't care, YOLO" attitude. If you can't beat 'em, join 'em. You stop caring about and become indifferent to following the rules. Let it be your little secret—there's no point in telling anyone; they weren't paying attention anyway. Or you flaunt it and find new friends who share the same approach. If other people don't care enough to honor what's real and what's right, why should you?

Another possibility is that you carve out special exceptions to the rules you've established. Rather than break them outright, you conclude that you've been good over here, here, and here, so it's okay to make an exception over there. This takes the shape of selective, self-justified hypocrisy. You tell yourself you're just being honest, which is a kind of Integrity, right? The rest of the world better not follow your example, though—they aren't allowed the same exceptions in your rulebook.

Under-Expressing: *Oblivious Hypocrite*

You've seen one too many people around you talk about what's important to them, what others should be doing, and then fail to follow their own rules. Unable to live a life of perfect Integrity yourself and highly aware that the rest of the world is incapable of doing so either, this shadow aspect is a product of you giving up the battle. Taking the high road feels pointless when no one else seems to value it, so screw it.

You get to have fun and live life free from the restrictions the high road of Integrity might impose, but, at times, you feel guilty about your

COMMON SHADOW ASPECTS:

- Tyrannical Dictator
- Oblivious Hypocrite

own lack of alignment and the experience of hypocrisy it creates. In order to accommodate for this guilt, you numb the feeling. Again, your self-awareness sinks below the level of your consciousness.

You give up, adopting a "Whatever, I don't care, YOLO" attitude. If you can't beat 'em, join 'em.

Your innate gift makes you great at pointing out the hypocrisy in others, but your guilt and shame keep trying to surface as you do so. This is why some people with the potential to embody Integrity often have a hard time doing so. Rather than being present to your greatness and holding it lightly, you are highly tuned in to your failures of Integrity. These drag down your sense of self-worth and can leave you defensive and touchy.

Obvious (But Ineffective) Fix: Get Right and Live Straight

Unable to live with your own experience of hypocrisy, you commit to "living right" and make grand, sweeping gestures to clean up the ethical messes in your life. Integrity is everything. If the first obvious fix is about leaning into the "bad" side of your binary relationship to Integrity, this one is about doubling down and recommitting to the "good" part.

You become hyper-vigilant of your behaviour and motivations, fastidious about living within the lines you've drawn. Life, of course, begins to shrink. Anything close to moral complexity or Integrity gray areas is unacceptable. It's all about being a good person or a bad one with no exceptions and no grace available for those who move in and out of Integrity (least of all yourself). You're living in a binary prison of your own making, constantly reassuring yourself that you're the good guy.

And yet—human beings are not perfectible, and deep down you know that. Even as you distract yourself by judging other people, you hear a small but persistent voice insist you're a hypocrite yourself.

Creating the Breakthrough

Your predictable relationship to Integrity tends to swing back and forth between rigidity and justified criminality. This largely arises out of your created belief that being in Integrity is "good" and being out of Integrity is "bad".

Your breakthrough begins when you let go of this moralistic approach to Integrity, and adopt a definition like this one (sometimes attributed to Gandhi):

Integrity is when your thoughts, your words, and your actions are all in alignment.

Free from moral judgments, this allows Integrity and your own alignment to simply be the source of your innate power. The places where you're out of Integrity represent power leaks, and the same is true for everyone else. That someone is hypocritical (meaning what they say is incongruent with what they think or do), may be annoying but it doesn't make them "bad." It simply means they have a power leak.

In this way, you can begin to relate to your Integrity like a mountain with no peak. You keep climbing and learn to love the climb. Rather than holding Integrity as something you have or don't have, you understand it as a lens through which to notice yourself, moment to moment, in all areas of your life.

Where are you currently out of Integrity in your life? Create a judgment-free list and find ways to bring yourself back into Integrity in those areas. Not because it makes you a good or better person but because it brings you access to your power.

COMMON SHADOW ASPECTS:

- Tyrannical Dictator
- Oblivious Hypocrite

Through this approach, you become better able to honor who you are at any given moment. You're a human, so you will inevitably fall out of Integrity from time to time, regardless of your best intentions. Releasing judgment about this allows you to get present to the impact of your Integrity. What you can own, you can release. What you cannot own owns you.

Leading and Working with People of Integrity

Members of your team with the gift of Integrity can create trust, intimacy, and truth on your teams. Their natural tendency to share the truth and all of the truth can be a beautiful gift and encourage the other members of your team to do the same.

You become hyper-vigilant of your behaviour and motivations, fastidious about living within the lines you've drawn.

It's important for you, as a leader, to learn how to work with this tendency, to walk the line between allowing someone to express themselves and inviting them to be responsible for their impact. While sharing one's complete truth can be a beautiful thing, there are times when it puts something problematic into the space that does little to move things forward. Just because your team member is bored doesn't mean they need to announce that fact loudly.

Your work as a leader is to notice how you hold this tendency to speak the whole truth and nothing but. Are you prone to sharing all the truth as well, or do you lean towards buttoning yourself up? Whichever your tendency, it's important to recognize and hold it in mind, so you can avoid unconsciously pushing your team members in that direction.

Ironically, members of your team who bring Integrity will show up at times as dishonest and sneaky. This doesn't come from malice but from the meaning they have attached to their Integrity. They may have learned that it was safer to hide the truth and need for support to bring themselves back into Integrity by sharing the truth. As a leader in this situation, your role is to model *being* with your own Integrity breakdowns without making it overly significant or wallowing in shame. This means sharing with your team where and how you're out of Integrity and doing the work to bring yourself back.

Bringing compassion to yourself and the members of your team when they share being out of Integrity will facilitate breakthroughs and allow problems to be addressed promptly instead of being driven underground. Celebrate the people on your team who are willing to own and honor their Integrity breakdowns.

Integrity

COMMON SHADOW ASPECTS:

- Tyrannical Dictator
- Oblivious Hypocrite

As you practise recognizing, acknowledging, and cleaning up your Integrity breakdowns with love and compassion, you'll notice increased access to power, more fluidity, and a great deal more ease in your life.

Practises

Get clear on your existing definition of Integrity.

One of the most powerful shifts for you, as someone with Integrity, will come from understanding and adjusting your definition of Integrity. Start by writing out that definition. What does being in Integrity mean to you? How important is it? How does it play out in your life, your decision-making, and the judgments you make of yourself and others? What does being *out* of Integrity mean, and how does that play out in your life?

For some people, being out of Integrity can be as heavy as dishonoring God. Consider the burden of significance they attach to their Integrity breakdowns!

Just because your team member is bored doesn't mean they need to announce that fact loudly.

Practise with a new definition.

Practise relating to Integrity using the definition provided above: *Alignment in thoughts, words, and actions.*

Returning to this simple definition will help you transcend the normative judgments that get you into trouble. You may have a persistent story that being in or out of Integrity means you're good or bad as a person. But you get to choose whether to be defined by that story or to adopt a different one.

Create an Integrity list for yourself.

List all of the places and ways you are currently out of Integrity. Rather than making this a yes-no question that ends your inquiry by jumping to judgment and blame (or avoiding it), create this list through the new definition I've provided, asking "Where am I currently out of alignment, and leaking power as a result?"

Use this list as an opportunity to reclaim your power. Take one item from your list each week and bring yourself back into Integrity.

Practise forgiveness and cleaning up messes.

There may be something to clean up when we share with someone how we've been out of Integrity. Practise releasing the self-judgment you feel around this, take accountability straightforwardly, and ask the people you've impacted if there's anything for you to clean up. Hold this as easily as if you're cleaning up a glass of spilled milk in the kitchen.

As you practise recognizing, acknowledging, and cleaning up your Integrity breakdowns with love and compassion, you'll notice increased access to power, more fluidity, and a great deal more ease in your life. Model this approach to Integrity in the world, and you'll notice the world begin to shift in partnership with you.

COMMON SHADOW ASPECTS:

- Tyrannical Dictator
- Oblivious Hypocrite

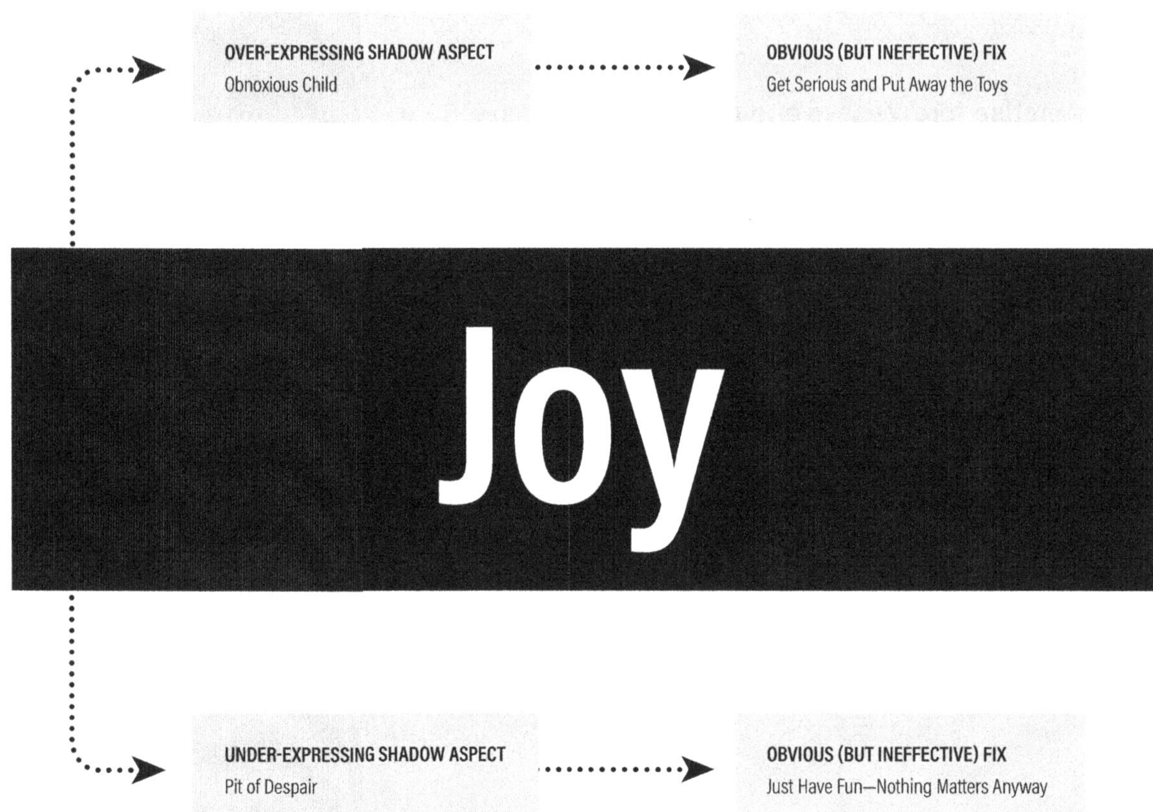
OVER-EXPRESSING SHADOW ASPECT
Obnoxious Child
OBVIOUS (BUT INEFFECTIVE) FIX
Get Serious and Put Away the Toys
Joy
UNDER-EXPRESSING SHADOW ASPECT
Pit of Despair
OBVIOUS (BUT INEFFECTIVE) FIX
Just Have Fun—Nothing Matters Anyway

COMMON DESCRIPTORS

Delight, Exuberance, Vitality, Vibrancy, Excitement, Energy, Effervescence, Joie de Vivre, Blissful, Exhilaration, Giddy, Happiness, Positive, Fun

The Quality

Your Gift

You are the gift of the fullest experience and expression of being human. You bring a sense of utter Joy into every space you walk into. The thrill of being alive is yours to experience on a daily basis. Along with the highs come the lows, and the experience of life that is your birthright includes a rich, broad spectrum of emotions.

Joy is not the absence of unhappiness, grief, anger, or the other emotions we learn to fear and avoid. It's the capacity to be with and experience them all. Consequently, you are more present to the rollercoaster that is life. Because of that willingness to experience and feel it all, you are present with far more happiness, delight, and pleasure than most people.

You are a delight to go exploring and to sample new things with, and take great pleasure in small miracles that others ignore.

On teams, you bring energy and vitality. Your teams are louder, more joyous, and more energized than most others. Boredom rarely comes up because there's always something to be felt and experienced. Your teams tend to *feel* into the right course of action rather than living and operating entirely from the head. You are imbued with a greater sense of intuition than those around you.

Joy

COMMON SHADOW ASPECTS:

- Obnoxious Child
- Pit of Despair

On teams, you bring energy and vitality. Your teams are louder, more joyous, and more energized than most others.

What is Predictable

Over time, you will experience the cost of your gifts. Feeling the absolute highs of life means you also feel the absolute lows. Because the world around you is less comfortable with sadness and anger than delight and laughter, you turn away from sharing your "negative" experiences and lean into feeling, or at least being perceived as all "positive"—even though your gut protests that in truth there is no negative or positive, only the full richness of being alive.

You avoid people and situations that leave you feeling those "negative" emotions. Over time, this leads you to dissociate from your immediate experience and to retreat into positive thinking. The world rewards you for finding the silver lining and sees you as having fewer "problems" and being less moody. Seeing the positive side of everything can be a gift—but when you do it automatically, as a way to stay safe from the experiences you fear, it becomes a crutch.

Coaches and leaders operating from this mindset find it difficult to empathize because they need everything to be "okay." As a leader, your team members don't feel they can bring you anything difficult because they know you'll start telling them why this isn't all that bad. You're right, in one sense—things often appear to be more problematic than they actually are. But if a team member has lost a loved one or failed embarrassingly at a project, they need to sit with and fully experience their emotions rather than trying to paint glitter on a turd.

Predictably, you will vacillate between disowning the downer parts of life and wallowing in sadness and anger when those parts become too much to wish away. People around you get the message loud and clear: Sadness and/or anger just aren't acceptable, and if they feel those emotions, it's time to get over it.

What is Possible

You represent the possibility of us finding Joy in all parts of this crazy existence. That doesn't necessarily look like gregarious laughter. It may be finding a deeper Joy in the experience of deep, clean grief for a lost loved one. It may be finding the Joy that comes from the purifying flames of anger (expressed responsibly).

You represent the possibility of us finding Joy in all parts of this crazy existence.

When you do the work to overcome your fears about the darker side of the emotional spectrum, you light the way for all of us to experience the parts of life we're most afraid of. By expanding your range and capacity as a leader, you hold space and give permission for all of us to do the same.

In this manner, you model that everything is okay *exactly as it is*—rather than telling yourself to look on the bright side. You don't need to tell people that it's okay to feel sad because grief is good for X, Y, and Z reasons. You simply let yourself grieve—deeply and with the sorrow it deserves.

Joy

COMMON SHADOW ASPECTS:

- Obnoxious Child
- Pit of Despair

When you approach life this way, others may feel a need to tell you it's going to be okay. But you know the deeper truth—it already is okay. You model the experience of things being okay by trusting what shows up and letting it exist in the moment.

Ironically, the less work you do to convince yourself and others that everything's great, and the sooner you let go of your need to return to a shiny, happy state, the sooner you move through whatever is showing up. Every dip on a rollercoaster is followed by a climb, and every climb followed by a dip. You embody the rollercoaster of life and the fullest possible experience of being alive.

Common Experience Coming of Age

You probably wondered in childhood why everyone was in such a hurry to grow up. "Guys, why are we suddenly finding reasons that playing tag isn't awesome?" This may have pushed you into either doubling down on the joy that seems to be slipping away but getting grief for it or by internalizing the message of "it's time to grow up" and stuffing down your emotions to fit in.

Having learned too well how the world responds to anger and grief, you shun them in order to live entirely through the "positive" emotions that are a part of your birthright.

Consequences of Owning Your Gifts

When you allow yourself to fully express your Joy, people may dismiss you as fanciful, silly, or vapid. Full expression entails a willingness to share openly *and* a full awareness of your impact on others when doing so. Your journey towards wholeness may involve owning how you sometimes come off and becoming intentional about it.

Shadow Aspects

Over-Expressing: *Obnoxious Child*

Having learned too well how the world responds to anger and grief, you shun them in order to live entirely through the "positive" emotions that are a part of your birthright. Over time, these "negative" emotions become like something locked away in the dark attic of your house. Now and then you hear thumps and knocks erupt from the space, but you just padlock the door and double down on pretending there's nothing in there.

What you cannot look at or process grows in power, as does your resistance to these aspects of humanity (yours and everyone else's). The more you disallow these emotions, the less capacity you have to handle them when they show up, so when they finally break through, they're explosive and none too pretty. In the aftermath, you're filled with remorse and embarrassment and more determined than ever to keep things positive.

The end result looks good—if people don't get too close. But resisting the parts of your life you don't want to be with means you can't be with them in other people. You insist on positivity, but it doesn't come from within. You no longer feel or embody authentic Joy. People tire of this lack of real experience or connection and move on. But no worries—it's all daisies and rainbows, anyway!

Obvious (But Ineffective) Fix: Get Serious and Put Away the Toys

At some point, trying to cover everything with happiness and fun feels a bit like painting turds with glitter. The grievances, upsets, and other emotions keep piling up, filling more and more of your emotional space. Like holding a beach ball underwater, it demands energy and you can only do it for so long.

You decide to give up on the "childish" joy you're known for. It's time to get real and be an adult, to stare life in the face and stop being so fanciful. Rather than learning to integrate and calibrate your access to Joy, you swing to the other end of the spectrum, shutting it out entirely.

You're on more of an even keel and begin to see positive results from the new approach. You're saving up for the big house and on track to get your promotion. But man, does it feel bleak, and your kids wish you still played with them the way you used to. Still, they'll never have to worry about money when they're older. Ruefully, you accept that they'll be the ones who get to live a joyful life—not realizing that they're more likely to emulate their newly serious, joyless role model.

COMMON SHADOW ASPECTS:

- Obnoxious Child
- Pit of Despair

Under-Expressing: *Pit of Despair*

If the first shadow responds to the challenge of being with heavier emotions by avoiding them, this shadow represents the other side—getting stuck in those emotions, unable to pull yourself up and out of the despair.

Because (in time) highs are inevitably followed by lows, you come to doubt your innate Joy. If every positive experience you have is followed at some point with sorrow or anger, how can you trust it? Better not to get your hopes up in the first place. At least that way you don't have so far to fall.

This shadow can also be created when you come of age and realize that people see your Joy as silly and frivolous. To earn their respect and achieve the success you're committed to, you set aside Joy and get serious. There's work to do and we're professionals. Even when you get home, you tackle the grown-up tasks rather than looking for ways to play. Joy becomes more and more compressed—who has the time these days?

You find yourself weighed down with significance and the heavier parts of life.

You show up as Eeyore, find reasons why things need to be this way, and plod through life. You notice you haven't been happy in some time and try leaving jobs, relationships, or locations, hoping a change of scenery will get your groove back. But, alas, external changes can't restore what you started shutting down internally so long ago.

Obvious (But Ineffective) Fix: Just Have Fun—Nothing Matters Anyway

On this side of the spectrum, you find yourself weighed down with significance and the heavier parts of life. You can't handle wallowing in the dark side of life any longer, so you turn up the Joy-meter to its highest setting. You find reasons and ways to be happy no matter what the cost. You may quit your serious corporate job in favour of dancing in the rain, deciding to be "who you are" and nothing else.

What you don't realize is that your previous success was also part of who you are, even though it was paired with so much heaviness. You've made this shift to a more joyful life contingent on eschewing everything about your old way of being—your drive, your commitment, and your visions for the future.

You're definitely happier. At the same time, something is missing. Surely, there's some way to experience Joy alongside commitment and achievement in life?

Creating the Breakthrough

The core of your breakthrough lies in recognizing that the Joy or lack thereof in your life has little to do with your circumstances. It results, rather, from the way you keep putting a lid on yourself. Absence of Joy usually reflects an inability to accept the other side of Joy—anger, sadness, and all the other emotions deemed unacceptable (or unproductive, depressing, unpleasant, or whatever label has been attached to them).

COMMON SHADOW ASPECTS:

- Obnoxious Child
- Pit of Despair

Flattening the emotional rollercoaster to avoid discomfort effectively flatlines all your emotions—including Joy. Moreover, when you resist those challenging emotions, they build up rather than having their moment and moving through you.

The breakthrough path for those who embody Joy lies in surrendering themselves to anger, sadness, or whatever emotion is there and practising how to have these experiences responsibly (rather than, for example, screaming and flipping the bird at people in traffic).

As you become more familiar and comfortable with anger and sadness, you will access self-assuredness and the understanding that while these emotions may be powerful, they will also pass, even if it takes time to work through them (you probably have a fair number of them backed up).

As you open yourself up to the possibility of your entire emotional range, Joy comes easily and authentically once again, along with a deep-rooted sense of ease.

Leading and Working with People of Joy

Members of your team with the gift of Joy reliably lift people's spirits, create a sense of fun and excitement, and remind everyone that having fun at work is as important as anything else. But such team members, sensing their role, may fall into a pattern of cheerleading exclusively.

Because Joy is your birthright, a lack of Joy in your life is rarely caused by people or circumstances.

A positive perspective is useful, but spouting positivity before setbacks have been processed can be jarring and counterproductive. Other members of the team, when told to pick up their spirits before they're ready to, may experience this as lack of empathy and downright insulting. For the cheerleader, that reaction to what they see as a gift feels frustrating.

One of the great risks for leaders who embody Joy is the tendency to label people as unwilling, complainers, and Debby Downers when their cheerleading falls flat. The problem becomes the team member rather than looking at how you show up, which may have created the problem.

A more fully embodied (and successful) approach on your part is to feel into the space and be with whatever is there. If sadness is the energy, what do people who feel that way need—as opposed to how can you cheer them up? If anger or resentment is in the space, what do people need to support them being with that? Are you giving them space in which to express these emotions before moving on to what's next?

If you're the one bringing Joy into the space, pay attention to what you may be unwilling to experience, and instead practise expanding your capacity to be with it. Note that some people, possibly you included, are comfortable with sadness but much less so with anger. For others, it may be reversed. Whichever the case, your job is to support people to be with precisely what is showing up for them rather than shifting them away from it.

Practises

Notice your inability to be with sadness and anger.
Part of the gift of Joy is a deep experience of the richness of human experience, but only if you're willing to hold space for all the emotions, including the ones that aren't so pretty.

Identify your strong suit and biases when it comes to the acceptable experiences people can have around you. Are you especially adept at being with people when they're sad? Angry? Resentful? Hurt?

Practise with people and situations that take you beyond your comfort zone.
It's important to understand that you absolutely do have a bias (this cannot be avoided) and that it's not a bad thing. Your bias simply tells you the emotional spaces you gravitate towards and where you try to shift people when they show up in a way that's uncomfortable for you. Practise being with people (including yourself) outside your comfort zone. If someone is sad and that's uncomfortable for you, practise simply being with them in their sadness.

COMMON SHADOW ASPECTS:

- Obnoxious Child
- Pit of Despair

Get clear on how you cap your Joy.

Because Joy is your birthright, a lack of Joy in your life is rarely caused by people or circumstances. More often it's the case that you clamp your Joy down or cap the amount of Joy you let yourself feel and express.

You could dig into why, but the bottom line is that it helped you survive and thrive and got you this far. Focus instead on noticing the specific ways you shut down Joy.

How do you cap or disallow it? What is your internal voice saying when you do so? How do you pre-emptively keep yourself from getting too excited?

For bonus points, practise letting go of those ingrained habits, incrementally if necessary, and allow yourself to feel and express the Joy that brings you to life.

One of the great risks for leaders who embody Joy is the tendency to label people as unwilling, complainers, and Debby Downers when their cheerleading falls flat.

Joy

COMMON SHADOW ASPECTS:

- Obnoxious Child
- Pit of Despair

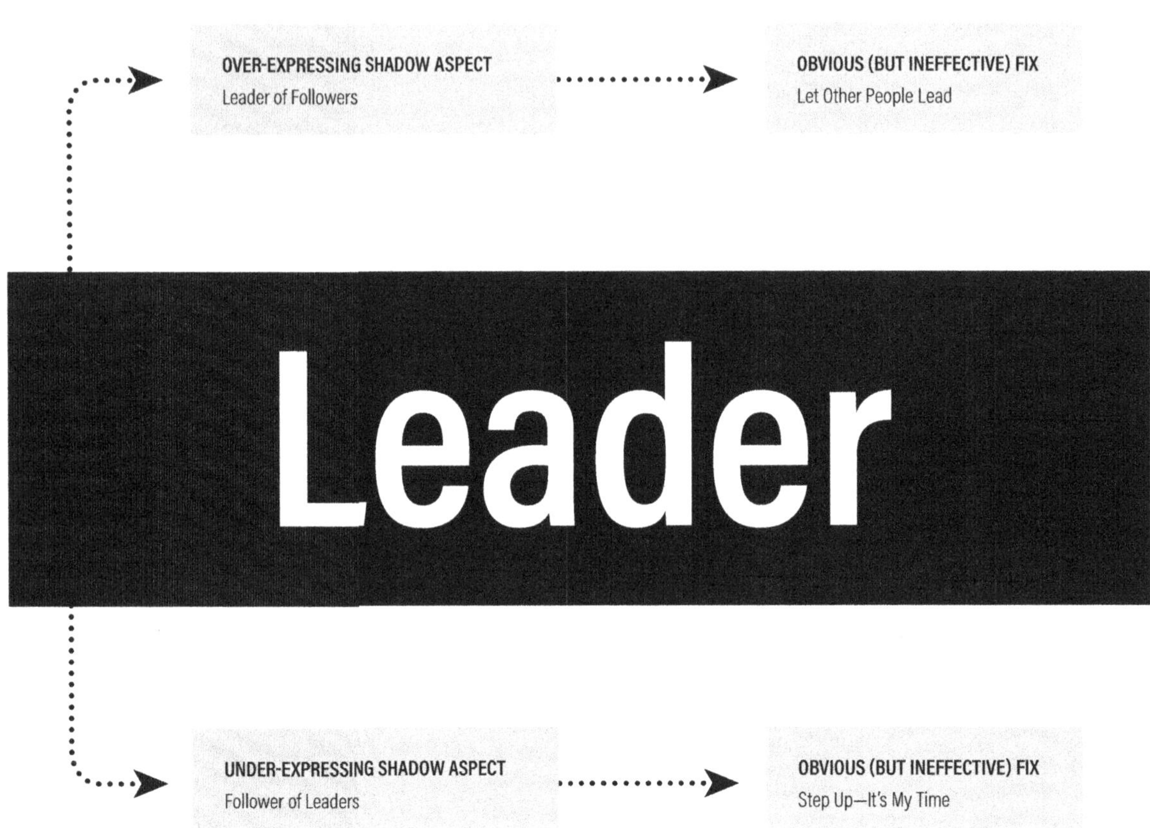
OVER-EXPRESSING SHADOW ASPECT
Leader of Followers
OBVIOUS (BUT INEFFECTIVE) FIX
Let Other People Lead
Leader
UNDER-EXPRESSING SHADOW ASPECT
Follower of Leaders
OBVIOUS (BUT INEFFECTIVE) FIX
Step Up—It's My Time

COMMON DESCRIPTORS

Pioneer, Front-Runner, Innovator, Trailblazer, Takes Charge, Guiding Light, Gets Everyone On the Same Page, Torchbearer, Influence, Motivation

The Quality

Your Gift

No matter what the situation, people turn to you for leadership. You step up naturally, enrolling them in visions and dreams they would never have imagined on their own, and directing them towards a common purpose.

You rally people around you easily, whether it's for a neighbourhood project, a benefit for your children's school or a project team at work. When you're in the picture, things just seem to get done. If a situation starts coming unravelled, people feel relief when you arrive. You're a godsend in the face of chaos, providing direction and forward movement when others feel panic.

You're more willing than most to lean over the edge and into the unknown, setting aside your fears to plumb the mystery that's there. Most of the time you lead projects from an easy, empowered place, although sometimes you step in because no one else seems up to the task.

COMMON SHADOW ASPECTS:

- Leader of Followers
- Follower of Leaders

What is Predictable

Those who are gifted as Leaders are naturally compelling, appealing, and magnetic to the world around them. Sometimes people see you

You rally people around you easily, whether it's for a neighbourhood project, a benefit for your children's school or a project team at work.

as fearless, amazed by your confidence, what you create and how you live your life.

Of course, no one is actually free of fear. You're better than most at hiding it, but deep down you have anxieties about getting it wrong, being challenged by someone with a better idea, becoming irrelevant and ignored, and so on.

For some, these fears morph into an overwhelming need for recognition. You need people to follow you uncritically, to remain in awe, not only at the beginning but right through the rough and tumble of getting things done. When you succeed at creating this aura of awe, you begin to look down on people for their lack of individuality or inability to make their own way. They're just mimicking you, and while that eases your deeper fears, it's hard to respect and wears on you over time.

You find yourself resenting your team members, without realizing that the cause of your resentment is that you've been creating followers rather than leaders.

No one can maintain the illusion of a fearless and flawless leader indefinitely, of course, and the projects you tackle suffer from a lack of diverse thinking and independent initiative in order to maintain the illusion.

Increasingly, the people drawn to you find themselves in a looping pattern. First, they're inspired by the possibility you represent and decide they want exactly that. Next, they align with you—hiring you, volunteering for your project, or finding some way to partner with you.

When the awe begins to wear thin, they're left wondering why they haven't become just like you—or rather, like the perfect game face you project. Disillusioned and feeling a bit betrayed, your followers stop trying so hard, and some drift away. This fuels your deepest anxieties and sends you in search of the next group of people drawn in by your aura.

What is Possible

The risk of Leader's shadows is that they turn mistakes and failures into one more shiny performance, further attracting followers to you. When you are supported to release all of the glamour and need for performance and simply show the muck that is as much a part of life as the glamour, you lead the way for people to embrace their own shadows as much as their light.

From this shift, your aura becomes something that enrolls people in the vision of their *own* lives—rather than being attracted to yours—and has them step more deeply into their purpose. You represent the possibility in all of us to discover leadership within.

When you release the need to have people in awe of you, it creates the freedom for you to show up in whatever way is true for you in the moment. And when you practise that, it creates the clearing for those around you to do the same. Ironically, the possibility of you unleashed in the world comes when you let go of the need to "perform leadership."

Instead of doing leadership the right way and making it look good, you model truth, integrity, and authenticity moment by moment. By releasing yourself from the precepts of your fears, life becomes free, easy, and effortless. The need to perform falls away, as does the need for others to honor and hold you in high regard. From this place, the possibility of everyone stepping into their leadership arises.

COMMON SHADOW ASPECTS:

- Leader of Followers
- Follower of Leaders

Common Experience Coming of Age

Always being the one chosen for leadership created a lot of pressure. Failure was very public and hard to live with. As a result, you may have found clever ways to fudge your results and sell what looked like failures as positive outcomes. You may have been surrounded by people who wanted to be with you, but lacking companions who felt like equals and might see you for who you were.

Consequences of Owning Your Gifts

Great leadership can be polarizing. When you take a strong leadership position and draw others to you, some will hate you for it. The ability to keep your heart open and humble to both is rarely created on our own. It's just easier to sell people a polished image or to stop caring about the naysayers—even if they may be reflecting useful information.

When you are supported to release all the glamour and need for performance, you lead the way for people to embrace their shadows as much as their light.

Shadow Aspects

Over-Expressing: *Leader of Followers*

The fears of Leaders are often about losing the awe, appreciation, and admiration of those around them. If they let people see who they really are, free of gloss and glam, it might prompt the adoring crowd to move on. Because that's unacceptable, they ensure that most of their outcomes look good. If they do look vulnerable or uncomfortable, those moments are carefully chosen and easy for their followers to forgive. Everything, ultimately, becomes a performance.

Over time, this pattern gains momentum and becomes more automatic, causing you to lose the ability to distinguish it. You don't believe or even realize that the way you share keeps you safe and attracts uncritical followers. You may even lament how people project greatness onto you—albeit without doing anything to dispel their illusions.

You end up with people who thoroughly admire you but do not (and cannot) challenge you to become your best self.

Consequently, you end up with people who thoroughly admire you but do not (and cannot) challenge you to become your best self. This limits the scope of your achievements and feels a bit hollow, but you're unwilling (or unable) to give it up. There's too much safety in being infallible.

On top of all this, it's possible you've used this shadow to create great results—there is a lot of money and impact to be made in this world from amassing a following and leading those followers.

At the end of the day, a leader's job is to create more leaders. You create more followers.

Leader

COMMON SHADOW ASPECTS:

- Leader of Followers
- Follower of Leaders

Obvious (But Ineffective) Fix: Let Other People Lead

As a Leader of Followers, you can't seem to find feedback that makes a difference for you, and you have the feeling you might be leaving something on the table. So, you vow to undergo some of your own work. You seek out Leaders who do things you greatly admire and call forth greatness in others.

Because your shadow compels you to avoid being with the disappointment, let down and muck of leadership, you are naturally drawn towards Leaders who project an even more polished way of expressing leadership than you do. Even their vulnerability and intimacy are performed exquisitely. It just looks so fabulous.

And so, you go and train with these leaders, learning how to do vulnerability the right way—not because that's what they teach, but because that's how they are being. You become impeccably vulnerable.

This feels like progress, but it's just a refinement of your existing shadow. As soon as vulnerability becomes performance, it is no longer vulnerability. You've simply shifted from being a Leader of Followers to a Follower of Leaders. How long will this iteration last before you get fed up and decide you've learned enough and it's now time to step back into the spotlight—without really having learned anything at all?

Fearing the consequence of stepping into leadership, you mitigate the risks by hanging out on the sidelines.

Under-Expressing: *Follower of Leaders*

Fearing the consequence of stepping into leadership, you mitigate the risks by hanging out on the sidelines. You're masterful at pointing out what should have been done, what was left on the table, and where the current leadership is going wrong.

Alas, most of your impact stays right there—on the sidelines. You may be a brilliant strategist, perhaps a *consigliere* to the brightest and best in leadership, but never really step into that role yourself. This protects you from your worst fear—public defeat and embarrassment—while still allowing you to express the Leader you are on some level.

You support great leaders who create great things. But, over time, you feel a brewing resentment. Why don't these people get it right? Why aren't they coming to you for more support? Why aren't they asking you to lead? The answer, of course, is that you've made it clear you aren't really interested. In the moment of contributing strategy, you're already stepping back, and looking to others to take it from there.

In its most extreme form, this aspect of your shadow becomes a complete avoidance of leadership. Because following someone will never be the truest expression of who you are, you follow one leader for a while then drift on to the next. When will you be willing to step forwards and run the show? Maybe you'll find just one more leader to learn from first.

Obvious (But Ineffective) Fix: Step Up—It's My Time

While great leadership creates more great leadership, the shadow of leadership creates more shadow. As a Leader who fears the potential public failure of true leadership, you naturally seek out leaders who collude with your shadow's tendency to follow. These relationships train you to do two things very well:

First, they train you to become masterful at learning and mimicking the work of other leaders, dressing it up as if it's a form of Leadership while continuing to operate in the role of follower.

Second, you learn how to convince your followers that you are developing them as Leaders. This, in part, is how your own shadow has drawn you to the leaders you've worked with.

As a result, you appear to step up into Leadership but without embracing the entire role—the vulnerability, nakedness, and truth that is your birthright. You create the performance of leadership rather than the being of a true Leader.

It looks great, and people hold you up as a model. You receive accolades and admiration, which feels good and encourages you to continue on the path you're on. And yet—a niggling voice in the back of your mind reminds you that you're bored and frustrated, that something is still missing.

COMMON SHADOW ASPECTS:

- Leader of Followers
- Follower of Leaders

Creating the Breakthrough

Your shadows are designed to avoid being with the cost of leading—disappointing people, being seen as a failure, letting down the people around you, and not living up to your promise. Your shadows allow you to either avoid those consequences entirely or find ways to bypass their impact.

You learn how to convince your followers that you are developing them as Leaders.

Avoidance is the easiest one to catch—it's simply you not stepping into the fullness of your Leadership, behaving instead as a Follower of Leaders. A sneakier expression of your shadow's aspect kicks in when you try to swing the pendulum in the other direction, creating drama and performance around the things you want to avoid. Disappointment, being seen as a failure, letting people down—all of these become ways to act out the performance of leadership. You turn these moments into another way to "succeed" and avoid just being with your real impact.

You do vulnerability better than anyone. When you fail, the world knows it, and you've got a beautiful way to share that failure, along with a story for it and just the right amount of crying. The world (and you) buys into the performance, keeping you at arm's length from the true expression of Leadership you crave.

Your real breakthroughs come when you allow yourself to be ordinary. No fanfare, no polish—simply going after things that matter to you and allowing yourself to be seen when you fail, just like when you succeed. Allowing yourself to fail and performing failure are two very different things. By embracing the former and letting things just be what they are, without spinning or faking it, you come into the integrity of being a real Leader. In so doing you create a clearing in which people see themselves more honestly, discovering their own power as they see you struggle without pretence.

You finally accept that while monuments and statues may be nice to look at, the greatest Leaders inspire us not by being larger than life, but by allowing us to see ourselves in their authenticity, vulnerability, and intimacy.

Working with People of Leader

Those with the gift of Leadership on your team will coalesce the rest and galvanize them into action. Leading those who bring the quality of Leader can be challenging. On the one hand, it can be intimidating when they naturally draw people's attention towards themselves instead of you. They already seem to have figured it out, and people around them are beginning to nod in approval. Should you just let them keep doing what they're doing?

The development of leadership requires a healthy measure of humility and vulnerability.

This is tempting, but it may leave them stuck in their shadow aspects and lead the team astray. Look more closely: Is this person being authentic and vulnerable in service of the team, or are they doing it in order to get their own needs met? This can be a subtle distinction and becomes easier to spot if you're doing your own work with the support of a good coach.

Leader

COMMON SHADOW ASPECTS:

- Leader of Followers
- Follower of Leaders

We draw people to us who reflect ourselves. If you find yourself with multiple Leader-type people on your teams, it may be that you have the gift of Leadership yourself. If so, their well-orchestrated performance will look a lot like your own shadow. Make sure you have the coaching support to recognize what's happening in yourself so you can notice it in them.

Keep an eye out for members of your team who challenge leadership frequently. This is often how the under-expressing aspect of Leader's shadow presents itself. Instead of trusting and empowering your leadership (or stepping into their own), they challenge and point out flaws in your direction.

The development of leadership requires a healthy measure of humility and vulnerability. Letting go of "already knowing" the answer is the key to breakthrough for those with the gift of Leadership.

Practises

Be on the lookout for how you may be performing leadership (as opposed to simply being Leader).
If you have been running these patterns for decades, they're probably invisible to you. Potential giveaways:

- People hold you on a pedestal.
- People relate to you with awe.
- People find you incredibly inspiring.

Letting go of "already knowing" the answer is one of the keys to breakthrough for those with the gift of Leadership.

These may be clues that you don't share the entirety of your truth. Or they may mean you share a more complete picture but in ways that leave you looking good no matter what.

Notice whether you jazz up your failings.
Where do you (consciously or unconsciously) package disappointment and let down in such a way that it still looks good?

Notice the ways you resist your own development as a leader.
Some common patterns of resistance:

- Rather than accepting someone else's leadership, you point out the flaws in it. You reserve the right not to empower them as a leader because they aren't doing it right.

- Rather than taking in feedback with an open mind, you instead ask yourself questions like, "Do I agree with this?" or "Is this true?"
- You avoid working with your own coach/leader or work with a *bunch* of them. The latter allows you to avoid the intimacy and openness of a deep, powerful relationship.

These approaches allow you to operate with the illusion of leadership ("I'm listening to feedback," "I'm just sharing my truth—that's leadership") without allowing in the messiness and vulnerability that come from receiving real feedback.

Notice the ways that you resist "ordinariness."
It's human to be ordinary (as well as magnificent). Notice when you add gloss and glamour to what you're doing and how you're showing up. In those moments, practise letting it go. See if you can allow yourself to be one percent more ordinary.

COMMON SHADOW ASPECTS:

- Leader of Followers
- Follower of Leaders

OVER-EXPRESSING SHADOW ASPECT
Cloying and Suffocating
OBVIOUS (BUT INEFFECTIVE) FIX
Just Stop Caring So Much
Love
UNDER-EXPRESSING SHADOW ASPECT
Cruel and Heartless
OBVIOUS (BUT INEFFECTIVE) FIX
Become a Being of Pure Love

COMMON DESCRIPTORS

Tender, Warmth, Adoring, Compassionate, Caring, Feels Like Coming Home, Empathy, Affectionate, Kind, Sensitive, Family, Open-Hearted

The Quality

Your Gift

You are Love personified. You have space in your heart for the foibles, greatness, and everything in between that is humanity. You fall in Love with people instantly, and people have the same experience with you. Many people envy the purity and freedom with which you express your Love.

Thoughtfulness doesn't tend to be something you have to pay attention to—it comes to you easily and without hesitation. Of course, you send people a card on their birthday and a bottle of wine when they buy a new house. Of course, you leave them a voicemail saying how much you love them. These things come as naturally to you as breathing.

You tend towards the romantic, and your heart tends to meet people from a place of deep openness. You fall in Love quickly, leading to whirlwind romances followed by deep feelings of betrayal when people don't live up to your idealized perception of them.

You struggle to understand it when people plunge into self-criticism, because in your world you accept them completely. What people dislike about themselves is just more to appreciate, love, and embrace.

COMMON SHADOW ASPECTS:

- Cloying and Suffocating
- Cruel and Heartless

You tend towards the romantic, and your heart tends to meet people from a place of deep openness.

What is Predictable

The punch you don't see coming is the one that hurts the most. In the context of your life, these figurative punches land on a wide-open, undefended heart. You tend not to see people's darker sides (which we all have) or to actively suppress your recognition of them.

As a result, you may often feel betrayed or find that the people around you keep falling from grace. You learn to protect your heart by closing it more quickly, rebuking and hitting back at the ones who hurt you. In some areas, your heart becomes hard and brittle, and you stop opening it up at all.

This is painful in and of itself, given your nature. In order to compensate for the existential pain this causes you, you layer Love and kindness atop your protected heart. People still experience a great deal of the warmth that is your birthright, and you feel a little better. But love provided from a closed heart often comes across like saccharine—it's overly sweet, and something about it rings false. You know that you have so much more to give, and on some level, there's never enough Love.

What is Possible

You represent the possibility of discovering Love *through* heartbreak (rather than by avoiding it). To love others fully, without holding back, you must be willing to walk through the gate of heartbreak over and over again. Like a parent who finds their way back to Love when their child says or does something hurtful, you teach us how to love the parts of ourselves that hurt us the most.

When you take on this work, you become a model for divine grace and forgiveness. We learn from you that Love isn't about never making mistakes or messes but about the healing work on the other side.

Your practise of allowing hurt, being left heartbroken, healing and then dropping deeper into Love and forgiveness, holds space for all of us to forgive each other and continue to find our way back to Love.

Jesus and Mother Theresa walked the same path that you do.

Often the people with the largest hearts erect the greatest walls to keep protecting themselves. The path back to Love requires summoning the courage to break down those walls, come what may.

Common Experience Coming of Age

Those who are Love tend to be a magnet for it. You probably had the experience growing up of being cherished and loved—by your peers but also regularly by adults. Having said that, some people may have seen this as a threat to their own importance and reacted by attempting to pull you down.

Consequences of Owning Your Gifts

Letting yourself love others fully leaves you more vulnerable than most to heartache and disappointment. Often the people with the largest hearts erect the greatest walls to keep protecting themselves. The path back to Love requires summoning the courage to break down those walls, come what may.

Love

COMMON SHADOW ASPECTS:

- Cloying and Suffocating
- Cruel and Heartless

Shadow Aspects

Over-Expressing: *Cloying and Suffocating*

Your natural ability to empathize with others makes you like an over-tuned antenna for people's suffering. The slightest discomfort in someone else becomes a quest that you, in your boundless empathy, must take on. Without realizing it, you commingle their pain with your own, leaving you both in need of relief.

You lose your ability to empathize freely and without agenda. Instead, you need the people you help to feel better and to behave in a certain way in order to alleviate the suffering your empathy causes you.

You're unable to let people have their own experience, and so you end up suffocating them. When your Love is rebuffed, it only increases your fear of not being enough and you compensate by redoubling your efforts.

You conclude that the problem is that you just care too much, and you need to learn how to stop caring.

You may end up in jobs supporting those who can't seem to support themselves or people who feel especially bereft of Love such as isolated elders. This over-compensation of Love is tinged with a need to prove to yourself that you *really are* kind and loving, and so you need a great deal of recognition and acknowledgment. Rather than giving yourself the recognition you need, you become ever more cloying or flip to the opposite aspect of your shadow, becoming resentful and cold.

Obvious (But Ineffective) Fix: Just Stop Caring So Much

You find that the first aspect of your shadow creates two problems: First, you end up feeling a great deal of suffering around people; and second, the love you do pour onto people goes unappreciated.

You conclude that the problem is that you just care too much, and you need to learn how to stop caring. Alas, the only way to really stop caring is to shut your heart off. To close it down and refuse to let people in. Rather than developing the ability to keep your heart open while simultaneously allowing people to own their suffering, you close down your ability to Love others—which of course diminishes your ability to feel their Love for you.

Life becomes less painful and more matter of fact. There's less suffering, heartbreak, and hurt in your life, so... maybe this is a good change? Except that the world now feels indifferent and a bit lifeless. What are you getting all of this work done for anyhow? What's the point?

Under-Expressing: *Cruel and Heartless*

Over time, you've learned that having your heart open means it will be hurt, and you will be left betrayed and heartbroken. This experience is coupled with the fact that people don't seem to appreciate the abundance of Love that you give them. When they do provide recognition, it's paltry in comparison to what you have provided, and so it furthers the let down and resentment you feel.

In response, you develop the habit of pre-emptively protecting your heart by closing it. You narrow the bandwidth of Love that you are able to provide and receive from others. This leads to a runaway effect in which you feel less and less love from others and ever more resentful about it.

And yet—you still have a tender, beautiful heart at your core and sometimes fall for people despite yourself. This leads to big swings between idealizing people and demonizing them. Those who you might Love most deeply are the ones you condemn most sharply, thus protecting you (to some extent) from the risk of heartbreak they represent.

You're able to get done what needs to get done and move through life fairly efficiently—but you can be left feeling cold and empty.

Obvious (But Ineffective) Fix: Become a Being of Pure Love

With your closed heart, you're largely able to get through life relatively unscathed. But you're left with a continual nagging feeling that there's more available. Life just feels empty and like you're missing something.

Desirous of richer relationships and a deeper experience of love, you try to be a more loving person. You look for ways of showing and demonstrating love and take to these approaches with gusto. Unfortunately, you enact these strategies overtop of a heart that remains closed and largely protected.

COMMON SHADOW ASPECTS:

- Cloying and Suffocating
- Cruel and Heartless

*You are left **doing** the actions of open-hearted love while **being** closed, safe, and protected. People are left with the unsettling experience of you acting loving while radiating something else underneath.*

Consequently, this fix tends to show up in a bizarre, cloying kind of way. Because this fix steps over the underlying resistance to having your heart broken (or breaking someone else's), you are left doing the actions of open-hearted love while being closed, safe, and protected.

People are left with the unsettling experience of you acting out love while radiating these buried emotions. They wonder how to connect and find that they can't seem to get it right. If they ask you what's wrong—which in and of itself makes you angry—you just double down on what already feels inauthentic. Your strategy leaves the people close to you feeling pushed away and attracts those who project the same kind of inauthenticity.

Creating the Breakthrough

Great love never shows up by itself. Because you're a person of deep feeling, other big emotions come with it—anger, despair, frustration, jealousy—and you probably feel these more than most. Your shadow aspects aim to rule out these less than angelic emotions or simply to stop feeling any emotion at all.

Your breakthrough lies in coming to terms with all your big emotions and seeing your humanity in their expression. When you can love yourself in anger and resentment and love others at their pettiest and most spiteful, you enter wholly into your gift.

This doesn't begin with you shouting out your anger in a crowded bus when something pisses you off. Rather, by owning that emotion quietly in your mind. Accepting the fury that comes up and letting it move through you without needing to justify it or judge it as a contradiction of your gift.

Justifying our emotions is a way of removing ourselves from the truth of them and simply owning what is so. You don't need to justify *why* you feel the way you do—your feelings don't require justification. They are true, exactly as they are, without any further information.

As you learn to see and honor what is showing up for you in the moment, you can start to get responsible for where you are, and then eventually, separate your feelings from whatever action to take next. In learning to honor whatever emotion shows up, at any given moment, you open the door for all of us to practise and experience unconditional Love.

Leading and Working with People of Love

Your team members embodying Love will be magnificent at forming connection and camaraderie on your teams. Like the glue that holds everything together, these team members will tend to be thoughtful, empathetic to how the rest of the members on your team are doing and quick to support the rest of their cohort when they are struggling.

Love

COMMON SHADOW ASPECTS:

- Cloying and Suffocating
- Cruel and Heartless

Because Love can tend towards the romantic, it's predictable that those who are Love will experience certain members of your team falling from their grace. When someone accidentally pushes the wrong button or does something that leaves your Love-based team member feeling hurt, the reprisal can be quick.

Once someone falls out of favour with your team member, it's almost impossible to find their way back into their good graces. Resentment, anger, and jealousy are the lenses through which your Love-based team member sees them, ensuring the pattern continues. Be alert for when the shadow aspect of Love shows up for a team member like this, in the form of resentment, anger, jealousy, as well as the experience of someone saying and doing Love without its underlying *presence*.

Your role as leader is to work with your team member to acknowledge when these feelings are real for them and to begin *there*. This will require a willingness on your part to hold space for your team members

Until your team member can honor the truth of all their feelings, they will forever be at the effect of them, needing to continue to pretend they aren't present, and layering inauthentic Love over top.

to simply acknowledge their upset, hurt, or resentment. Your job is not to fix this or jump on it with the intention of making these feelings go away. Doing so actually perpetuates the problem as a replication of the internal dynamic happening for your people.

Until your team member can honor the truth of all their feelings, they will forever be at the effect of them, needing to continue to pretend they aren't present, and layering inauthentic Love over top. Hold space for your people to own what's real for them and then to support them in seeing what might be next, past their reaction.

To support your team members this way, you must take on your own emotional state. If you operate with a belief that getting angry is unacceptable, you can't hold the clearing for your team members to come to acceptance. Notice where and how you shut down your own difficult feelings and work with a coach to broaden your emotional range.

Practises

Notice when and where you are closed to Love (yours and others).
Where do you resist Love? Where do you close your heart and bat away Love or insist you don't need it?

One of the most pernicious ways to do this looks something like raising a bet in poker. When someone offers you Love, your go-to response is to come back at them with an even greater show of Love. This allows you, in the guise of being extremely loving, to avoid opening up.

Notice the situations in which you are unwilling to give Love.

Under what circumstances do you prevent yourself from expressing love to the person in front of you or wrap it in a barbed-wire blanket of conditions? For bonus points, notice how you justify this. How do you make closing your heart feel like the right thing to do?

An absence of Love in your life is often a function of resisting the shadow that comes with it.

As you continue this practise, try releasing those justifications when they come up and acknowledging the simple truth of the moment: You've closed your heart and are resistant to opening it up.

Get to know and embrace your shadow.

An absence of Love in your life is often a function of resisting the shadow that comes with it. Practises that allow you to understand and embrace your shadow aspects can really set you free.

Love

COMMON SHADOW ASPECTS:

- Cloying and Suffocating
- Cruel and Heartless

One of the simplest approaches is an *anger on purpose* exercise. Choose a time every night to feel *all* the anger within you. Set aside some time (two minutes is a good starting point) to be alone, put a pillow over your face, and scream out your anger for the next two minutes.

This may be anathema to many people with the gift of Love. Initially, you might see it as silly and forced or even impossible—you have no anger to express! With continued practise, however, anger almost always breaks the surface, often surprising in its vehemence. In the aftermath, as anger clears its channels, you will often feel relief and ease, and may even begin to laugh at yourself. In so doing, you find a new freedom to open your heart and express Love unreservedly.

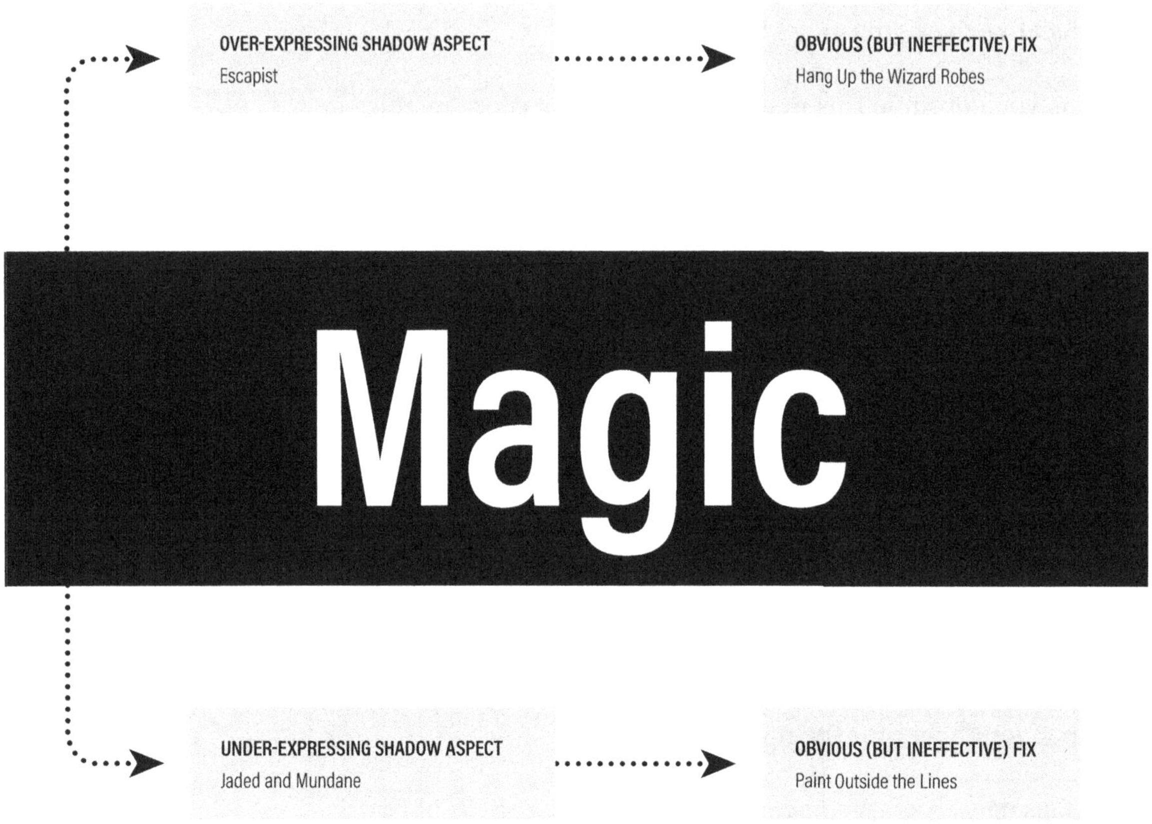

OVER-EXPRESSING SHADOW ASPECT
Escapist

OBVIOUS (BUT INEFFECTIVE) FIX
Hang Up the Wizard Robes

Magic

UNDER-EXPRESSING SHADOW ASPECT
Jaded and Mundane

OBVIOUS (BUT INEFFECTIVE) FIX
Paint Outside the Lines

COMMON DESCRIPTORS

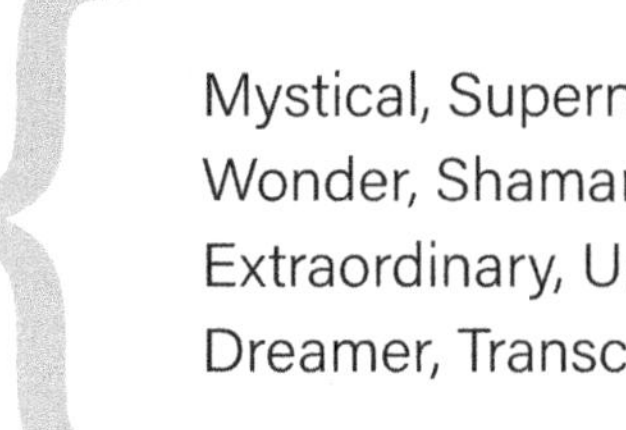

Mystical, Supernatural, Sparkle, Wonder, Shamanistic, Uncanny, Extraordinary, Unique, Enchanting, Dreamer, Transcendent, Otherworldly

The Quality

Your Gift

You are the embodiment of Magic and the possibility of miracles existing. In your presence, people feel that anything is possible. They lose themselves in the childlike wonder that epitomizes this way of seeing the world.

Visionaries like Walt Disney, Elon Musk, and other blue-sky thinkers all embody this trait—a commitment to seeing what could be and a willingness to continue holding that dream in the face of a world that pulls back towards stark reality.

When you join a team, you imbue its members with a greater degree of vision and greater access to belief that those larger visions may come to fruition. The gift of Magic is not simply the ability to dream big—it's the ability to create that Magic moment by moment, out of thin air, as you pursue that vision.

People often wonder how you make that happen. Sometimes you're as perplexed as they are. You just kind of let things flow and the Magic unfolded. As a result, the gift of Magic and possibility can be frustrating at times. You'd like to map out your process, but you're not entirely sure how you arrived at a given magical result. You just kind of surrendered to your process and trusted things to happen.

Magic

COMMON SHADOW ASPECTS:

- Escapist
- Jaded and Mundane

Children love spending time with you, as they still possess easy access to the Magic that you embody. Tea parties, magic tricks, and events all come alive in your presence.

In your presence, people feel that anything is possible.

What is Predictable

The world based on pragmatism and rational calculation can feel cruel to someone with the gift of Magic. You can see what others can't, but that doesn't mean they trust you. Perhaps it's no surprise: The art of Magic can be unpredictable and fickle, which makes it hard for you and others to trust. They'll laugh, call you a dreamer, and insist you play *their* game on *their* terms.

One predictable outcome is that after hearing this enough times, you concede they must be right and buckle down to their approach. You "grow up," shut down your Magic, then systematically go about shutting it down in others. We can't afford to dream or to trust that something wonderful might be created here. We need to work with data, spreadsheets, and reality!

You learn to generate results predictably and reliably, becoming a steady workhorse, and make things happen in a way that makes sense to the rest of the world. Life becomes more predictable, and you miss the thrill of feeling Magic pour through you—but at least you're no longer being laughed off.

Alternatively, when the world demands that you face facts and be pragmatic, you rebel, escaping into fantasy and daydreams. Following this path lets you feel true to your gift, but along the way you lose your ability to stay rooted in reality. You can dream and create magical visions, but that's where it stays. When it's time to operationalize your vision, exposing it to the harsh glare of the pragmatists, you lose interest and retreat into more visioning and fantasy.

The abundant possibilities that come with your Magic remain just that—possibilities and little more. Magic becomes an escape from reality rather than something that animates and partners with it.

As you do your work to hold space simultaneously for the pragmatic and the miraculous, you enlarge our belief in the scope of what is possible.

What is Possible

The possibility you embody is that of all of us discovering our own Magic. As you do your work to hold space simultaneously for the pragmatic and the miraculous, you enlarge our belief in the scope of what is possible. A willingness on your part to stand for Magic while anchoring it in down-to-earth practicality makes you the kind of leader who blasts through paradigms.

Being the embodiment of Magic sometimes leaves you crestfallen and disappointed when what you can imagine isn't noticed or taken seriously by others. When you feel scared and urgently need a particular kind of result, trusting in the ephemeral and spiritual way can feel tough.

Magic

COMMON SHADOW ASPECTS:

- Escapist
- Jaded and Mundane

The natural response to this experience of disappointment is to show up in such a way that you avoid that feeling in the future. But when you do your work to open back up and be with these moments of disappointment, you discover an ability to bring Magic to the world regardless of how it is received. You stay open in the face of what life brings and learn how to marry the pragmatic and the magical. This integration of capabilities becomes the fullest expression of who you are.

People sometimes feel let down when they're shown how a magic trick was performed. They've lost sight of the Magic that exists when someone is willing to practise a simple sleight of hand for years on end until it becomes perfect. This is the possibility you represent—the ability not only to create Magic in the spur of the moment, seemingly out of nowhere but to revel in the Magic of each moment, no matter how mundane its origins.

Common Experience Coming of Age

Growing up, you may have found yourself labelled a dreamer, laughed at for the fantasies you created and sometimes (in the eyes of others) became obsessed with. Meanwhile, you struggled with the mundane and the minutiae your teachers and parents told you to focus on. If you persisted in exploring your Magic, you may have been written off as distracted, lazy, and difficult.

Consequences of Owning Your Gifts

Over time, you develop a ferocious allergy to pragmatism, fearful it will clip your wings and destroy the gift you love so deeply.

You inspire some people, but others want to drag everything out of the realm of Magic into a nuts-and-bolts model that they can easily grasp and replicate. If you can't, which is often the case, they regard you with raised eyebrows and skepticism. Earning these people's trust—without abandoning the Magic you are—sometimes just feels like too much work.

Shadow Aspects

Over-Expressing: *Escapist*

Growing up, the world's insistent demands that you bring yourself back down to earth and "get real" felt like an increasingly frustrating violation of who you were. Eventually this frustration peaks and becomes a refusal to play their games.

You try to fit in at first, doing as you're told and explaining your actions in terms that are comprehensible to the skeptics. But over time, you develop a ferocious allergy to pragmatism, fearful it will clip your wings and destroy the gift you love so deeply. You become an escapist, unwilling and then unable to spend time considering how to implement your dreams.

You take refuge in jobs where your ability to envision wonderful things is highly regarded, but implementation is handed off to people willing to roll up their sleeves and problem-solve.

This isn't necessarily a bad thing. All our shadows can be worked with, and the world creates careers and jobs that work in partnership with our shadows. The drawback is that it leaves you unable to move past the visioning phase. If you have a project you truly wish to bring into reality, you have to find someone else to get it done, making inevitable compromises along the way that might leave your project unrecognizable by the end.

More so, if you wish to deepen into your own leadership, it requires an ability to broaden your range, and it is in the area of implementation that your range is cut off. You're great at blue-sky thinking, but that's it.

Obvious (But Ineffective) Fix: Hang Up the Wizard Robes

You're tired of having a million great ideas and nothing to show for it, and frustrated at not being taken more seriously. Your life just doesn't look the way it's supposed to.

You decide it's time for a change, and to "grow up." The catalyst for this shift might be someone leaving you, a loved one getting angry at you for not "growing up", one too many rejections for the career you've been aiming towards, or something else.

Whatever it is that leads you here, you commit to living grounded, in the real world. In the process, you slaughter the Magic at the altar. Rather than getting supported to create the breakthrough that would allow you access to both Magic and realism, you trade one in for the other.

COMMON SHADOW ASPECTS:

- Escapist
- Jaded and Mundane

You may well create areas of whimsy and possibility in other places in your life, as a trade-off and a way of maintaining balance with the places you've set aside the Magic, but it's still a zero-sum game you're playing.

As you make these trade-offs, you will certainly begin to see results, and this will feel good, initially. The only problem is that you've created these results by trading in part of what is innate to you. Over time, you're left wondering, "Does it have to be this dry and mundane?"

Under-Expressing: *Jaded and Mundane*

Remember that leadership is about expanding your team's and your own range rather than operating within everyone's comfort zone.

Growing up, you learned the hard way that Magic was neither appreciated nor praised. This training may have come from your peers, parents, teachers, or guardians. Wherever it came from is not the issue—it's simply worth knowing that you came by this tendency honestly.

You internalized the voices around you, discovering that when you focus on getting the job done and doing what is possible, people acknowledge and reward you. Over time, this stops being a choice you make in the moment and becomes automatic—a habitual way of showing up and succeeding in life. It's just not worth feeling the pain that comes up when you let yourself dream.

At this point, you've identified with the aggressor and begin policing the visions and dreams of others, inviting them to get real and focus on the job at hand. You squeeze the life out of Magic, externally and internally. Life moves forwards and you create results. They just seem to be... a little mundane. Didn't life once feel more vibrant and filled with promise?

Obvious (But Ineffective) Fix: Paint Outside the Lines

Wasn't life filled with Magic, once upon a time? You remember feeling more fun and open, with less heaviness and weight spread throughout the day. You look around you and notice life seems to have taken on shades of gray rather than the vivid colors you remember and adored.

Wasn't life filled with Magic, once upon a time?

You throw away the blueprints and the plans. Let's get reckless and pursue something fantastical! This time it's going to be different. There are many places you can create these kinds of changes. You may look in the realm of career, your relationships, your friendships, the kinds of vacations you take, or anywhere else.

You create a whimsical experience of Magic in these areas, but it comes on the heels of an all-or-nothing approach to the way you previously showed up. Pragmatism and reliability are thrown out the window, in service of whimsy and possibility.

You're like a leaf blown about by the wind. In the areas where you adopt this way of showing up, life is one magical experience after another—it's just that it doesn't have a lot of direction or consistency.

Magic

COMMON SHADOW ASPECTS:

- Escapist
- Jaded and Mundane

Creating the Breakthrough

Your shadow aspects are designed to save you from the heartbreak of being a unicorn amongst horses. But they are also your curse, pushing you towards the extremes of all Magic or none, neither of which is satisfying or wholly productive.

Rather than bouncing between the two, your breakthrough will occur when you combine your ability to dream in magical colors with a "let's get this done" approach. A magician creates successful tricks with an inspired idea *and* a willingness to practise it thousands of times. In that mundane practise, Magic is fully realized. The moment arrives when you finally understand that you are both horse *and* unicorn and find joy in every aspect of this truth.

Leading and Working with People of Magic

Members of your team with the gift of Magic will be inspirational in the brainstorming and blue-sky phases of a project. They have a natural talent for seeing far beyond the limitations of traditional project design. But they may also struggle with logistics and execution, jumping ahead impatiently to a new project or idea. Watch for their tendency to "chase the squirrel"—that is, to jump ahead to a new project or idea when the existing one is no longer novel and fresh.

One way to address this is to delegate implementation and operational work to other team members, leaving the ideas people to push the boundaries. But remember that leadership is about expanding your team's and your own range rather than operating within everyone's comfort zone.

Notice your reluctance to accept responsibility for day-to-day planning and implementation.

Your opportunity is to invite your magicians to remain focused and on task, even when the magical feeling begins to fade. In a willingness to stay the course, they discover that Magic is always available, even if they have to generate it from within.

As the Zen saying goes, before enlightenment we chop wood and carry water. After enlightenment... we chop wood and carry water. Invite your team members to combine their scope of possibility with the day-to-day work of chopping wood and carrying water.

In the meantime, keep an eye out for the under-expressed shadow of Magic. If you see team members who seem hopelessly bogged down in the details of implementation, check in with your intuition. Might they be resisting their Magic? If so, acknowledge this part of their being and help them recognize the impact on both themselves and the team. Stand up for the value of the entire gift they have to offer rather than settling for half.

Practises

Notice where and how you snuff out your experience of Magic.
Many people who embody this quality see their experience of Magic as a function of their circumstances. If they aren't feeling the Magic, they resign themselves to its absence or frantically rearrange their circumstances to bring it back. Both efforts miss the deeper point—that their Magic is inherent, and they can bring it to any given situation. If they have lost the experience of magic, they are snuffing it out themselves.

As the quote attributed (apocryphally) to Lewis Carrol goes: "Everyone wants a magical solution for their problem, and everyone refuses to believe in magic." It doesn't matter how much Magic you are attempting to layer on top of life if you are actively sabotaging it and snuffing its possibility.

Practise noticing when you resist the experience of Magic. Notice the ways you resist, sabotage, or pre-emptively shut down the Magic that is innately yours to experience. Practise releasing this impulse.

Notice when you shirk the work of implementation.
On the other extreme, notice your reluctance to accept responsibility for day-to-day planning and implementation. What kind of excuses do you make, and where do you hide out in your mind? What delicious fantasy suddenly calls to you? Ask yourself how you can create Magic at precisely this moment.

Rather than simply working on the vision or theory of your project, plan out the design as well, and take the lead for implementation.

COMMON SHADOW ASPECTS:

- Escapist
- Jaded and Mundane

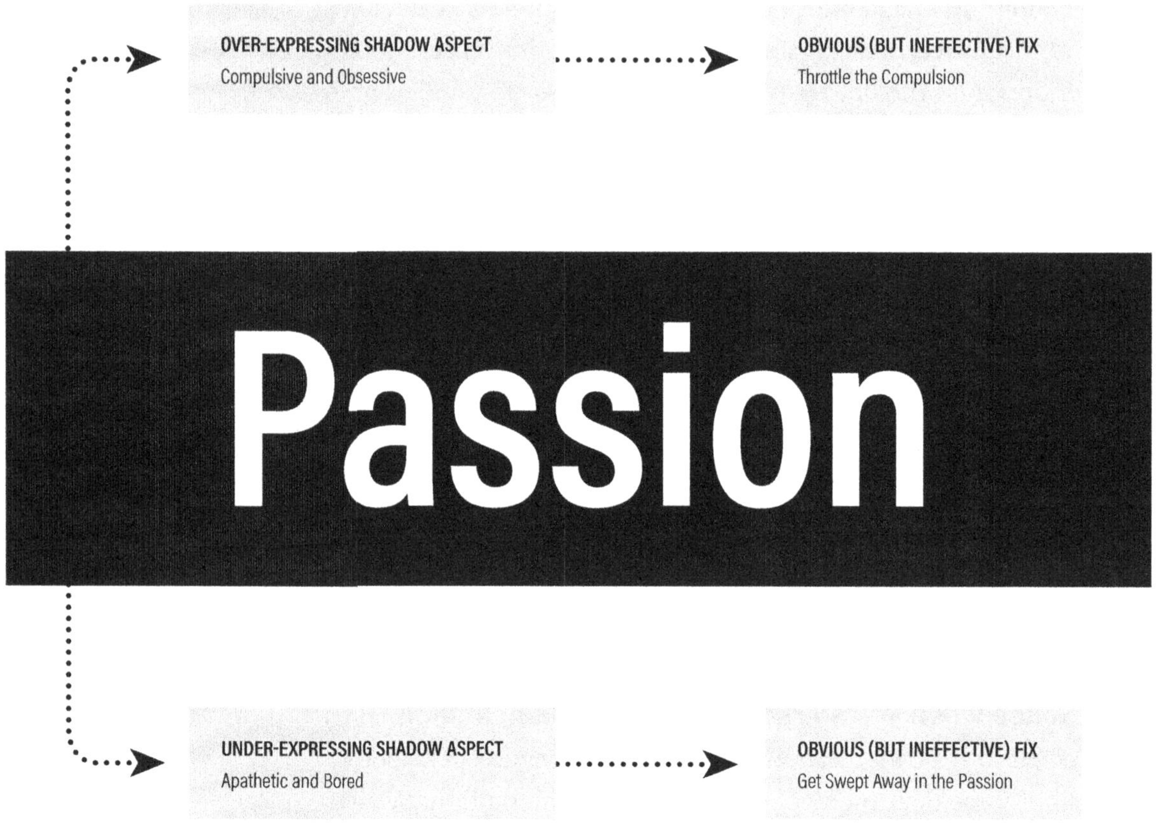

OVER-EXPRESSING SHADOW ASPECT
Compulsive and Obsessive

OBVIOUS (BUT INEFFECTIVE) FIX
Throttle the Compulsion

Passion

UNDER-EXPRESSING SHADOW ASPECT
Apathetic and Bored

OBVIOUS (BUT INEFFECTIVE) FIX
Get Swept Away in the Passion

COMMON DESCRIPTORS

Intense, Fervent, Fiery, Zealous, Heartfelt, Eager, Excited, Spirited, Fierce, Enthusiastic, Fixated, Obsessive, Infatuated, Keen, Focused, Absorbed

The Quality

Your Gift

It's not that you have a lot of passions—you *ARE* passion. Whatever you put your thoughts towards, you pick up with an enthusiasm and fascination that people around you envy. You do not simply like things—you love the crap out of them and obsess over every single aspect of whatever currently holds your attention. Your Passion provides rocket fuel to your commitments, and you become a master in many areas.

Your excitement and enthusiasm inspire others to do better and go deeper than they might otherwise have done. Passion is infectious—your team members are excited about the work they take on and continue talking and thinking about the project long after they've gone home.

You might self-describe as having a "geek-gene." You don't take things lightly—you take them on head first. When you want to learn about a particular topic, you take scads of books out of the library and recite fascinating (and at times, tedious) details about it. Deep immersion is your home territory.

Passion is the motivator that keeps things moving forwards long after pain, pressure, and "should do's" have worn off. People who bring Passion into the world often take a given initiative further than almost anyone else would have.

COMMON SHADOW ASPECTS:

- Compulsive and Obsessive
- Apathetic and Bored

It's not that you have a lot of passions—you ARE passion.

What is Predictable

Passion's shadow aspects can look like obsession, addiction, or (paradoxically) apathy. When you lose yourself in your pursuits you may also lose touch with the world around you and other parts of yourself that matter.

Paradoxically, your Passion may cause you to be seen as flighty or unreliable, as you drop projects you once cared about and jump into brand new projects you're fired up about.

Over time, you may notice diminished human connection in your life. The joy of Passion has been eclipsed by a myopic pursuit of perfection. You become ever more fixated on achieving mastery above all else. As everything else recedes into the background, obsession makes sense. History is littered with people to whom we owe great debts for their discoveries made in this manner—but at great cost to their own experience of life.

You do not simply like things—you love the crap out of them and obsess over every single aspect of whatever currently holds your attention.

You may find yourself diverting into illicit pursuits—substances, sex, affairs—driven by a need to restore personal balance and connection with the world. But you go after these with the same tunnel vision, and they inevitably fall short. Eventually the joy and exhilaration of your Passion wane entirely, leaving you with not much more than stubborn persistence. You rigidly complete your tasks but take little pleasure in doing so. The external trappings look the same—long hours, late nights, nonstop work—but as you march grimly onward, you're left feeling apathetic, the polar opposite of Passion.

Knowing the high cost of diving into something wholeheartedly, you may choose the opposite approach. Keeping everything at arm's length, you carefully choose pursuits you can engage in without losing yourself. This gives you a life that's more orderly and balanced, at least on the surface. But you're bored most of the time and feel distaste at how mundane your existence has become.

What is Possible

You are the possibility of living a life on fire. When you do the work to integrate Passion with the other parts of yourself and the world around you, you help us all see that it's possible to love life deeply and passionately rather than simply liking it. The path is rocky and requires a willingness on your part to be vulnerable and confront the darker facets of your Passion, like apathy, obsession, and compulsion.

Your path involves learning to stick with your interests and commitments through both inspiration and boredom, learning to generate yourself and your Passion from within. Doing so often requires noticing the ways you've shut down your Passion and choosing back into what is innate for you, in the moment.

Rediscovering and generating yourself this way require a willingness to slow down and sit with the moments where you notice your Passion has vanished. It's in these moments that your work can really be taken on.

Perhaps, when you were young, staying engaged once your initial burst of excitement wore off meant that you got in trouble for putting too much time into something. Maybe you were told you were stupid if you weren't continually learning. Maybe this was the point where you learned you could receive new accolades by jumping ship and choosing a new venture to excel in. The particular reason isn't important; what is important is a willingness to stay in the discomfort that comes in these moments, and rather than dutifully plodding along, allowing the Passion that is already present to be expressed.

Passion

COMMON SHADOW ASPECTS:

- Compulsive and Obsessive
- Apathetic and Bored

Common Experience Coming of Age

Growing up, you may have been labelled as a geek, prone to obsession, and out of touch. You may have felt that those around you were only interested in the surface level of things, which you found the least interesting. Other people's interest in what you were saying tailed off just when you were getting to the good stuff.

You may have been the kid who wore bird-watching t-shirts to school because you didn't care about anything else and didn't understand why that wasn't cool. The world isn't always kind to those who are different, and you may have learned to keep your Passion to "acceptable" levels around those who did not share your level of enthusiasm.

You might self-describe as having a "geek-gene." You don't take things lightly—you take them on head first.

Consequences of Owning Your Gifts

Owning your gifts and sharing your Passion is just too much for many people. You may get labelled a geek or overhear things like, "Don't get them talking about..." You find it frustrating that other people are willing to be mediocre when you can only pursue things to the deepest level.

Shadow Aspects

Over-Expressing: *Compulsive and Obsessive*

Passion from a wide-open heart is a beautiful thing, but from a fearful, closed heart, afraid of being mediocre or tepid, it becomes obsession. Given your ability to go deeper than almost everyone else, you see the possibility in things and chase that potential to the point of compulsion.

You lose sleep, health, friends, relationships, and family, demanding perfection in yourself and others. This part of Passion's shadow can tend towards addiction. We rarely achieve total perfection in life or in our pursuits—but we *can* feel perfection, at least briefly, through substances or sex. At a minimum, we find temporary reprieve from the impossible demands of perfection.

Operating from fear, the compulsive aspect of Passion can often lead to missed or last-minute deadlines and resentment when others are unwilling to put in the same level of effort as yourself.

Micromanagement can also fall under this part of the shadow, out of an insistence that things be taken "all the way" to completion. Delegating can feel like giving up to you, and so you meddle in the affairs of those to whom you've delegated.

The results this aspect of your shadow can generate makes it especially challenging to set down. It may be costing you a great deal, but you're creating results and receiving accolades. Getting support in the face of this can be especially challenging.

Obvious (But Ineffective) Fix: Throttle the Compulsion

Frustrated by an inability to moderate the tunnel-vision obsession with which you pursue things, you set up systems of control and arbitrary sets of rules that seek to allow the "appropriate" expression of Passion. The result is an existence in which you steer clear of almost everything you give a damn about.

Ultimately you throttle your Passion, and consequently, your own self-expression—either by preventing it from being manifested or leaving it so wrapped up in red tape that you give up before you start. You feel safer and appreciate having what passes for greater self-control, but it comes at a steep cost: You're bored and apathetic.

COMMON SHADOW ASPECTS:

- Compulsive and Obsessive
- Apathetic and Bored

Under-Expressing: *Apathetic and Bored*

By rigidly controlling your Passion with a set of rules and strategies, you are able to ensure you never get too immersed in anything and thereby avoid Passion's darker natures of obsession and compulsion.

Knowing the high cost of diving into something wholeheartedly, you may choose the opposite approach. Keeping everything at arm's length, you carefully choose pursuits you can engage in without losing yourself.

You live a tidy, modulated life, leaving work at the stroke of five, but you often feel empty and a little frustrated. Is this all there is? You may indulge in secret binges from time to time, but then you shake your head and renew your commitment to controlling this part of yourself.

If the first aspect of a shadow is designed to compensate for not having enough of a good thing, this second aspect is about compensating for having too much.

This side of your shadow also aims to address your tendency to jump from pursuit to pursuit trying to keep your Passion aflame. You decide that you never finish things and want to take them all the way through, so you force yourself to finish the task at hand, losing sight of the real game. Instead of putting your attention on generating and rekindling your Passion as you finish a project, you make finishing the project the sole goal, leaving you bored and apathetic.

Obvious (But Ineffective) Fix: Get Swept Away in the Passion

The boredom and mundanity you feel in life becomes too much. Your Passion, dammed up for far too long, floods over you, leading to an epic binge in your existing obsessions or rapid-fire jumping from one new obsession to the next. Before long, of course, the messes you create lead you to clamp down again.

Your competing shadow aspects lead to pendulum swings back and forth between controlled apathy and unapologetic binges. You manage to make this work, but life feels chaotic and extreme, and you feel like there must be a deeper level of expression and freedom to be had.

Creating the Breakthrough

Yours is the gift of being able to create and create and create, so much so that you never really need to stay rooted. There is always a new pursuit that will allow you to feel the exhilaration of your Passion. Because of the immediate fascination and desire for depth that Passion creates, you tend to learn new things quickly and effectively, then grow bored and move on. There are great gifts available to you in choosing to stay with a particular pursuit rather than jumping ship when things get hard or boring.

Rather than avoiding boredom, steer towards it. Can you find Passion in the plateaus that exist between those exciting moments of breakthrough and integration? Consider that your fears and shadow have led you into avoiding aspects of life that you struggle to be with.

When you notice yourself swept away by Passion, check in with yourself. Are you trying to avoid something boring and challenging? If you slow down long enough to sit with that (instead of immersing yourself in that exciting new project), can you find acceptance and ease? What might be causing you to shut down your Passion for what's right there in front of you? What is available to reengage with in your current project? Remember: Your Passion is *always* available.

Keep track of the rest of your life. What are your foundations, and can you ensure these are honored while in the delight of your Passion? Places to look include: Your well-being, the health of your relationships with your partner and family, your career, your finances, and your social life. You may be resistant to honoring these parts, seeing them as obstacles between you and whatever your Passion pulls you towards. Remember that these are the things that allow your Passion to be sustained and find ways to create balance within your pursuits.

COMMON SHADOW ASPECTS:

- Compulsive and Obsessive
- Apathetic and Bored

While many people will benefit from recovery work, your natural addictive tendencies are especially served by the fellowship and grace that twelve-step and similar programs provide. In sobriety (of any and every kind) you are able to bring your deepest Passion to whatever is showing up in the moment.

Leading and Working with People of Passion

Remember that we are often more present with someone's shadow aspects than we are with their light. We are more likely to experience frustration with someone's lack of energy (their apathy) than we are to be inspired by their Passion.

Passion from a wide-open heart is a beautiful thing, but from a fearful, closed heart, afraid of being mediocre or tepid, it becomes obsession.

Members of your team with Passion will tend to be excellent starters and catalysts until at some point they either settle into obsessiveness or dump the existing project in favour of the next bright, shiny thing. If you wish only to manage them (and their shadow aspects) effectively, you can put them in charge of the early phases of a project. However, if you wish to develop their leadership, you will need to do more than simply play along with their shadow. Setting up structure and creating a container for commitment provides an excellent support for Passion to work *through* the boredom and restlessness that comes from plateaus while keeping them from getting lost in myopia.

This kind of structure is necessary but not sufficient to create a breakthrough. If they are only held accountable for getting things done on time they may do so with boredom and apathy, leaving out the magic and delight with which they launched the project.

The gift of structure in this case provides regular check-ins for you and your team member. The question to bring is not "Is this person meeting their deadlines and moving the project forward?" Rather, it is "Is this person sticking with their commitment, AND are they embodying their Passion as they do so?"

If the answer to this question is no, your work is to go deeper. What might they need to reengage their Passion on the project—as opposed to taking on a new project altogether or resigning themselves to push it through apathetically?

Be on the lookout for burnout and excessive hours. Team members with Passion may suffer in silence because of the contributions they make with their epic spurts of productivity. It takes a leader to stand for something different, even if it means reducing productivity in the short-term. In the long-term, you will be developing a team member who can bring sustainable passion and create results far greater than short-term explosions.

Remember that fear causes these patterns, and so that's what you must look for with your team member. Simply insisting that someone "stop doing something" only addresses the immediate problem. When you see someone in the throes of manic Passion, help them distinguish and address any fear that may be at play rather than being driven by it.

Passion

COMMON SHADOW ASPECTS:

- Compulsive and Obsessive
- Apathetic and Bored

Instead of putting your attention on generating and rekindling your Passion as you finish a project, you make finishing the project the sole goal, leaving you bored and apathetic.

Practises

Engage in fellowship and partnership.

Passion tends to get "drunk" on things. Whatever you're currently enthralled with, you drink deeply and frequently. To ensure your sobriety without cutting away your Passion, engage in fellowship and partnership. By including other people along the way, you gain useful perspective and reduce the risk of burnout.

Intentionally choose areas to act out your obsessive tendencies.

Your shadow aspects aren't bad—they're like a familiar itch that feels good to scratch. There's nothing wrong with empowering these parts of yourself, and in fact, there are times when they will serve you. The game is in learning to *choose* your shadow aspect rather than having it run on automatic and *use* you.

Audit where your Passion does and does not show up.

Create a list of areas in your life where you feel deep Passion and another list where you feel apathetic. Examine both lists one item at a time. What might you be avoiding, whether it's through your apathy or obsession?

Create long-term projects, and get the support you need for them

Creating longer-term projects and getting support by someone to take them all the way can greatly open things up for you.

When you are held accountable to a project of greater scale, you'll be forced to confront both your apathy and your desire to chase after new projects. This will help you move *through* your fear rather than manoeuvring around it. When you use the structure of a project to tackle your fear this way, you'll discover it opens up entirely new realms of possibility.

QUICK TIPS

- Rather than avoiding boredom, steer towards it.
- Be on the lookout for burnout and excessive hours.

Passion

COMMON SHADOW ASPECTS:

- Compulsive and Obsessive
- Apathetic and Bored

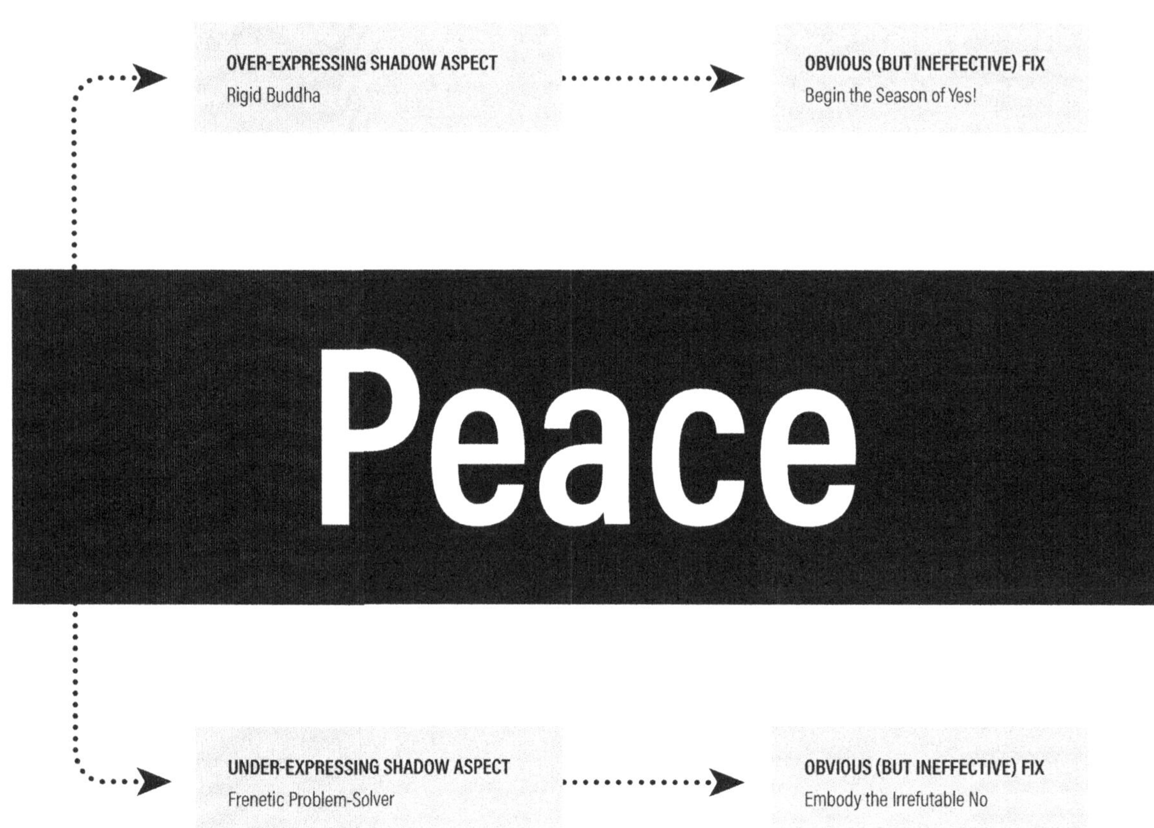
OVER-EXPRESSING SHADOW ASPECT
Rigid Buddha
OBVIOUS (BUT INEFFECTIVE) FIX
Begin the Season of Yes!
Peace
UNDER-EXPRESSING SHADOW ASPECT
Frenetic Problem-Solver
OBVIOUS (BUT INEFFECTIVE) FIX
Embody the Irrefutable No

COMMON DESCRIPTORS

Tranquil, Calm, Placid, Restful, Oasis, Stillness, Serene, Calm in the Storm, Unworried, Untroubled, Unruffled, Harmonious, Grace Under Pressure

The Quality

Your Gift

You are the calm amidst the storm. When things become intense, crazy, or unmanageable, people know you will provide a haven—a place for them to simply show up and be. You bring peace to every space that you enter, restoring comfort and ease, and allowing people to recover their belief that things will work out, no matter how improbable that seems. Ironically you may find yourself in places of turmoil more often than most, as that's where your innate Peace has the greatest impact. You are great at rapid-fire dealmaking, hostage negotiation, and other high-pressure roles that require coolness under pressure.

When leading teams of people, your team probably exudes calm regardless of what's happening. You may even seek out storms because you enter your strength when weathering them and because they provide a beautiful contrast between the world around you and your inner Peace. Your composure amidst chaos means you see emerging patterns before others do and excel at creating opportunities out of crisis. You are the leader who can rally the troops when the chips are down and things look hopeless.

You represent the opportunity for all of us to find beauty and inspiration in the solitude and quiet of life. In your presence, we remember that we don't need TV, alcohol and drugs, video games, sports, work, or

COMMON SHADOW ASPECTS:

- Rigid Buddha
- Frenetic Problem-Solver

You are the calm amidst the storm.

any other form of artificial stimulation. Instead, we discover the poetry and awe that comes from gazing out over a lake in the morning sun.

What is Predictable

You will probably become frustrated with the world's endless challenges, which disrupt those moments when Peace might naturally be expressed. Your gift is the ability to manifest Peace at any given moment, *regardless* of your circumstances. But, over time, you begin to see your ability as a *function* of those circumstances. Accordingly, you begin to impose increasing amounts of control over your environment, fencing out potential conflict to protect the Peace you crave.

Slowly but surely, you contract from life, creating an existence that is simple, elegant, and quiet but simultaneously leaves you feeling somewhat irrelevant. Your misplaced belief that circumstances dictate your ability to experience Peace translates into a careful, limiting leadership style. You end up stepping back precisely when your gift of Peace would most be welcomed.

This may sound like you deciding to stop forcing things in life, saying no to more things, or making your decisions a function of what feels good in the moment rather than your deepest purpose and commitment to your legacy. Ironically, in an effort to protect your gift, you rule out the opportunities to deepen your capacity for its expression.

The flip side here comes from fearing that you are too peaceful and might leave your legacy on the table. You plunge into challenging circumstances, tough conflicts, and get significant and hurried about everything you take on. In doing so, you lose sight of the Peace you embody, take on more and more work, say yes to everything, and find yourself utterly exhausted. You may create results, but you no longer even recognize yourself as Peace and are left confused when people reflect this quality back to you.

The pendulum may swing back and forth between these two extremes, leaving you to grapple frantically with life for several years before throwing your hands up, calling it quits, and jealously guarding your newfound Peace. Or you cordon off your life such that work is your arena of frantic action, and the rest of your life exists in (rigidly protected) Peace.

Your misplaced belief that circumstances dictate your ability to experience Peace translates into a careful, limiting leadership style.

What is Possible

You are the possibility that Peace is available no matter what the circumstances. When you do the work to expand yourself and bring your natural Peace forward, no matter what's happening around you, you teach us that we don't have to wait for retirement to love the life we are living.

You are also here to teach us that we don't have to control our circumstances to find the ease that we desire. Many people find mountain hideaways, take extended vacations and sabbaticals, and all manner of things to rediscover their experience of Peace, then dive back into their daily lives. Your role as a leader is to model that we don't have to escape our day-to-day lives to embody the Peace we seek.

COMMON SHADOW ASPECTS:

- Rigid Buddha
- Frenetic Problem-Solver

This isn't meant to discourage you from building that remote cabin in the woods as your perfect hideaway. Rather it's to encourage your understanding that Peace is always available, no matter what life puts in front of us. With that realization, the remote hideaway becomes another expression of who you are rather than a compensatory mechanism to deal with the burden and aspects of life that drag you down. In other words, you *are* the hideaway in the woods. Peace isn't something to be contrived, but rather coming home to who you have always been.

Common Experience Coming of Age

Growing up, your embodiment of Peace may have been misconstrued as indifference. Teachers, parents, and peers may have mislabelled you as distracted, spacey, or uninterested in what was going on. In truth, you may be paying close attention, just doing so without becoming ruffled. When you show up as restful and relaxed, those around you decide you're just out of touch.

Growing up, your embodiment of Peace may have been misconstrued as indifference. Teachers, parents, and peers may have mislabelled you as distracted, spacey, or uninterested in what was going on.

Amidst this judgment and the world's uproar, you may have polarized towards your two shadow aspects. On the one hand, you choose avoidance, manipulating your circumstances to maintain Peace. On the other, you take on the story that you're uncaring and double down on *significance.* You push your Peace aside and lunge towards creating solutions.

Consequences of Owning Your Gifts

When you allow your Peace to manifest naturally, it can be frustrating for those around you who equate agitation with productivity, connection, and empathy. They're frustrated when they feel like they're losing it, and you—rather than empathizing and understanding—seem to think their concerns are no big deal.

Shadow Aspects

Over-Expressing: *Rigid Buddha*

You have seen the cost of a lack of Peace and fight hard to arrange life to prevent that from happening. Avoiding tough challenges becomes your goal rather than figuring out how to fully express your gift and making the impact you are here to create.

Possibility and fear tend to show up in equal and opposite measures to one another (because possibility exists in the realm of the unknown, and the unknown is what triggers our fear). Because your fears tend to revolve around the loss of your Peace now that you have found it, your capacity to expand beyond the world you have created is limited and hamstrung.

You successfully create a pocket of Peace for yourself, but you and those around you are left with a sense that there must be more to life. Life is lovely and placid, but in the absence of the storms you've come to fear, there is a corresponding lack of new possibility available.

Obvious (But Ineffective) Fix: Begin the Season of Yes!

While you're able to maintain yourself as an ocean of calm through controlling your surroundings and circumstances, you feel a bit like a boat caught without wind.

Tired of floating and not making quite the difference you are committed to, you decide to take on more projects and step into a bigger life. Maybe you accept a promotion or enter a relationship that demands more of you.

Because these changes are made on the surface, in the circumstances of your life rather than the underlying relationship you have to those circumstances, the impact is inevitable. While you initially feel good about creating something more significant than you had before, over time, you start to feel harried and frantic.

You remember the doldrums you left behind and don't wish to return but are left with a degree of resignation. You're having the kind of impact you want to have, playing the game of leadership, and working with powerful people and missions, but you suppose it just has to come with this frantic feeling.

COMMON SHADOW ASPECTS:

- Rigid Buddha
- Frenetic Problem-Solver

Under-Expressing: *Frenetic Problem-Solver*

This shadow aspect is borne of internalizing the feedback that Peace equates with laziness and indifference. To prove that you are not these things, you dive into the fray, tirelessly trading your Peace for frantic or belligerent action. Life, along with the opportunity to experience the Peace you are, becomes about getting everything done.

Of course, this is an impossible task, as the world is abundant and there is always going to be more to do. Further, because of the disempowered relationship you've created with Peace, even the moments of respite are simply a sign that the other shoe is going to drop.

Eventually you burn out—tempted once again to put up walls and retreat behind them, using the Obvious Fix to swing back to the other side of your shadow aspect.

While you're able to maintain yourself as an ocean of calm through controlling your surroundings and circumstances, you feel a bit like a boat caught without wind.

Obvious (But Ineffective) Fix: Embody the Irrefutable No

You notice that life seems to be a lot of frantic action and a constant managing of everything that gets thrown at you. Frustrated by the constant busy-ness, you attempt to change your circumstances around you so that you no longer have to do so much.

Taking stock of everything you've said yes to, you downshift your life: Maybe you fire a bunch of clients, take on a less demanding job, or get rid of possessions and try to simplify.

It works at first, as you have reduced the scale and size of the life you are living, but there's been no internal shift—you've simply changed the external circumstances in your life.

Over time, life starts to become about controlling and managing the world around you to ensure your Peace. You've reduced your circumstances, but because you haven't created the breakthrough that would allow you to be with *whatever* life is putting in front of you, you are forced to trade in the possibility and impact you'd like to create for the controlled calm of your shadow.

Creating the Breakthrough

Your strategies are set up to abandon the concept of Peace altogether or to limit your circumstances such that nothing interferes with your Peace. Both approaches ultimately leave you in reaction to your circumstances and prevent you embodying your gift fully.

The breakthrough lies in realizing that you are Peace and can access that way of being in any and every moment. From this place, changing your circumstances becomes less important.

The breakthrough lies in realizing that you *are* Peace and can access that way of being in any and every moment. From this place, changing your circumstances becomes less important. Your circumstances are not your adversaries but a useful set of mirrors, reflecting when your gift isn't yet fully expressed.

Transformation happens when we expand our capacity to *be with* whatever life provides us, without trying to control or hide from it (both of which shrink the full experience of being alive). By noticing when you generate frantic behaviour and anxiety, you can practise setting down that behaviour. Your breakthrough doesn't come from changing your situation, but by realizing the obstacles to your inherent Peace lie within.

Peace

COMMON SHADOW ASPECTS:

- Rigid Buddha
- Frenetic Problem-Solver

Leading and Working with People of Peace

Members of your team with Peace are an incredible gift amidst the chaotic energy of transformational work. As these team members deepen their leadership, they become like lighthouses for the entire team—beacons of rest, peace, and tranquillity. They are quietly reliable at getting things done without adding to the general chaos.

And yet—when they struggle with their gift, trying to do it all, they may inject the opposite kind of energy, becoming frantic and breathless. This sets up traps for you, as leader. The first trap is when that frantic energy gets picked up by the rest of the team. They may get everything done but can't seem to slow down when reporting in meetings, giving everyone the sense that they too should be running faster, thus spinning up the entire dynamic of your team.

An inexperienced leader witnessing this may feel compelled to pull this team member back from work that generates this dynamic, thereby removing their opportunity to deepen their leadership. The team member is more at ease, but they cease to grow—and someone else has to pick up that work. The other side of this leadership trap is to conclude that frenzied energy is "just who they are," and becoming resigned to it as the cost of getting things done. This approach may include efforts to quarantine other team members from the chaos.

Leaders need to stand for the leadership of their team members rather than their comfort.

Leaders need to stand for the *leadership* of their team members rather than their comfort. Watch for members of your team who generate high anxiety and remember this may reflect a shadow aspect of their innate Peace. Support them in recognizing who they truly are and the disconnect with how they're showing up in the moment. Help them understand that their opportunity for growth lies in their *relationship* to their workload, not the workload itself.

Share with these team members how much you value their presence, and support them as they open up into their embodied expression Peace.

Practises

Identify the storyline when Peace disappears from your life.

Notice when you erupt with reactive energy and when you don't. Recognize that this energy comes from within, not from the circumstances. What story are you telling yourself about these people, places, and things? Are there voices from the past you're trying to please or prove yourself to? How do you relate to the things around you that *don't* trigger your harried energy?

The story you tell yourself is at the heart of your journey as a leader. Get familiar with it and consider that you will be confronting it over and over as you deepen into your true self.

Notice the ways you actively create busy-ness and whip up frenzy.

The power in this practise comes in you getting responsible for the ways in which you create the very thing you are trying to avoid. By getting clear on this, you can take back your power. If you can see how you are actively creating the kind of energy you are trying to avoid, you can start to do something about. As long as you operate under the belief that your experience of life is a function of the world around you, your only option is to try and avoid these circumstances.

Put your attention on the experience you'd like to create in your life.

Building the tranquil lakeside cottage to escape to each year is a beautiful thing, but if you create that through your

COMMON SHADOW ASPECTS:

- Rigid Buddha
- Frenetic Problem-Solver

chaos and franticness, it's kind of missing the point, isn't it? If the cottage becomes an escape from all the chaotic energy you surround yourself with, it's not really serving you to deepen—only to escape what you are creating on a regular basis.

How could you create the results you're committed to *and* simultaneously create a deeper experience of Peace than ever before?

Building the tranquil lakeside cottage to escape to each year is a beautiful thing, but if you create that through your chaos and franticness, it's kind of missing the point, isn't it?

Peace

COMMON SHADOW ASPECTS:

- Rigid Buddha
- Frenetic Problem-Solver

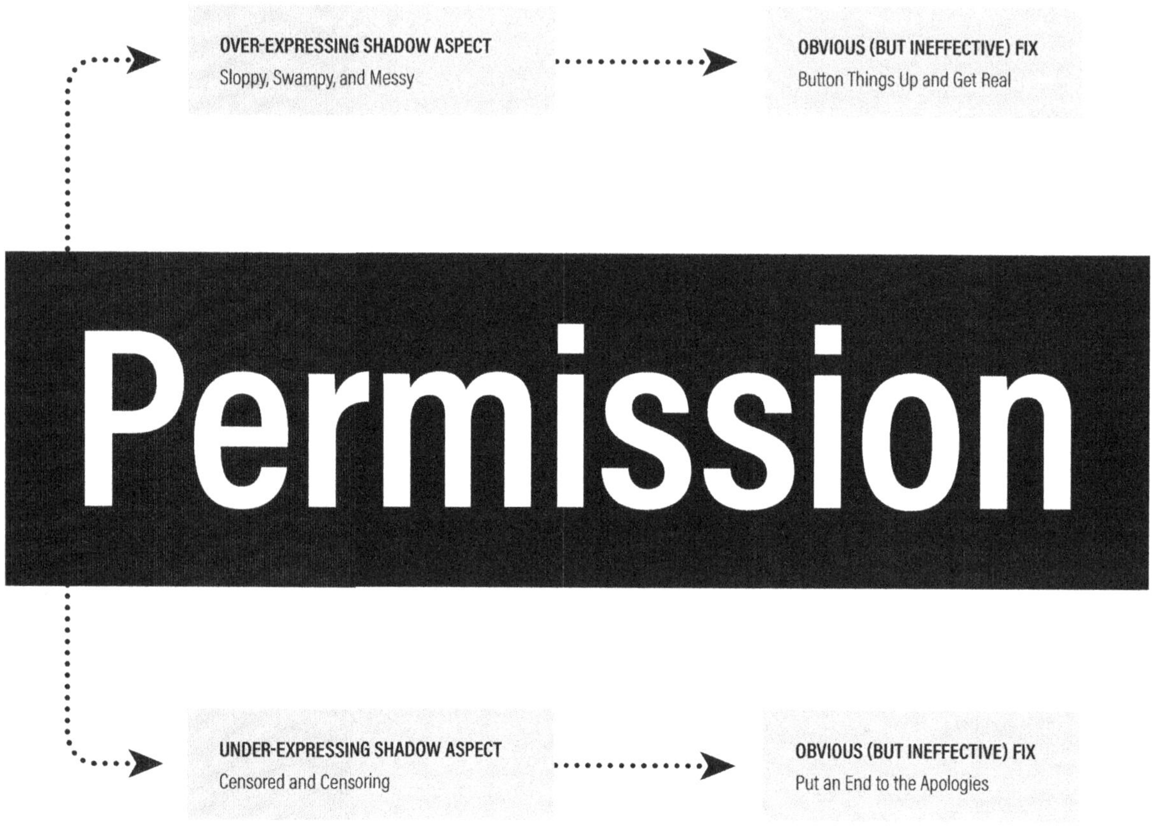

OVER-EXPRESSING SHADOW ASPECT
Sloppy, Swampy, and Messy

OBVIOUS (BUT INEFFECTIVE) FIX
Button Things Up and Get Real

Permission

UNDER-EXPRESSING SHADOW ASPECT
Censored and Censoring

OBVIOUS (BUT INEFFECTIVE) FIX
Put an End to the Apologies

COMMON DESCRIPTORS

Approving, Acceptance, Freedom to Be Exactly as I Am, Allowance, Receptive, Open-Minded, Safety, Feel Like I Can Be Myself, Intimacy

The Quality

Your Gift

In your presence people feel Permission to show up exactly how they are, wherever they are, in each and every moment. The gift of Permission is healing to people. You create the space for them to experience and allow all of who they are. Your acceptance allows people to find within themselves greater ease and creativity, to access what they long ago took away from themselves. With you, people feel safe and empowered to speak fully with their own voice, to honor their body, to dress as they want to dress, and to express the opinions they have.

When people meet you for the first time, they may share more intimately and deeply than they normally do. A natural consequence of Permission is a tendency to fall into the role of confidante. This isn't something you aim to do, although you love it when people are willing to share their deepest truths with you. It's a natural byproduct of the acceptance and permission you create in your presence.

The teams you lead embody a greater degree of trust by virtue of the permissive space you clear for them. They feel safe to express themselves in ways they never have with their previous leaders. Your team members are more likely to share their truths openly and less likely to harbour resentments, making it easier for things to be cleared up.

COMMON SHADOW ASPECTS:

- Sloppy, Swampy, and Messy
- Censored and Censoring

With you, people feel safe and empowered to speak fully with their own voice, to honor their body, to dress as they want to dress, and to express the opinions they have.

The innate Permission you bring into the world overlaps with the quality of Integrity, in that it allows you to be yourself. You probably dress, carry yourself, and speak to people in ways that feel good to you. You follow your own path and want more than anything to empower others to do the same.

What is Predictable

Yours is the gift of a natural freedom of expression. Unfortunately, much of the world is not prepared nor appreciative of this particular quality and will respond by attempting to teach you prudence.

In doing so, you are trained in two distinct patterns (manifested in your shadow). The first is that what comes most naturally to you is *wrong*. The innate Permission that exists within you is not to be trusted, and consequently, you need monitor it in both yourself and, over time, others.

The second pattern you're trained in is that, given the world attempts to constrain and control your freedom of expression, you need to defend it vigorously.

As these two conflicting aspects of your shadow are developed, your life becomes a tension between the two extremes.

In some places you insist on people following the rules and tend towards paternalistic, highly structured approaches. These approaches do double duty, ensuring that people don't get too permissive with themselves, and in other situations, that we don't take any action that might take away from someone else's freedom of expression.

You become a contradiction in terms, simultaneously fighting for the right of people to express themselves with one hand while you shut down expression with your other.

Leaders with the gift of Permission excel at allowing people to make mistakes and create messes without fear of being blamed. But your fear of making people wrong and shutting them down means you struggle to bring rigour and accountability to your teams.

You give everyone the freedom to express themselves fully ***and*** *to take responsibility for cleaning up any mess this creates.*

As a result, your teams tend to be places where people fail to take responsibility or clean up their messes. What initially seemed to be a growth edge eventually keeps them from actual growth.

What is Possible

When you learn that Permission isn't something to be bestowed or held in check but a gift you bring to every space, you free yourself from compulsively breaking down doors, eliminating rules, and protecting other people (regardless of whether they need or want protection).

The true gift of Permission comes from being willing to make a mess (the first stage of Permission) and then cleaning up the impact of the messes you make (the second stage of Permission).

This gives everyone the freedom to express themselves fully *and* to take responsibility for cleaning up any mess this creates. When you marry love and responsibility in this manner without bringing blame into the picture you become the kind of leader who generates leadership in others.

Permission

COMMON SHADOW ASPECTS:

- Sloppy, Swampy, and Messy
- Censored and Censoring

Other leaders will look at you and wonder why your teams work together so efficiently and effortlessly. Isn't there supposed to be more friction and jostling along the way?

Common Experience Coming of Age

Growing up, there's every chance you got into trouble by embodying Permission. As a child, total freedom to explore isn't necessarily desirable or safe and may have led your parents and teachers to come down hard on what came naturally to you. Permission became unsafe, and you learned it was safer to wrap yourself in rules and restrictions.

When rules and structure become the enemy of your shadow, your life becomes less and less structured.

Alternatively, you may have learned that guarding your innate freedom was essential and constantly at risk of being taken away. Self-expression and Permission became all-important.

Consequences of Owning Your Gifts

As you start to embrace and embody more of the Permission you are, you will likely create messes and interpret the reaction to these messes as an indication that you need to shut yourself back down. There is a gift in you learning the difference between censoring yourself or apologizing and being responsible for your impact.

Shadow Aspects

Over-Expressing: *Sloppy, Swampy, and Messy*

Taken to the extreme, your mission becomes about protecting and embodying Permission in all its forms. You act out against any rule or norm that restricts your freedom or the freedom of others.

There are many ways you might act out, including promiscuity and substance abuse. Rules are made to be broken, after all, and you don't need Permission from others to do what feels right.

When rules and structure become the enemy of your shadow, your life becomes less and less structured. You may get things done but flail along the way for lack of a structured process. You have Permission to do anything and often say yes to more than you should. At times, you notice yourself wishing for a slightly more linear path to walk but dismiss this quickly.

Because of the training and conclusions you put together growing up, responsibility gets equated with censorship, making people wrong, and an imposition on our right to simply be as we are. This leaves you unwilling (and unable) to take ownership for what you create and for your impact along the way.

You tend to be left by people unwilling to sit in the messes you create and end up surrounded by people who create similar messes.

Obvious (But Ineffective) Fix: Button Things Up and Get Real

Realizing one day that the promise of Permission for all isn't getting you what you want, you decide it was a nice idea but that now you need to tighten up. A big part of this is that you want to have more people around you, and the way you were showing up seemed to drive them away.

You slowly but surely stuff down your impulses, desires, and everything else that Permission makes available. You go from being a "truth-teller" who has trouble fitting in to someone who is likable because they act like everyone else.

You start to judge yourself and others for being reckless. While people are willing to be around you and you seem to make fewer messes, you feel a growing resentment that you only have friends and get invited to things if you keep yourself (and subconsciously others) from showing up too much.

COMMON SHADOW ASPECTS:

- Sloppy, Swampy, and Messy
- Censored and Censoring

Over time, you evolve from resenting people for being unwilling to accept you as you are into resenting yourself for the self-censorship you've imposed to be accepted.

Under-Expressing: *Censored and Censoring*

When the gift of Permission is reflected by others as something negative (e.g., "Nothing ever gets done when people do whatever they feel like"), you shut it down, withdrawing Permission from everyone and everything.

There are correct ways to behave and correct ways to show up, and your job is to discern what's right and wrong. Over time, this becomes the code you live by.

There are correct ways to behave and correct ways to show up, and your job is to discern what's right and wrong. Over time, this becomes the code you live by. Permission, by its nature, becomes a dangerous thing you must keep buttoned down.

This feels like a successful approach, but you become the victim of your own rules, censoring yourself and doing almost anything to avoid negative impact. Life becomes a bit dry and boring, but at least you're not getting into trouble.

One of the ways your shadow will convince you that everything's all right with this approach is by shrinking your world. It's a little bit like a bird flying into an atrium in a building and then creating an experience of freedom inside those confines. Permission is available for all here, provided you stay within these prescribed rules.

In this way, your shadow keeps itself hidden, clothing the strict conformity it demands in what looks like Permission. You fully believe that you stand for Permission and draw it out in those around you, remaining blind to the small enclosure within which Permission is allowed.

Obvious (But Ineffective) Fix: Put an End to the Apologies

Tired of censoring and apologizing for yourself, you declare mightily to the world that you are done with all that and will no longer conform and clean yourself up to make other people feel comfortable.

Unfortunately, that leaves you creating messes and resentment in your wake. Resentment not for who you are as a person but because you're unable and unwilling with this new approach to be responsible for your impact.

This obvious fix conflates taking responsibility with accepting blame. You feel great without all those restrictions but notice people starting to withdraw. Unable to own your impact on other people and to take responsibility for that impact, you blame others. They just can't handle the real me, you tell yourself.

Because they often learn in childhood to hold back on their natural instincts, those with Permission tend to reach this point later in their life. They're left to choose between censoring who they are, or showing up as themselves but being unwilling and unable to hear about the impact they're having and grow correspondingly.

Your leadership is confined to your own self-awareness. Because this aspect of your shadow leaves you closed to reflection from others about the impact you may be having, you are unable to grow beyond what you already know.

COMMON SHADOW ASPECTS:

- Sloppy, Swampy, and Messy
- Censored and Censoring

Creating the Breakthrough

Your strategies are ultimately a function of how you collapse blame and responsibility into one. Be yourself and get blamed or button everything up to avoid blame. With this perspective, your only option is to keep swinging back and forth between these two undesirable shadow aspects, spending just enough time in one to get sick of it then jump back to the other.

The gift of Permission becomes open and available when you are willing to be with your impact and practise setting aside the blame *you* create around that impact.

Your leadership is confined to your own self-awareness.

Part of the challenge here, as with the shadows of all qualities of being, is that you create a world that reflects your shadows back to you. Even though you are the final arbiter of making someone wrong (yourself included), you have created a career, family, and friends who reflect that same belief. This forces you to live with the feeling of being made wrong before you can break through into true Permission.

When you become willing to sit with the feelings of blame and being wrong and find support to release them, responsibility becomes tolerable and then easily available. From this point, you can live freely and support others to do the same.

The Permission that is your birthright comes alive not through avoiding blame but by trusting your ability to show up as who you are, clean up any messes that's created, and move forwards cleanly from there.

Leading and Working with People of Permission

Members on your team with the gift of Permission will be magnificent at creating bonds of trust and empathy with their teammates. They have an innate ability to draw out deeper truths with their team and become confidantes for the leaders of the teams they're on.

While this trust and intimacy is a tremendous gift, it brings its own issues that will challenge unprepared leaders. Team members with the gift of Permission will likely be zealous critics when others are held accountable for their actions. Confusing responsibility with blame, they will implicitly sabotage leadership efforts to establish rigour and responsibility. Rather than working around their tendency to interject themselves as fierce defenders, address it directly.

Taking responsibility for something that didn't go well is not the same as being to blame for it.

Doing so requires you to have done your own work to move beyond blame and to stand for Responsibility instead. Bring this to your coach and work through it. Saying that you don't blame someone when blame is clearly leaking through in your tone will just worsen relations with your Permission-type team members.

Bring the distinction between responsibility and blame to your Permission-type team member and invite them to distinguish the two. Help them understand that taking responsibility for something that didn't go well doesn't automatically confer blame. Invite them to see how taking responsibility means they step into more and more of their power. Help your team members self-inquire regarding their motivations for leaping to others' defence.

If a Permission-type personality leads one of your teams, you may end up with close-knit teams that operate in dysfunction but are incredibly accepting within that dysfunction. Be clean and clear with yourself about distinguishing blame and responsibility and stand for your team leader to step into responsibility for correcting the problems.

Permission

COMMON SHADOW ASPECTS:

- Sloppy, Swampy, and Messy
- Censored and Censoring

Your Permission-type leaders need to move beyond simply accepting (and defending) everything that happens and bring rigour to their teams. Help them recognize that their work includes holding their team members' and direct reports' feet to the fire, not by blaming and shaming, but by inviting them to be responsible for their impact and to take the next steps necessary to moving forwards more productively.

Practises

Distinguish responsibility from blame.

One of the most valuable practises to begin taking on is distinguishing responsibility from blame. Sit down and write out your definitions of the two concepts and how you would distinguish them from each other. How do you hold responsibility? How is it different from blame? If you notice that these two things go hand in hand, you may need to do some work to pull them apart.

How do you hold responsibility? How is it different from blame?

The more resistance you have to pulling these two concepts apart (even if the resistance is just getting stuck with "I don't know"), the greater your opportunity to learn from this.

Notice all the ways you see the world through a lens of blame.

Those who are Permission are quick to insist that they would *never* place blame on someone for how they show up. This insistence is a perfect hiding spot for our ego and shadow aspects. Practise noticing all the situations in which you apportion blame.

If you find yourself getting stuck here, consider that the first place to look might be when you blame someone for not giving another person enough Permission to be who they are. Intolerance of someone else's intolerance is still intolerance. Can you give Permission to those who take it away from others? This is the highest level of practise.

Get curious and expand your capacity to be responsible. Notice the places where you're unwilling to apologize for how you've shown up, and instead, get curious about what you can be responsible for.

A leader is always looking at how they can become responsible for *more* of what has been created rather than less. Notice when you resist taking responsibility and practise pushing through that resistance. How can you broaden your ability to own what has been created? How can you take one hundred percent responsibility for what has occurred?

COMMON SHADOW ASPECTS:

- Sloppy, Swampy, and Messy
- Censored and Censoring

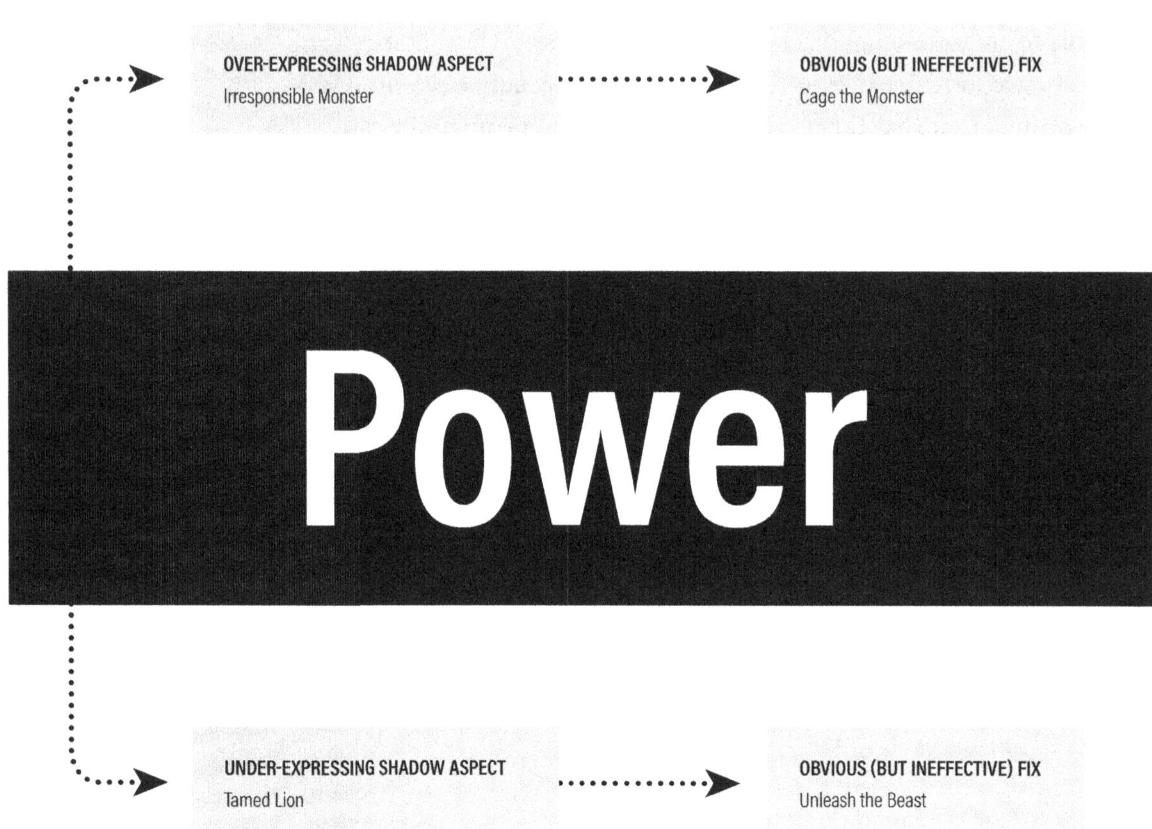
OVER-EXPRESSING SHADOW ASPECT
Irresponsible Monster
OBVIOUS (BUT INEFFECTIVE) FIX
Cage the Monster
Power
UNDER-EXPRESSING SHADOW ASPECT
Tamed Lion
OBVIOUS (BUT INEFFECTIVE) FIX
Unleash the Beast

COMMON DESCRIPTORS

Authority, Commanding, Sovereignty, Sway, Leverage, Clout, Forceful, Strength, Might, Vigour, Intensity, Potent, Impactful, Fortitude, Guts

The Quality

Your Gift

Putting you on a project imbues that project with unstoppable momentum. There is no force strong enough to keep you from creating what you want. Once you've set your sights on something, you will let nothing get in your way. Conversations with you often leave people charged up, unsure why something was getting in their way before, and quite clear that it won't do so anymore. You move through life with an intention and a potency that many admire and envy.

Your Power is not a function of what you say or do, nor how you say or do it. You don't need to shout or take robust action for people to feel the Power you embody. You can make a request in a whisper, and people still feel the impact as a function of your underlying being.

Your gift lends itself naturally to leadership, though that is not a necessity for you to align with your natural state. You can bring Power to how you follow another leader or to the simple act of reading a book.

In martial arts, the Power delivered by a punch is a function of how well aligned someone's fist, wrist, forearm, elbow, and shoulder are. Similarly, your gifts are closely related to your integrity and alignment. The flip side of this is the lack of Power you feel when caught in a situation that doesn't align with your deepest truth.

COMMON SHADOW ASPECTS:

- Irresponsible Monster
- Tamed Lion

You don't need to shout or take robust action for people to feel the Power you embody. You can make a request in a whisper, and people still feel the impact as a function of your underlying being.

What is Predictable

Embodying Power can be a dangerous thing, especially when you're still figuring out how to use it responsibly. Like a superhero who hasn't yet learned how to harness their special abilities, you may cause damage and leave people upset.

This ability to impact people powerfully is a function of your gift. The reality is that human beings impact each other all the time, for better and for worse. However, you in particular are told that your impacts are just too big, to the point of being a danger to others.

To resolve this, you probably went down one of two predictable paths. The first path is deciding that your Power just can't be trusted, and so you routinely cage and hobble yourself. You become oversensitive to the possibility that you might be reprimanded for causing harm and end up feeling powerless and like a wimp. On the plus side, you feel safe in the knowledge that you don't hurt people anymore. That's a noble trade-off, in theory, and it comes from a heartfelt place, but it leaves you feeling inadequate and unfulfilled.

The other path is deciding that if people let themselves get hurt that's their problem and has nothing to do with you. Your job is to live your life as you see fit. How people feel about that isn't up to you to manage. In going down this path, you experience your Power more fully but at the cost of disconnecting from people. You leave anger and hurt feelings in your wake, and some of the people you liked now avoid you, but you're unable or unwilling to address it. After all, you're just being who you are.

What is Possible

The possibility you represent for all of us lies in fully expressing who you are while simultaneously being responsible for the impact of that expression. When you begin doing your real work—taking ownership of your impact and cleaning up any mess you create, intended or otherwise—you discover a level of Power that goes deeper than mere strength.

The more you integrate Power with responsibility, the more you model for the world that it's okay to make mistakes and that there is no mess we cannot make right.

The more you integrate Power with responsibility, the more you model for the world that it's okay to make mistakes and that there is no mess we cannot make right. In so doing, you develop a deep affinity and trust for yourself and deepen your intimacy and connection with others. They trust that when you create a mess, you'll clean it up. Through this practise, expressing your innate gift transcends dominance or pulling your punches. You earn people's trust, establishing comfort with and appreciation for your embodied Power.

As you deepen in your journey, you will notice that not only is more Power available but also more love. Each time you create a mess and clean it up, you open the doors for more intimacy and trust between you and the person you are cleaning up with. And as you deepen intimacy and trust with someone, you also open the door for a deeper expression of Power. You are the possibility of Power wielded benevolently, with an open heart.

Common Experience Coming of Age

COMMON SHADOW ASPECTS:

- Irresponsible Monster
- Tamed Lion

Growing up, you may have wondered why things kept going wrong and people kept getting hurt despite your good intentions. The heartbreak you felt over this led you to hold back instinctively—or to toughen yourself to other people's pain. You may have excelled in sports and gotten into fights, situations that rewarded your strength and ferocity.

Consequences of Owning Your Gifts

When you rely on Power alone, you get your way but at the expense of bulldozing people. Some will go along with you, so long as it suits them, but they understand the bargain they've made—to take your shit or get out of the way. You may end up the kind of leader who rarely looks for a win-win solution and gets things done by inspiring fear in their allies as well as their enemies.

Shadow Aspects

Over-Expressing: *Irresponsible Monster*

Seeing the collateral damage you cause is painful, and at some point, that pain becomes too much to bear. You make the empathic pain you feel the problem and shut that part of your heart down.

The shadow aspects of Power emerge as a result of the innate impact you have on and in the world. Your impact is larger than most and can tend to create collateral damage.

Possessing Power doesn't necessarily mean you lack empathy. Seeing the collateral damage you cause is painful, and at some point, that pain becomes too much to bear. You make the empathic pain you feel the problem and shut that part of your heart down. You decide that what people make of you is their business, not yours; you never volunteered to be their babysitter, after all.

Over time, this strategy works in the sense that you get things done without having to second-guess yourself. When people get hurt in the process, you fall back on maxims like, "My way or the highway," and "If you can't take the heat, get out of the kitchen."

By shutting your empathy off, you become less able to feel the impact of your actions and consequently, lose the ability to be responsible for them. Your need to distance yourself innocently ends up turning you into a monster in the eyes of many people.

Obvious (But Ineffective) Fix: Cage the Monster

As much as you've managed to shut down your heart and operate over top of your impact, you remain a caring, loving person. On some level, you still feel the collateral damage you cause, and eventually, you decide it's too much to bear. You strive to be a better person.

You conclude that your problem is the impact your actions have—and so you set about containing their breadth, scope, and power. Rather than getting responsible for your impact and cleaning up the messes you've made, you instead try to avoid ever making a mess in the first place.

You hold back how you feel, keeping your Power in check so that others are not hurt by you.

You hold back how you feel, keeping your Power in check so that others are not hurt by you. Over time, you start to resent everyone around you. They seem happier, but things take longer. You feel like you're held in check, ineffective and weak.

Predictably, it's only a matter of time before the volcano explodes again because you haven't addressed the underlying issue; you've just found new ways of avoiding it. When a full blowout doesn't happen because you no longer allow it to be directly expressed, you may unconsciously find indirect ways to express Power by undermining people, cutting them with sarcasm or subtly taking control of whatever situation you find yourself in.

COMMON SHADOW ASPECTS:

- Irresponsible Monster
- Tamed Lion

Under-Expressing: *Tamed Lion*

This shadow aspect takes the opposite approach to dealing with your outsized impact. Whereas the first operates by you avoiding and dismissing your unintended impact, this second aspect operates by attempting to avoid making any impact in the first place. If you constantly pull your punches, you're assured of never hurting anyone again.

You show up like a lion terrified of its strength. The internal restraint this requires is exhausting. Feeling in conflict with yourself, you unleash internally, becoming ruthless with yourself. Occasionally, this spills over onto other people where either a degree of anonymity or familiarity makes it safe to do so (e.g., shop clerks, people in traffic, or romantic relationships and friendships).

Your breakthrough begins with the willingness to show up in the fullness of your Power—and consequently being willing to receive feedback from those you may hurt and clean up any messes you create.

When this ruthless, powerful side of you leaks out, you're horrified by the impact and double down on holding yourself in—leaving those around you to wonder at the incongruity between those prodigious explosions and the tamed lion who normally shows up.

Obvious (But Ineffective) Fix: Unleash the Beast

Having put yourself and your Power in a cage, you've managed to create a life free of upsetting or hurting people. But you often feel like a wimp (or at least as though you're perceived as one). Tired of this experience, you decide it's time to turn over a new leaf and commit to telling people how you really feel or showing up in the world with all of your Power expressed.

When you do so, the impact is overblown and dramatic. You have zero practise with this new approach, and so you spew molten lava. This impact, caused because you're practising something different, isn't a problem in and of itself. The problem is how you relate to it—that it's wrong and shouldn't be happening. From here, you have little capacity to let someone share with you what impact you've had. Instead, you push towards making your impact someone else's problem.

You do this by hardening your heart so you can forge forwards or by doubling down on your commitment to hide your power to keep the world safe. In either case, you're pushed back out to one of the two poles of your shadow.

Creating the Breakthrough

You see your gift of Power purely through the lens of its impact, and your shadow's responses are to either diminish that impact across the board or diminish your capacity to care. Both are deeply unsatisfying and unsustainable. What they have in common is avoidance.

Your breakthrough begins with the willingness to show up in the fullness of your Power—and consequently being willing to receive feedback from those you may hurt and clean up any messes you create. Over time, you will learn to express your Power with greater precision and accuracy. Spilling milk in someone else's kitchen is only a problem if you are unwilling to clean it up.

The more you take responsibility for and receive feedback about your impact, the more you are able to learn about what does and does not work, and the more deftly you will wield your Power.

By the way, don't get too caught up in whether someone's complaint about your impact is right or fair. Accept the generosity of that feedback regardless of how artful or artless its delivery.

Leading and Working with People of Power

Team members embodying Power will bring potency and determination to the table. With them on board, projects are less likely to go down rabbit holes or become exercises in navel-gazing. Having said that, these team members may create their own breakdowns—trampling on other people's feelings and blowing up at obstacles, unable to manage their anger.

COMMON SHADOW ASPECTS:

- Irresponsible Monster
- Tamed Lion

Your work involves supporting these people to see and acknowledge their impact as it happens and to work in partnership with them and the people whose feelings they've bruised. This won't get you a win the first time you try. The bruisers won't want to slow down, and the bruised may be too shy or conflict-avoidant to share.

In order to avoid making a mess, you often have to exert a lot of control, either over yourself and your expression or on the situation and those around you.

To succeed in this mediation, you need to be doing your own work, such that you can articulate someone's impact without blame or making them wrong (which will only trigger defensiveness.) Remember that they may already be making themselves wrong for this, and that your job is to support them in taking responsibility *free of blame.*

Pay attention as well to members of your team who come across as unusually powerless. These may be Power-types who have learned to operate from the other side of their shadow. Get curious about what lies underneath and what they would be saying or doing if they didn't worry about how it would land. Stand for them and encourage this expression. Only when they begin to express themselves fully can you invite them into a conversation about responsibility. Their path to leadership may require an awkward blurt-out phase before moving towards responsibility.

Practises

Notice the places where you hold your Power in check. What do you hide from the rest of the world—and from yourself? Are there ways you pull your punches to avoid fully expressing Power? If you find yourself doing this, begin by simply vocalizing what you see. For bonus points, practise expressing one percent more of what you're holding back.

Look for the ways you control a given situation and what you sacrifice to do so.

In order to avoid making a mess, you often have to exert a lot of control, either over yourself and your expression or on the situation and those around you.

Notice when and what you're controlling in any given situation and get clear on what it's costing you. Is it tiring to do so? Do you feel disconnected from those around you? Perhaps you're often left frustrated.

Practise releasing your control as access to that one percent more expression described above.

Ask people for feedback on your impact.

Be in the practise of asking people for feedback about your impact. Here's a simple question to try: "Hey, how did that land for you?" Listen to how they respond without needing to justify what you did or make them wrong for how they received it. The more you're willing to sit with people and listen in this way, the more responsibly you can wield your choices and your Power.

Don't apologize and fall on your sword.

Be careful about apologizing too quickly. One of the best ways to avoid getting really present to your impact is to attempt to immediately apologize for it so that it goes away and is resolved. Avoid the temptation of falling on your sword and writhing in apologetics to escape. Instead, simply sit in the discomfort that may come up. This is your path to truly responsible Power.

COMMON SHADOW ASPECTS:

- Irresponsible Monster
- Tamed Lion

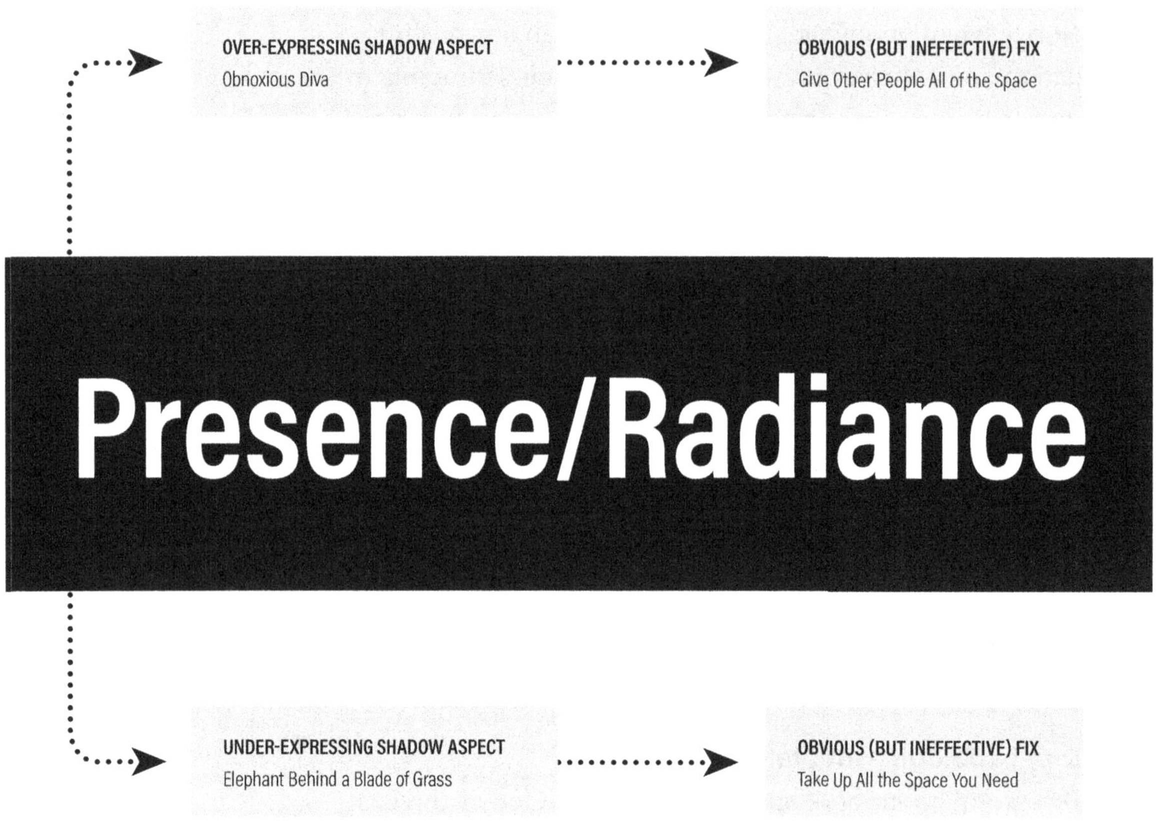

OVER-EXPRESSING SHADOW ASPECT
Obnoxious Diva

OBVIOUS (BUT INEFFECTIVE) FIX
Give Other People All of the Space

Presence/Radiance

UNDER-EXPRESSING SHADOW ASPECT
Elephant Behind a Blade of Grass

OBVIOUS (BUT INEFFECTIVE) FIX
Take Up All the Space You Need

COMMON DESCRIPTORS

Charisma, Vivid, Individuality, Get Noticed, Magnetism, Take Up Space, X-Factor, Handsome, Attractive, Beauty, Dazzling, Style, Fashionable

The Quality

Your Gift

No matter the event, room, or space, you are a lightning rod for attention. You're noticed when you enter the room and when you leave. You have the gift of innate Presence. You can take up space like nobody's business—wherever you find yourself, people are watching.

In this chapter, I present Presence and Radiance interchangeably. They're essentially the same quality, although for individuals identifying as men, we tend to relate to it as Presence; for individuals identifying as women, we tend to see it as Radiance. Those with Presence or Radiance have the celebrity factor. People with this gift naturally draw our eyes. They are also highly sensitive to what draws the attention of others, and what pushes it away.

Those with Presence or Radiance are often good-looking, although not necessarily in the sense of being physically attractive. They are good-looking in the sense that they're interesting and satisfying to look at, in the way you might describe a city as "good walking." Adam Driver, known for his portrayal of Kylo Ren in Star Wars, is a great example of this quality.

Because those with Presence and Radiance are highly attuned to the attention of others, they tend to have a gift for aesthetics, production,

COMMON SHADOW ASPECTS:

- Obnoxious Diva
- Elephant Behind a Blade of Grass

Those with Presence or Radiance have the celebrity factor. People with this gift naturally draw our eyes.

fashion, and art. As artists, photographers, and directors, they put this gift to work by expressing the beauty of the world.

What is Predictable

You love the spotlight and love the positive feedback you receive in the form of people's attention, which satisfies your need for approval and recognition. Having said that, all those people turning their heads towards you becomes a lot of energy to hold and receive. Some people may be triggered by your ability to take up space, dismissing you as an attention hog and deliberately turning away—which leaves you bereft of the attention that affirms you and may drive up your fear of being irrelevant. Moreover, those around you who *also* possess Presence/Radiance may feel the need to compete, either by turning their light way up or diminishing yours.

You take all this feedback as a clear message that you're just too much and dial down your light. You become careful not to take up space when others might want it. You find some refuge in this diminished aspect of your shadow, but it stokes your fears of being invisible and irrelevant. And in fact, the rest of the world sees you like an elephant hiding behind a blade of grass. People wonder, "When are they going to take the stage?"

At the other extreme, you find yourself stealing the show entirely, taking up *all* the space in a conversation. As this approach comes from fear, there's an element of desperation in this effort, and, as noted, it sparks resentment and disapproval in some. Predictably, you find yourself resenting others—both when they take up too much space and when they're unwilling to do so and complain about how you do.

The lesson you end up teaching the world—regardless of which shadow you embody—is that it's not okay to shine our light as brightly as we can.

What is Possible

You represent the possibility of everyone discovering and becoming the stars they are. When you release your fear of being irrelevant, it frees you from the need to compete for the spotlight or see it as "your territory" to defend. Radiance/Presence becomes a natural expression of who you are rather than a means to get approval or recognition.

Human beings are the embodiment of paradox, and part of the paradox you carry is a fear of being either too much or not enough. Expressing one aspect of this shadow alleviates one of these fears until that becomes too much, and you swing to the other side to compensate.

The possibility of full expression becomes available to you when you come to terms with your fears of irrelevance *and* of sucking the oxygen out of the room. This isn't necessarily a flaw—it's just evidence that you're a human being who sometimes slips out of balance. When you can accept that, you open the gates to the free expression that is your birthright.

As you become more conscious of—and willing to receive feedback about—when you dim your light unnaturally and when you turn it too far up, you develop better instincts about when to take centre stage and when to hold it open for others. People learn simply by being around you that everyone has the capacity for Presence and Radiance.

Presence/Radiance

COMMON SHADOW ASPECTS:

- Obnoxious Diva
- Elephant Behind a Blade of Grass

Common Experience Coming of Age

Growing up, you probably heard comments like, "Stop showing off," and "Give someone else a turn." While some people were delighted by your natural attraction, powerful voice and energy, others were triggered. Unable to recognize their own internal struggle with Presence/Radiance, they pressured you to diminish your light.

Your natural tendency to attract attention meant that you got more feedback than most, making you especially vigilant about how people perceive you at any given moment.

As you become more conscious of—and willing to receive feedback about—when you dim your light unnaturally and when you turn it too far up, you develop better instincts about when to take centre stage and when to hold it open for others.

Consequences of Owning Your Gifts

When you show up fully, some people create meaning about themselves and/or you ("I'm not enough," "She's too much," etc.). Either way, the message is the same—they don't like or approve of you when you express yourself naturally.

Shadow Aspects

Over-Expressing: *Obnoxious Diva*

A core fear for those with the gift of Presence/Radiance is that of irrelevancy—the painful sense that "I'm not enough, and I don't matter." In reaction to this fear, they become like an addict who needs a fix. The attention they receive naturally isn't enough because no amount of attention can disprove this persistent fear. As a result, your shadow becomes ever more needy and demanding of attention.

You own centre stage by whatever means necessary, sometimes becoming obnoxious and overbearing. It all becomes a one-man show with you as the star.

Ironically, this becomes isolating. Because you suck the oxygen out of the room, you preclude others from reflecting your impact. Either they compete for the limelight (which leads you to clutch for attention even more), or they shrug and give up, letting you have your time until they can move on.

You're definitely an entertaining show. It's just that people don't want to spend their whole lives watching a show. They want connection, dialog, and (like you) a chance to have an impact.

Growing up, you probably heard comments like, "Stop showing off," and "Give someone else a turn."

Driven by your core fear, you become masterful at hiding in plain sight. You appear to be sharing a great deal about yourself, but on some level, you know it's all part of the show.

Obvious (But Ineffective) Fix: Give Other People All of the Space

Over time, you get tired of the work involved in proving, forcing, and performing your Presence/Radiance constantly. You don't love competing with other people or experiencing their resentment. It's exhausting always being on. Situations where you can relax and simply BE feel few and far between, and you crave a break.

So, you start holding yourself back. You sit quietly and give other people all the space they want. And yet this doesn't feel right either. You're biting back your natural expression, and everyone else is waiting for you to jump in and say something. Whereas you used to feel the exhaustion of always being on, you now feel the exhaustion of actively resisting your expression.

Sometimes you just can't help yourself—you jump back in, stealing a punchline or abruptly kicking someone off stage just when they're getting comfortable.

In the end, as people watch the inconsistent way you hold yourself, they're left with the sense that you just won't let yourself be real. You may give up the spotlight, but it's only a matter of time before you lunge in and grab it back. People begin to feel awkward around you, which just exacerbates your deepest fears.

COMMON SHADOW ASPECTS:

- Obnoxious Diva
- Elephant Behind a Blade of Grass

Under-Expressing: *Elephant Behind a Blade of Grass*

Terrified of being too much or filled with judgment about those who are, you overcompensate by pulling a hood over your light. As long as you remain dim and contained, no one can accuse you of taking up too much space.

Driven by your core fear, you become masterful at hiding in plain sight. You appear to be sharing a great deal about yourself, but on some level, you know it's all part of the show.

When you enter a room, people notice and then forget you. Later, they're puzzled when they notice you again and wonder, "Why did I forget this person?" By refusing to take up space, you create a bizarre experience for people. They sense that something's off about your behaviour, which is distracting and takes up its own kind of space.

A simple model here is when someone in a meeting speaks softly, explains they don't have too much to say, then talk at great length. Paradoxically, if they were willing to project their voice and take up the room, there would be less attention and energy directed towards them. As with all shadows, we tend to create the very thing we are seeking to avoid. In this way, your attempts to stay hidden actually force people to notice you.

You may become a champion for other people's light to shine brightly. Because you ARE Radiance/Presence but won't step into that yourself, you find proxies and support them as they step into their own light. People operating predominantly from this shadow aspect often find themselves in careers devoted to getting other people seen, such as directors, producers, agents, and more.

Obvious (But Ineffective) Fix: Take Up All the Space You Need

You've been squelching your Radiance/Presence for far too long and swing to the opposite extreme: "From now on, I'll take up all the space I need!"

But during those years of atrophy, you've lost your ability to calibrate how you take up space, and your attempts land awkwardly and cause embarrassment. Others may see you as obnoxious, overbearing, or simply clumsy, and you may feel inauthentic and awkward as you learn to flex those withered muscles.

When this awkward, all-or-nothing approach shows up, you are left feeling embarrassed and uncomfortable with all the stage lights shining on you. Rather than relating to this as a practise and sitting with the discomfort that comes from learning something new, you distance yourself from the discomfort, insisting that you just need to learn to be okay with all eyes on you, all the time.

By refusing to take up space, you create a bizarre experience for people. They sense that something's off about your behaviour, which is distracting and takes up its own kind of space.

You white-knuckle your way through to the shift you are hoping to create. As a result, you end up at the other side of your shadow, taking all the air out of the room, and, because you've distanced yourself from feeling this impact, you're unable to acknowledge or do anything about this new tendency of yours.

Creating the Breakthrough

The gateway to breakthrough for Presence/Radiance is often a willingness to be with those moments when you overdo or underdo it without over-compensating in the other direction. You may come across as irrelevant and/or obnoxious once in a while, but so what? In letting yourself do so—and in willingly considering the feedback you get—you're learning to calibrate and adjust your presence (and corresponding impact) to what best suits the situation.

Presence/Radiance

COMMON SHADOW ASPECTS:

- Obnoxious Diva
- Elephant Behind a Blade of Grass

Practise noticing your impact. Are you taking up a lot of space? Any space? What would best serve this moment? What about the team? In this moment, does the team need someone to show up and really model taking our space, or do they need someone to hold space while others shine?

Be willing to get the feedback that you're being too much, and then take a look and see where and how it's true (there's almost always a truth to this feedback, even if it's rarely the one that the person giving the feedback is insisting upon).

Leading and Working with People of Presence/Radiance

Your team members with Presence/Radiance are naturals for presentations, teaching, and other positions that involve owning the spotlight. Make sure these people are given opportunities that allow them to make the most of their natural talents.

You are a special, unique human being who occasionally shows up as irrelevant or loud. The more you come to terms with and make friends with what you fear, the less reactive and compensatory you need to be.

If you have team members operating from the under-expressed pole of their shadow, they may come across as hidden and avoidant. In such cases, they usually find ways to draw attention to themselves indirectly, in ways that don't require owning their need. When you identify these team members, acknowledge them for the gift of Presence/Radiance they bring, and invite them to step into the spotlight. They may insist they aren't ready or admit they're afraid to do so. Your job is not to force them but to invite them into becoming who they already are.

Your team members operating from the other pole of their shadow will work too hard to be the centre of attention, leading others to turn away and ratcheting up their fear of being ignored. It's important for you to honor this fear, affirm their Presence/Radiance, and invite them to notice the impact they're having.

Don't let them pretend the impact isn't there. Because this may trigger defensiveness on their part, be sure you reflect this pattern to them in private. As time goes on and they become enrolled in you supporting their breakthrough, you can be a be little more pointed, asking them what they notice about their impact on the room in the moment.

Practises

Notice where and how you keep yourself small.

How and when do you dim your light and around what kind of people? Ask yourself why you're doing so, and practise allowing one percent more of your light to be expressed. Remember that you don't need to "work" at this but, instead, to release your resistance. Your goal is to allow the light that's already there to shine through.

How and when do you dim your light and around what kind of people?

Notice how and when you take up too much space.

When you catch yourself taking up all the space in the room, ask yourself what this may be protecting you from. What fears are currently being protected or managed?

Remember that this may not look like talking loudly and aggressively. Some people steal the attention in the room by speaking quietly, forcing others to lean in and pay attention. They may take too long to get to their point, capturing others and giving themselves the opportunity to share everything they want to share.

If this description resonates with you, it's worth considering that you will also have places where you act out the diva aspect of your shadow.

Sit with your fears of irrelevance and obnoxiousness.

Notice when your fears of irrelevance and obnoxiousness flare up. Rather than trying to convince yourself those fears are wrong, practise simply being with them and letting your reactivity settle.

COMMON SHADOW ASPECTS:

- Obnoxious Diva
- Elephant Behind a Blade of Grass

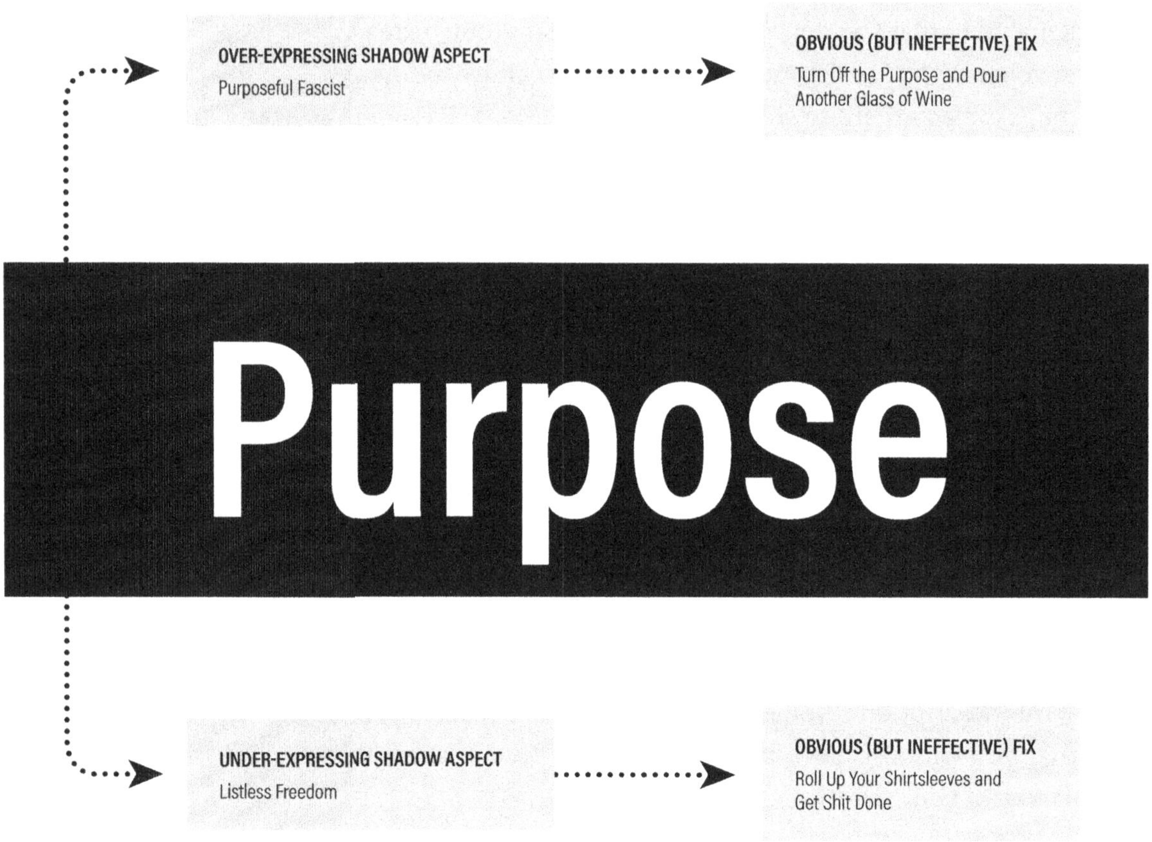

OVER-EXPRESSING SHADOW ASPECT
Purposeful Fascist

OBVIOUS (BUT INEFFECTIVE) FIX
Turn Off the Purpose and Pour Another Glass of Wine

Purpose

UNDER-EXPRESSING SHADOW ASPECT
Listless Freedom

OBVIOUS (BUT INEFFECTIVE) FIX
Roll Up Your Shirtsleeves and Get Shit Done

COMMON DESCRIPTORS

Determined, Resolute, Firm, Steadfast, Ambitious, Enterprising, Motivated, Driven, Striving, Sense of Direction, Know Where You're Going, Go-Getter

The Quality

Your Gift

You are like a compass for every team, project, and opportunity you find yourself in. No matter what is being done, you imbue it regularly with a renewed sense of purpose, a direction for things to move toward. You're fantastic at creating order out of chaos and marrying blue-sky thinking with on-the-ground pragmatism.

You don't necessarily create Purpose through your words (although that is often a part of your magic). It is simply inherent in the way you are in any given situation. In your presence, people are less inclined to go down rabbit holes and more likely to bring themselves back on track quickly. When you're in the room, there seems to be more clarity and intentionality available.

Projects and meetings that you run tend to be efficient and purposeful with fewer digressions. You are focused and reliable in moving towards your goals. While others struggle to find their way through the chaos of life, you're clear on what's to be done and more than capable of making it happen.

You are highly sought after and excel in roles like project management and managerial consulting, as well as executive leadership. You bring the gift of cutting through the superfluous and getting to the matter at hand.

Purpose

COMMON SHADOW ASPECTS:

- Purposeful Fascist
- Listless Freedom

When you're in the room, there seems to be more clarity and intentionality available.

What is Predictable

Over time, Purpose may morph from a gift to a fundamental need. Moving forwards without intention or direction goes from merely unpleasant to outright offensive. The fact that life does not come with a built-in purpose (beyond procreation and survival) turns into an ongoing challenge you have to overcome for yourself and for others.

When Purpose becomes a need rather than a choice, things like connection, intimacy, and play become superfluous and pointless. You find it harder and harder to sit in conversations that are simply about connecting with another person. In relationships, you may get frustrated when your partner just wants to be heard or to connect. You're always looking for a problem to solve—even when your partner tells you that problem solving is the last thing they want. You hear yourself thinking, "Okay, but what's the point? And here's what you need to do."

You may become overbearing and abrupt in relationships (romantic, familial, friendships, etc.). You're masterful at drawing a straight line towards your goal, but intimacy is often about being at ease with whatever shows up and going wherever that takes you. Instead of enjoying that ride, you feel ill at ease. Your need for an intention overrides the polarity that creates spark and delight in relationships.

Consequently, relationships become tedious and frustrating. Why can't your partner get to the point or listen to your advice? Out of sheer frustration, you may bulldoze over them. Or, noticing that this approach makes you unpopular, you decide you have to tolerate a certain amount of wasted time as the cost of being in relationship or doing business. You try to listen to your partner, thinking you're doing the right thing by pretending to engage with what they're saying—even though it's evident to them that you're jiggling your knee and checking your watch until the allotted time is up.

Work takes up an ever-increasing amount of your time and energy. Friends and marriage(s) fall away. You become a performer of the highest calibre with a personal life that's agonizingly lonely between projects.

What is Possible

The paradox of being human is that we are driven to discover meaning in a universe that is fundamentally without it. No inherent purpose is handed out at birth other than surviving, procreating, and passing down our genes. Beyond that, Purpose is what you choose to make it.

Your gift to the world lies in your innate understanding that Purpose is something to be chosen freely, moment by moment. You probably learned growing up that lack of Purpose was something bad to the point of being intolerable, dismissing people who lacked purpose as useless and uninteresting. Direction and forwards movement became as necessary to you as breathing. Your gift opens up for the world when you do the work to release that compulsion. When you allow yourself the freedom—and a little bit of leisure—to *choose* a Purpose that serves you and those around you.

As part of this process, you deepen your capacity to trust yourself regardless of the state you're in, and be at ease with whatever shows up. In that moment of freedom, you and those around you begin to hold Purpose as a creative act.

From this place, your Purpose stops showing up like an aggressive taskmaster and instead becomes a lightning rod around which you and your teams can coalesce. You draw out the Purpose in each person you lead, not frantically, in order to fill an urgent need, but as a wellspring for what happens next.

COMMON SHADOW ASPECTS:

- Purposeful Fascist
- Listless Freedom

Common Experience Coming of Age

Growing up, you may have been called "bossy" or "pushy" and found it challenging to play games with other kids. Their fanciful desire to have fun and explore ran directly counter to your desire to get on with the game (obeying the rules, of course) until someone wins—preferably you. *What else is the point of playing?*

Relationships and intimacy were probably challenging, given their essentially purpose-less nature and lack of a clear outcome. There's nothing to do but be there with your partner as they show up in the moment, which you may have found tedious and infuriating.

The fact that life does not come with a built-in purpose (beyond procreation and survival) turns into an ongoing challenge you have to overcome for yourself and for others.

Consequences of Owning Your Gifts

When you show up and stake a Purpose in the ground, it can make you a target. People may disagree, point out flaws, and withhold their support—even when your choices are the right ones (for you) in the long run. Standing strong for your Purpose can remind others of their own indecision; they may resent you for making choices that they were unwilling to make. If things don't turn out the way you had hoped (which happens inevitably, from time to time), they pounce with "I told you so."

Shadow Aspects

Over-Expressing: *Purposeful Fascist*

This shadow aspect evolves from being taught growing up that it was wrong to be idle. Idle hands are the devil's work, and you are unwilling to do the devil's work. Purpose ceased to be something you chose deliberately and became a compulsive need for intention in everything you do. Feeling purposeless, no matter how briefly, is existentially painful.

To avoid this pain, you enforce Purpose nonstop and give up your ability to be with the unknown and sit with ease in the moment. The very notion of downtime makes you impatient. You wish you could let your team arrive at their own conclusions, but you usually last about ten minutes before jumping in and setting direction.

Growing up, you may have been called "bossy" or "pushy" and found it challenging to play games with other kids.

You tend to listen with a bias towards reaching conclusions: *What needs to happen? How do we solve this? What's the bottom line?* People are often left with the experience of not feeling heard by you. You don't listen to hear or to empathize with people—you listen for Purpose and to get the ball rolling.

Because solving problems presents a clean, purposeful path that you find immensely satisfying, you construct your life direction out of doing so. You may be highly sought for roles in which you resolve tough issues as a matter of course. One downside is that when there are no problems at hand, you unconsciously go about creating them just to have something to fix.

Obvious (But Ineffective) Fix: Turn Off the Purpose and Pour Another Glass of Wine

You have bulldozed a lot of people to get things done and notice that your incessant drive leaves you angry, frustrated, and lonely. It begins to feel like too much of a sacrifice—your life is getting away from you!—and so you decide to change it up, removing yourself from the stressors that drive your internal dynamo. You back away from expressing your Purpose.

Having eased off across the board, you give people around you all the space in the world. Rather than providing them support in their choice of what's next, you relinquish direction entirely, letting go of how things should turn out and relaxing into early retirement (figuratively, if not literally.)

COMMON SHADOW ASPECTS:

- Purposeful Fascist
- Listless Freedom

When there are no problems at hand, you unconsciously go about creating them just to have something to fix.

One of the dangers of retirement is that people swing to the extreme far end of their shadow. Having spent most of their life over-expressing their shadow, which left them fed up, out of balance, and exhausted, they swing to total under-expression,

Stress levels come down, which is a relief. And yet with no fire in their belly, they're left feeling directionless and pointless. They wonder if their choices have to be this binary: Purposeless drift without upsetting yourself or anyone else or relentless drive to create something at the cost of your relationships?

Rather than sit with that paradox, you pour another glass of wine, kick back, and avoid those things about which you "care too much." You're vaguely uneasy and unfulfilled, but at least you don't feel the stress and frustration of your former life.

Under-Expressing: *Listless Freedom*

This shadow stems from your reaction to the heavy weight of Purpose placed on you when growing up. Perhaps your parents drove you too hard from their own Purpose-based shadow. Maybe you noticed that when you embraced Purpose, you became increasingly intense and annoyed with the world.

Life is good enough, comfortable, and fairly boring. But, hey, things could be worse.

Whatever the reason, like all shadow aspects, you came by this one honestly. Rejecting your innate Purpose, you choose instead the freedom of being purposeless. You clamp down on the part of you that is driven and determined, opting instead for blissful drift.

You may fantasize about early retirement or find ways to simulate that experience now, moment by moment. From this aspect of your shadow, life is relatively stress-free and easy. You go along to get along.

None of this is bad, mind you—it's just that hanging out in a directionless peace leaves you expressing only a fraction of who you are.

You feel like a drifter or a lazy tourist. You sometimes wish to create more, knowing you have a destiny to fulfil on this planet (more so than most). But you're unwilling or afraid to confront everything that would require. Life is good enough, comfortable, and fairly boring. But, hey, things could be worse.

Obvious (But Ineffective) Fix: Roll Up Your Shirtsleeves and Get Shit Done

After way too much time resisting your innate Purpose, you decide to finally stand up and own your power. You trade in your boat for a briefcase and turn the dial up to eleven on expressing your Purpose. It's been so long since you expressed this part of yourself that you have little ability to calibrate it, and switch from easy-going to absolute tyrant.

The tyranny may be reserved for yourself and contained within, at least in the beginning. Your newfound Purpose provides direction and meaning to your life, but also generates urgency, frustration, and anger when things are out of alignment with that Purpose. Because you care about people deeply and are committed to not belching fire on them out of anger, you may direct and contain most of your ire inwards. As time wears on, however, your ability to contain the fire wears thin. Feeling yourself start to crumble under the weight of everything you are holding, your anger either explodes onto others or you retreat from it, back to the safety of a life with little Purpose.

Creating the Breakthrough

Your shadow is designed to protect you (and others) from the tunnel vision and intensity your Purpose generates and to help you brush aside people who don't get on board.

Your breakthrough comes when you stop avoiding these things and begin to work *through* them. Lean into the part of you that becomes obsessed and impatient. See yourself trampling on people's ideas and

Purpose

COMMON SHADOW ASPECTS:

- Purposeful Fascist
- Listless Freedom

contributions in your rush to get things done. Notice how you justify this by, as you tell yourself, *focusing on what matters* and how easily you dismiss people as distractions. To achieve your breakthroughs, you may need to enroll people who are willing to point out this tendency as it shows up. And you will need to drop your resistance to pausing and looking at what they've brought to your attention.

Your breakthrough happens not by avoiding your upset or taking it out on the people around you but by allowing those feelings to show up without being triggered into an immediate response.

In those moments, see if you can expand your being and awareness to allow for a Purpose greater than the one you're fixated on right now. Is it more important to have things go forwards the way you think they should, or to broaden your scope, taking time to get everyone on board even if that means adjusting your plan? Which of these will have the larger and longer-term impact?

As you continue down this breakthrough path, don't be surprised at getting upset and frustrated sometimes. Your breakthrough happens not by avoiding your upset or taking it out on the people around you but by allowing those feelings to show up without being triggered into an immediate response. Instead, move *through* the feelings patiently until they ease. Practise releasing those emotions in responsible ways (e.g., waiting until you're alone and shouting into a pillow). Work with a coach to get complete on what is showing up, so you can begin creating from a clean slate. With that larger perspective, you can get back to Purpose and work.

Leading and Working with People of Purpose

If a member of your team embodies Purpose, they will be a powerful motivator, a beacon calling your team towards its collective Purpose. If one of these team members becomes fixated on a particular approach and way to achieve it—insisting people do things their way, making threats, or berating them when they don't—recognize they have shifted into the fascist aspect of their shadow. Your role as a leader is to support your Purpose-type team member in identifying this tendency and moving through it.

How do you go about this? First, help them recognize that fear is the ultimate driver beneath this shadow. It may show up in disguise—as anger, frustration, resignation, or any number of other things—but ultimately, it's the fear of being seen as useless and worthless, their worst nightmare. As you support your team member through this realization, hold space for them to express what they are feeling.

Many management approaches aim to curtail a team member's frustration by helping them *not feel* what they are feeling. This just forces the emotions further below the surface and ensures the pattern continues. Only when we allow ourselves to freely express what we are feeling can we move through and transcend those feelings.

Part of your job in these cases is to let go of your own need for your team members not to get angry. It's important to recognize they're already operating with the story that they shouldn't feel the way they do. If you pile your need on top of theirs, it pushes them even farther away from breakthrough.

You may also encounter team members who show up as listless and lackadaisical, demonstrating the other side of Purpose's shadow. Resist your first impulse, which is to dismiss them as having no value. Relate to them instead by recognizing their innate Purpose as the gift it truly is and invite them to bring forwards this part of themselves.

At first, this may feel forced to them. They may have spent a lifetime shutting down this part of themselves, so that's okay. Be loving, patient, and compassionate while continuing to stand for them to express their potential.

COMMON SHADOW ASPECTS:

- Purposeful Fascist
- Listless Freedom

Practises

Notice where in your life you feel listless and lacking in Purpose.

From the under-expressed aspect of your shadow, your immediate experience may not be one of idle drifting, at least on the surface. If you spend half of your life wrapped up in the intensity and drive of Purpose, the areas where you feel listless might feel like a welcome respite.

What would it look like to be a little more purposeful without giving up the relaxation and rejuvenation that serves you well?

You may feel downright defensive of the places where you've laid down the burden of Purpose. This defensiveness will get in the way of your ability to see your shadow as it shows up. Check in with yourself about those areas, doing so with greater patience and ease until your deeper truth emerges.

Practise bringing one percent more Purpose.

Where you are under-expressing Purpose, practise bringing one percent more intention and direction to bear. What would it look like to be a little more purposeful without giving up the relaxation and rejuvenation that serves you well?

As you learn to integrate Purpose with downtime, you will find that it leaves you feeling even more resourced than when you check out of Purpose altogether.

Lean into what you normally avoid for fear of becoming over-intense and myopic.

What are you unwilling to take on out of fear that you may lose yourself in the ferocity of Purpose? Where and how do you prevent this from showing up? For example, if you avoid playing sports you love for fear that you will become too competitive, lean into this fear rather than avoiding it.

Remember, the breakthrough for you as a person of Purpose is not to avoid the situations and people that stimulate your over-expressed shadow. Your breakthrough lies in *leaning into* these situations and getting the support you need to avoid being taken over by the constriction and obsessiveness you fear will show up.

In taking on this work and through your willingness to walk courageously into the heart of this fire, you will slowly but surely develop an ability to live on Purpose without the messy shadow aspects that used to be the price of doing so.

Broaden the scope of your Purpose

Those with the gift of Purpose easily fall into the trap of turning everything into a to-do list that measures how well they're succeeding at life. Push your list aside, breathe deeply, and allow the scope of your Purpose to broaden. (You can always go back to the list later.)

For example, if you were to take on improving your well-being as a worthy Purpose, you would probably create a running to-do list of things that need to be completed and crossed off along the way. Over time, checking off those items before you go to bed at night becomes the real Purpose of the project and you wrap your sense of self-worth and achievement into whittling that list down.

Slow down and remember your deeper Purpose. Throw away the to-do list if necessary and check in every night instead with your sense of well-being. How would you relate to your to-do list differently if you held your deeper Purpose in mind?

COMMON SHADOW ASPECTS:

- Purposeful Fascist
- Listless Freedom

OVER-EXPRESSING SHADOW ASPECT
Spiritual Bypass

OBVIOUS (BUT INEFFECTIVE) FIX
Abandon God and Walk with the Mortals

Spirit/Divinity

UNDER-EXPRESSING SHADOW ASPECT
Faithless Cynic

OBVIOUS (BUT INEFFECTIVE) FIX
Ladle on the Piety

COMMON DESCRIPTORS

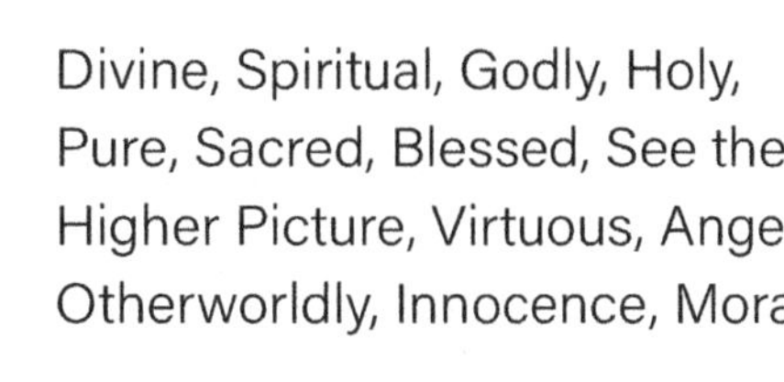

Divine, Spiritual, Godly, Holy, Pure, Sacred, Blessed, See the Higher Picture, Virtuous, Angelic, Otherworldly, Innocence, Moral

The Quality

Your Gift

Being with you is like being with angels. The way you show up reminds us all of the existence of something greater than ourselves—regardless of what we choose to call it or how we relate to it. Your presence in a given space or moment imbues it with a connection to the divine.

You serve as a reminder that we are spiritual beings having a human experience and that spirituality isn't something to achieve or get to at the end of our journey through this mortal coil. You bear witness that the spiritual aspect of existence is present in each and every moment.

In your presence, we find ourselves letting go of our innocent and innate selfishness and becoming present to the majesty of existence. Your ability to discover grace and transcendental truth, even in the most trying circumstances, serves you and others beautifully.

You have a natural talent for rising above our attachment to the pettiest aspects of humanity and remembering that on a divine level everything is perfect. You help us rise above our daily upset and heartbreak, invoking our spirituality and in so doing raising our spirits.

Your gift is unrelated to any particular religious belief. You may reject religion as a whole or at a minimum reject the dogma that comes with it. You know in your bones that Spirit is present in every moment, no matter how profound or profane.

COMMON SHADOW ASPECTS:

- Spiritual Bypass
- Faithless Cynic

Your presence in a given space or moment imbues it with a connection to the divine.

What is Predictable

Predictably, your connection to the Divine will lead you into suffering and disappointment. Grappling with the baser nature of humanity, you attempt to sever those aspects from the purity of the divine. No matter how hard you try, however, the humanity inherent to our dualistic nature persists. You find it challenging to be with this aspect of your humanity and everyone else's.

Predictably, you will learn to do one of two things:

1. Condemn the weakness on display around you, and retreat into the safety of spiritual bypass or religious righteousness. You may decry the grasping humanity in others—shunting your own humanity into blind spots in the process—or float away on a meditative cloud, refusing to let yourself be soiled by the real world.
2. Alternatively, you may adopt an "If you can't beat 'em, join 'em" attitude. Since you can never outrun your humanity, you stop trying and accept that our base nature is a basic truth. You might as well embrace that fact and move forward, even if it means becoming a bit cynical and calloused.

The irony here is that some of the most spiritually gifted among us can be found living depraved and profane lives, acting out as gang members, convicts, con artists, and so on. When you look for those who most radiate spirituality, keep an eye out for those who show up as completely devoid of it.

What is Possible

Remember how we're spiritual beings having a human experience? Well, you represent the possibility of integrating that duality. When you do the work to finally accept and love the fullness of your human experience with all its faults and failures and go deep into forgiveness and healing—rather than trying to rise above it all—you find your way home to grace.

When you do your own work and learn to expand (rather than contract) in the face of our humanity, you model that our spiritual connection is available in every moment. Superficially, this approach would mean rising above any given moment and simply being unwilling to let it impact you. But the real work comes from being willing to be fully impacted by our humanity, at large, and then finding your way back to forgiveness.

By resolving the either-or paradox—that is, being spiritual or human but never both—you make it possible for all of us to embody spirituality in every moment.

Common Experience Coming of Age

Growing up, you may have felt a bit like an alien. Unable to understand the cruelty and selfishness going on around you, you found it difficult to fit in. Your innate ability to transcend the immediacy of the moment may have made it easier for you to connect with adults, at least some of whom were operating with a broader awareness than your childhood peers.

You may also have struggled with religion, unable to comprehend how spirituality could be reduced to petty, quarrelsome dogma. Alternatively, you may have closed your eyes to religion's flaws and dove into believing in one religion over the rest. You may have become a rabid atheist on one hand or a religious zealot on the other.

COMMON SHADOW ASPECTS:

- Spiritual Bypass
- Faithless Cynic

Consequences of Owning Your Gifts

People can be cruel, and owning your gift may open you to ridicule and being taken advantage of. Proposing a transcendent approach to a real-world problem may strike some as affected and whacky. Your teachers and peers may see you as unrealistic, pious, or a bit off the deep end.

Shadow Aspects

Over-Expressing: *Spiritual Bypass*

You may decry the grasping humanity in others—shunting your own humanity into blind spots in the process—or float away on a meditative cloud, refusing to let yourself be soiled by the real world.

The cruelty of the world around you—and the cruelty you discover within—are too much to bear, and so you retreat into the clouds. Because everything is divinely chosen and meant to be, there's nothing for you to get upset about and no pain to feel. Spiritual bypass is available to people of all stripes but is especially accessible for those with the gift of Spirit.

Detachment feels good initially, allowing you to show up and be with all of what life puts in front of you. But, over time, you start to pay more and more of a cost for this approach. As you disconnect from the harsh realities of life—all that the trauma and disappointment—you become reluctant and eventually unable to empathize with those around you. You also sever yourself from your emotional range. By ruling out heartbreak, betrayal, and hurt, you give up joy, ecstasy, and love.

While you get to maintain a sense of elevation and "above-it-all"-ness, you can no longer connect easily with others. People begin to feel like it's a little pointless or even impossible to really be in relationship with you. Because you've let go of your humanity, there's no impact to be made and little left to connect with.

Obvious (But Ineffective) Fix: Abandon God and Walk with the Mortals

Yes, you're untouched by the world around you, and yes, it's nice not to feel all those messy emotions your peers do—but you feel isolated from the life experience you once hoped for. Dwelling in Spirit turns out to be overrated. You abandon it in pursuit of your lost humanity.

Proposing a transcendent approach to a real-world problem may strike some as affected and whacky.

Revelling in life, you express yourself with the nuance of the Titanic slamming into an iceberg. You may launch a career that requires you to get your hands a little dirty, but the world's beyond saving anyway, so what the heck—let's party while the ship is going down.

The material and tangible successes you wanted in your previous life are now readily available and at your disposal. Never mind that your pursuits sometimes feel a little hollow or that what you're willing to engage in sometimes tugs at your conscience.

Under-Expressing: *Faithless Cynic*

Bitten one too many times by the cruelty of fate and humanity, you disavow the promise of Spirit and dive headfirst into profane cynicism. Sure, it's a cruel world, but you expect it to be and find ways to excel in that acceptance.

The moments when the clouds do part are temporary and you know this better than anyone. You give up the hope of transcendence, trading it in for faithless cynicism. Life becomes a vicious, cruel world, but you aren't overly hurt by the fact—rather, you accept it and excel in your acceptance.

Having shrugged away Spirit, you decide the way to get ahead is through wealth, success, and material possessions. These things provide you with relatively shallow, short-term fulfilment, but, hey, you're a success now and you get results even if life now feels a little gray and emotionless.

COMMON SHADOW ASPECTS:

- Spiritual Bypass
- Faithless Cynic

Obvious (But Ineffective) Fix: Ladle on the Piety

Pursuing wealth and success on the material plane has gotten you ahead, no question about it. But you notice an inner emptiness that won't go away. You may not be able to put your finger on what's missing, describing it as "greater presence," "deeper connection," or "purpose." Whatever it is, you're eager for something more.

Bitten one too many times by the cruelty of fate and humanity, you disavow the promise of Spirit and dive headfirst into profane cynicism.

Because our shadows are linear, compensatory, and binary, they don't allow for much nuance in our behaviour. So, you swing to the opposite extreme and start over, selling the Ferrari to become a monk or your particular version of that approach.

Whatever your response, it's important to realize that there's nothing wrong with your desire or intention—it's simply that the broad brushstroke with which it's implemented means you rule out a good deal of who you are. Meditating on that skimpy pillow is satisfying in all kinds of ways—but is figuratively living alone in a cave really the only way to recover your spiritual self?

Creating the Breakthrough

The shadows of Spirit and Divinity are rooted in an inability to be with the profanity that comes with being human. Take a look at the state of the world. Divine gifts, incredible technology, and profound beauty live side by side with poverty, filth, and depravity. Both are a part of our human nature.

The shadow aspects of this gift aim to mitigate the core problem: That we are spiritual beings having a human experience and cannot separate the two, no matter how we try. Breakthroughs become available through a willingness to be with the profound and the profane simultaneously without judging or rejecting either one. When you accept and embody this natural tension, you begin walking the path that you are here to walk.

Down this path, your life becomes filled simultaneously with more reverence *and* irreverence. You learn to see and be with the sacredness of our existence while simultaneously being in on the cosmic joke of it all (after all, none of us gets out of this ride alive).

Leading and Working with People of Spirit

Members of your team that embody the gift of Spirit can be challenging to support at times. If they retreat to the haven of a higher spiritual plane, they lose touch with the rest of the team and may come off unconsciously as condescending, righteous, and aloof. Bypassing their down and dirty human nature comes at a cost.

Your role as a leader is to stand for these team members in owning and honoring the natural anxiety, fear, or disappointment they want to rise above. As you model being present with all your emotions, you help them step into their own leadership.

On the flip side, don't overlook those Spirit team members who have adopted their under-expressing shadow (the Faithless Cynic). They may be especially potent at generating results but at a cost to the vision, commitments, and ethical boundaries of your organization. Recognize and acknowledge the results they create while inviting and encouraging them to operate in alignment with the company's (and their own) principles and vision. They may grumble at this but will actually feel better about themselves for doing so. And watch out for your behaviour if you notice yourself getting caught up in short-term gain at the expense of longer-term growth and commitments.

Spirit/Divinity

COMMON SHADOW ASPECTS:

- Spiritual Bypass
- Faithless Cynic

Be especially wary of your own fear, scarcity and neediness when working with this aspect of Spirit's shadow. Because this approach is effective at generating results, it's easy to assume that your team members who take this approach have everything handled and focus instead on the *lower-performing* members of your team. Remember that *everyone* has a leadership edge to step into and help your Faithless Cynic team members find that edge

Practises

Be in the here and now.

There is a scene in the movie *Fight Club* where the antagonist, Tyler Durden, has induced a chemical burn on the back of the protagonist's hand. While the protagonist tries to meditate and escape the pain, Tyler Durden slaps him across the face and demands he stop checking out and remain present with the agony.

Your life becomes filled simultaneously with more reverence and irreverence.

In many ways, this is half the battle for those with Spirit. Don't check out. Don't disconnect. Don't escape to the safety of the heavens. Be here, now, on Earth, and be with everything that life presents. Provide a little more love than Tyler's character does while being every bit as firm with yourself.

Give yourself permission to have judgments.

One of the ironies inherent in the holier-than-thou shadow aspect of Spirit is the tendency to hold yourself above other people while simultaneously insisting you don't judge them or need them to change. As a practise, take on noticing your judgment as it shows up, even—and especially—if you're certain you don't have any. To be human is to judge. To believe otherwise is to actively bypass a part of your humanity.

Get clear on where you've abandoned Spirit.
Perform an audit on your life to identify where and when you do whatever's necessary to generate results, foregoing Spirit in the process. Also look to the other pole of your shadow and identify where and when you gave up on results in order to rise above your humanity. What's going on when you swing from one of these extremes to the other?

Consider for each of these extremes how you might practise bringing the other side into the mix. For example, if you're a yoga teacher who has decided you're happy with a relatively small income, what if you got creative and asked yourself how to create more? How could you enjoy wealth *and* spirituality?

Take on noticing your judgment as it shows up, even—and especially—if you're certain you don't have any.

Spirit/Divinity

COMMON SHADOW ASPECTS:

- Spiritual Bypass
- Faithless Cynic

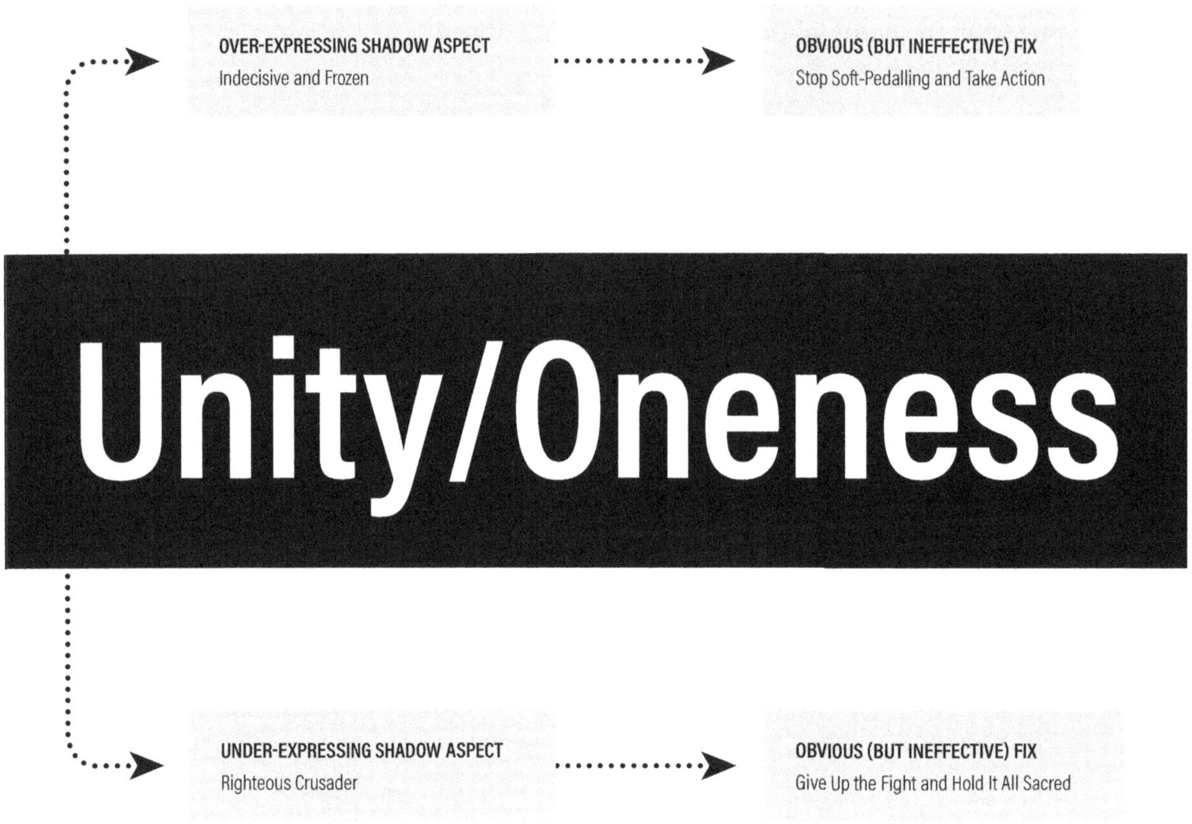

OVER-EXPRESSING SHADOW ASPECT
Indecisive and Frozen

OBVIOUS (BUT INEFFECTIVE) FIX
Stop Soft-Pedalling and Take Action

Unity/Oneness

UNDER-EXPRESSING SHADOW ASPECT
Righteous Crusader

OBVIOUS (BUT INEFFECTIVE) FIX
Give Up the Fight and Hold It All Sacred

COMMON DESCRIPTORS

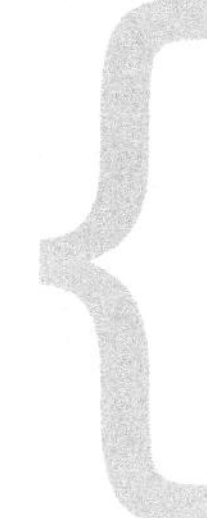

Selfless, Harmony, Wholeness, Love for All, Cohesion, Universal Love and Consciousness, Balance, Cooperation, Inclusive, Welcoming, One Love

The Quality

Your Gift

You are a safe space and hold acceptance for everyone you come in contact with. Cultures, races, sexual orientation, dietary preferences, and every other aspect of human individuality are accepted and loved in your presence. You represent the possibility of love for all creeds and cultures. You are the Oneness of humanity.

You are the gift of peace on earth. The gift of each of us being in partnership together—not despite our differences but *through* and *as* our differences. You are a walking, embodied celebration of our uniqueness and the collective Unity that is possible.

What you bring into the space goes deeper than simple acceptance, however. Your very being is an invitation for the uniqueness of each individual to be expressed and for the people around you to express their individuality more deeply. When you enter a space, you bring the possibility of us simultaneously being different from one another and unified in harmony.

A given harmony is made up of different notes played together that, in unison, create a sound greater than the sum of the individual parts. This is the possibility you carry within you and into every project, organization, and relationship you are a part of.

Unity/Oneness

COMMON SHADOW ASPECTS:

- Indecisive and Frozen
- Righteous Crusader

You bring the possibility of us simultaneously being different from one another and unified in harmony.

What Is Predictable

Every human has within themselves the capacity for great love and kindness, as well as great cruelty and heartlessness. We admire the loving parts and judge the nasty parts, but each of us has the capacity for the entire range of human expression.

This a challenge to those with the gift of Unity/Oneness. Reconciling the Oneness and love that you know is possible with the baseness and pettiness that is also part of human nature becomes a personal challenge. As is so often the case, the traps we fall into and our potential breakthroughs are both tied up in this paradox.

The hardest place to reconcile this tension is within yourself. You passionately believe in and embody Unity and Oneness, and yet you know you have the capacity for anger and judgment, which sometimes come out. This realization can be challenging or even terrifying. Remaining open and loving towards everyone is so hard when some people show up as unloving and cruel. For you, in particular, it creates heartbreak.

Over time, recurring heartbreak can reach a breaking point, turning you callous and hardened to the world. One of your predictable paths is that you begin to pick and choose the places where you express your Oneness and generosity. The rest of the time you are harsh and judgmental, jaded by your own species, which seems to be unwilling to enjoy the Eden it has been offered.

Another pitfall for those with Unity is codifying your gift into a set of rules for correct behaviour and expecting everyone to show up in in observance of the rules. In doing so, you may reduce the collective harmony of a symphony to a bunch of musicians playing the same note.

What is Possible

You represent the potential for amnesty and acceptance for everyone on the planet—even those who behave in ways that are broken, depraved, or cruel. One example would be the mother of a murdered child who finds forgiveness for the murderer, and the two of them speaking out together about forgiveness.

The gift of Unity inevitably brings heartbreak. When you become willing to go into this heartbreak, allowing yourself to fully feel the devastation and find your way back, you begin to realize the promise of your gift.

This begins with the work of accepting your own shortcomings, judgments, and anger. As you do so, you develop the capacity to hold space for others to do the same. You recognize that your judgment and righteousness will never help other people transform into their better selves. Instead, your ability to love them exactly as they are creates a space in which they can choose to transform.

Your deepest realization is that we don't need to be the same to be deserving of love—that love is available for all, in our best moments as well as our worst.

In a world that is constantly trying to shape us into someone different than who we are, your possibility fully expressed creates something truly unique and divine.

Common Experience Coming of Age

Growing up, you may have been bullied or hurt by other children and felt the need to distance yourself. Your purest self would have a hard time comprehending the cruelty of kids: "Why can't everyone be nice? Why can't I hug everyone?"

COMMON SHADOW ASPECTS:

- Indecisive and Frozen
- Righteous Crusader

You may also have found competitive games frustrating. Why are we competing ferociously with one another when we could all be doing something fun together? Classes and hobbies that allowed for greater expression of harmony—music, dance, drama, and the arts—may have been much more your style.

You represent the potential for amnesty and acceptance for everyone on the planet.

Consequences of Owning Your Gifts

Truly owning your gift may lead to you getting a lot of grief for being "too nice" and too liberal. For those who believe nice guys finish last and who adopt a hard-nosed, "realistic" approach to life, you're hopelessly naïve. Moreover, if you truly embrace Oneness and unconditional love, you may feel required to defend people who others (and you) wish to condemn—a position that can earn you fire and scorn.

Shadow Aspects

Over-Expressing: *Indecisive and Frozen*

Unity/Oneness, in its over-expressed aspect, becomes about ensuring that you never hurt anyone's feelings, and no one ever feels left out, denigrated, or marginalized. This is a noble aspiration but trying to create a life in which you never have this impact is impossible. Those feelings are a fundamental part of the human experience. There's no escaping that sometimes we will feel left out, and that's not necessarily a bad thing.

Truly owning your gift may lead to you getting a lot of grief for being "too nice" and too liberal.

In your attempts to live the "perfect" version of Oneness, you circumscribe your action and the scope of your impact in the world. Terrified of upsetting or treading on anyone, you land in existential analysis paralysis. Because any choice will inevitably include some people and exclude others, you have very few options.

Ultimately, this shadow aspect leads you to stay small. By playing a small game, you limit your impact and ensure you can always include those who matter to you.

Alternatively, you can commit to playing a bigger game in life, but at the extreme of this shadow aspect, every decision requires careful deliberation. How do you possibly ensure that everyone is included and all their feedback is considered, when, say, you are running a festival for thousands of people?

Decisions take longer and occupy more and more of your attention. At some point, you realize it's impossible to run a large project effectively without *someone* feeling offended or excluded. Overwhelmed, you find yourself tempted to go back to being small, letting the promise of Unity die within you when you do.

Obvious (But Ineffective) Fix: Stop Soft-Pedalling and Take Action

Tired of treading so lightly and feeling like you're not creating the stir you want, you decide to start showing up powerfully. You train your sights on and criticize the most obvious targets, projecting into the world the very things you're unable to own, integrate, and bring love to in yourself.

At first, it feels freeing to be able to speak your mind and share your truth. You've been holding yourself in check for so long that airing your dissatisfaction, expressing judgment, and denouncing those you see as wrong is like dumping an incredible weight off your shoulders.

Alas rather than doing the difficult internal work of processing that weight, you've shifted it onto others and dehumanized them. You fail to see that you're showing up in ways that are similar to those you say you despise, and, over time, this new freedom begins to feel slightly toxic. You feel righteous that the hate is justified, but some part of you understands that you're perpetuating what you abhor. You struggle to shake it off though. Unity and collective love sound good, but they just don't work out in the real world. At least you don't feel frozen anymore, right?

Under-Expressing: *Righteous Crusader*

Equality and love for all! Except for those who tread upon the equality of others. For them, punishment and disparagement! Your stand for Unity shifts to a zealous belief in the *right* way to accept and experience other people. The opportunity for people to hold a variety of beliefs is ruled out by your strict definition of Unity, leaving you as exclusive and judgmental as those you criticize.

Decisions take longer and occupy more and more of your attention.

This approach is particularly tempting because it relieves you of the need to include everyone. People displaying ignorance, bigotry, prejudice, and other kinds of affronts to your Unity are *out*, period, dehumanized as the targets of your anger and indignation.

To be clear, bigotry, prejudice, and ignorance cause varying degrees of harm in the world and are not to be celebrated. The problem is that these are common human responses from fear—and this aspect of your shadow ends up creating the expectation that people not show up afraid. Or at least they can only do so in the ways you have decided are acceptable.

The upshot is that you rule out people showing up as they are in the moment, and as they're moving *through* their fear. Either their fear needs to look like yours does, or they need to have it handled in advance. This shadow aspect of your gift turns Unity from love for all humanity into an exclusive club, and you end up becoming as exclusive and hurtful as those you condemn. This just perpetuates the cycle that keeps the promise of Unity from being realized.

Obvious (But Ineffective) Fix: Give Up the Fight and Hold It All Sacred

Playing the role of Righteous Crusader gives you a degree of freedom and ability to act in a non-unified world, but it keeps taking a toll over time. Paradoxically, venting your anger and disapproval on others doesn't leave you feeling any better or lighter. In fact, you feel rising levels of anger and frustration—plenty of which goes towards those you judge as deficient, but the greatest amount targets yourself.

Exhausted, you decide to take a step back, and try to hold everyone as sacred. From now on, you will exclude no one, hold people in the highest regard, and love unconditionally. You feel certain that you're coming into alignment with your true self.

And yet despite your noblest intention, you find yourself white-knuckling through mounting degrees of frustration around certain people. Unable to see that your inability to be with them is the work you need to unfold into, you suppress your anger, holding it in for as long as you can before belching hot fire, often about some trivial offense. This leaves them—and you—stunned and horrified. Rather than learning from this, you tell yourself you just have to try harder to forgive, which works until, predictably, it happens again.

Creating the Breakthrough

Your shadow aspects are designed to prevent you from acknowledging that your human makeup sometimes encompasses being selfish, judgmental, and narrow-minded. This is just too painful to comprehend, given your sense of yourself as a person of acceptance and Oneness. And it's why you so violently dislike these traits in other people.

The truth is that until you accept these capacities in yourself, you will be unable to hold them lovingly in anyone else. Your breakthrough usually involves allowing the tyrannical, judgmental parts of yourself

COMMON SHADOW ASPECTS:

- Indecisive and Frozen
- Righteous Crusader

to come to the surface, seeing them for what they are, and loving them (and yourself), anyway.

You feel rising levels of anger and frustration—plenty of which goes towards those you judge as deficient, but the greatest amount targets yourself.

Accepting the full extent of who you are can be especially challenging for those with the gift of Unity/Oneness. You have probably gotten very good at keeping those undesirable parts of yourself under wraps. You may have constructed elaborate justifications for why your behaviour is correct, even when it looks pretty similar to what you're judging harshly in someone else.

The second way to keep this in your blind spot is to avoid the situations that would drive up this part of yourself you'd rather keep hidden. By avoiding commitments, situations, and people that drive up your own selfishness, judgment, and so on, you never have to be with any of it. Unfortunately, this also limits your ability to be and create with the full abundance of life.

Practise being with the prejudice, ignorance, and pettiness you encounter in yourself and in the world. Practise opening your heart with compassion. It is worth reminding yourself that for the most part, people are not malicious—they are simply hurt, afraid, and unaware. Just like you.

Leading and Working with People of Unity/Oneness

Members of your team that exhibit high levels of Unity and Oneness will be fantastic at leading charges for inclusion and celebration. They will also be alert to and call out instances of bullying, clique development, and other forms of "you're in and you're out" behaviour that are antithetical to the Unity of a team.

These team members will often serve as glue for your teams, ensuring cohesiveness and bonding. In one of their shadow aspects, however, they may create an "us versus them" dynamic: If you're on the team, you're among the good people. Everyone else can fend for themselves.

Your Unity-type team members can become hypervigilant around issues of safety and anti-dominance. These are important to address, but one's antenna can be over-calibrated to the point of spotting false positives. In practise, these team members may feel an urgent need to rescue or protect anyone they see feeling discomfort of almost any kind. Discomfort doesn't necessarily mean lack of safety, and someone's powerful stand in service of a team member's breakthrough can be confused with dominance.

If one of your team members leaps reflexively to others' defence, help them understand that they may be, with all good intentions, getting in the way of that person's breakthrough. What if the breakthrough that person needs is to stand up for themselves?

Help your team member see through this lens and learn to pause in their discomfort long enough to understand what's going on and choose from a different place than reaction. Are they going to the assistance of someone genuinely in need? Or are they assuaging a need of their own?

Your willingness to hold space powerfully thus becomes a crucible for leadership development for these team members, teaching them when to allow discomfort in the service of what's next.

Unity/Oneness

COMMON SHADOW ASPECTS:

- Indecisive and Frozen
- Righteous Crusader

Practises

Practise being with the prejudice, ignorance, and pettiness you encounter in yourself and in the world.

Notice your relationship to your own anger and frustration.

This is often the first sign that you are losing access to your Unity and Oneness. It's important to note here that the game isn't to avoid becoming angry or upset or to never let it happen. This may already be one of the shadow games you're playing with yourself.

Instead, get clear on your relationship to these feelings. Here's a helpful writing exercise to bring that forth. At the top of the first page, write, "Anger is..." and describe everything that is true about anger. On the next page, write, "Other people's anger is..." And finally, "My anger is..."

Acknowledge it when you become angry.

This practise is simply to notice when you are angry. For Unity/Oneness, it's often easier to judge other people's anger than to become responsible for your own. Responsibility, in this case, doesn't mean not getting angry. It means rather, that you can acknowledge and hold it when it's there instead of instantly transferring your attention to its target. To get angry is human—to be responsible for it is to be a leader.

The more you can identify and coexist with your anger, bringing compassion to yourself in the process, the more space you will have for the anger in other people. From here, this opens the place to bring people the healing experience of openness and love when they are at their most hurtful and petty.

Bring Compassion to yourself and others.

Practise finding your way to compassion, especially with those you despise. Can you find a place in your heart to bring one percent more love to them? Note that finding a way to open your heart is not the same as condoning their actions. You don't have to agree with someone's choices or beliefs to hold them with love and compassion. In truth, those you disagree with represent the most powerful places to practise your gift.

For Unity/Oneness, it's often easier to judge other people's anger than to become responsible for your own.

COMMON SHADOW ASPECTS:

- Indecisive and Frozen
- Righteous Crusader

OVER-EXPRESSING SHADOW ASPECT
Self-Satisfied and Oblivious
OBVIOUS (BUT INEFFECTIVE) FIX
Play the Jester and Join the Party
Wisdom
UNDER-EXPRESSING SHADOW ASPECT
Foolish and Ignorant
OBVIOUS (BUT INEFFECTIVE) FIX
Grow Up and Get Wise

COMMON DESCRIPTORS

Wise, Old Soul, Contemplative, Thoughtful, Deep, Introspective, Reflective, Common Sense, Understanding, Insightful, Discerning, Perspective

The Quality

Your Gift

While Brilliance is like a beam of sunlight cutting through the mist, your Wisdom is like a forest glade and the stream of water running through it. Wisdom is the quality of deep, inner knowing, transcending time and space to see the deeper meaning behind everything at play.

When people spend time in your presence, they leave knowing more about themselves the world, and in a more contemplative state. Part of the gift of Wisdom is humility and lack of pretence.

You have the gift of elevation—the ability to see the greater picture and larger meaning in a given situation. You are less likely to get bogged down in the minutiae of life. The momentary setbacks of the day are less upsetting to you than they might be to those around you, and you're often able to provide solace and comfort to yourself and others. Those who are Wisdom have the capacity to rise above the immediacy of the moment.

You embody seeing beyond the immediate moment to discern deeper purpose, meaning, and vision. Your presence on a team ensures that progress and projects rise out of the weeds and keep moving towards their targets. When things go sideways, your sense of perspective makes it easier to pivot and incorporate life as it shows up rather than trying to bulldoze through.

COMMON SHADOW ASPECTS:

- Self-Satisfied and Oblivious
- Foolish and Ignorant

You are less likely to get bogged down in the minutiae of life.

What is Predictable

We are all spiritual beings having a human experience. While much of life is transcendent and beautiful, it can also be cruel, banal, and foolish. These baser aspects of human nature, both in others and yourself, stand in contrast to the Wisdom you bring.

This is your gift, but it creates a tension that can be difficult to resolve. On one hand, you see the Wisdom available in all of us. On the other, you can't seem to escape the foolishness that seems to be an inextricable part of being a human. Rather than resolving this tension by simply being with human Wisdom *and* foolishness, you may retreat into the safety of greater meaning—and in so doing avoid being impacted by the current moment. Rather than being with embarrassment or anguish, you pull up the ladder to your lofty place of Wisdom and become untouched and unaffected by the world.

Alternatively, when you can't seem to figure out how to be with the boorish shortsightedness that is human nature, you decide that if you can't beat 'em, join 'em. This shadow aspect can lead those with great Wisdom to behave as if they are foolhardy and ignorant. This brings its own kind of relief, as you are released from the burden of considering higher truth and rising above the daily foolishness around you.

In the first case, life becomes as elegant and smooth as the surface of a glassy lake. You float above it all, giving up your desire to create meaningful impact in the world. In the latter case, you deliberately play the fool, resenting yourself and those around you for not taking your gift more seriously.

What is Possible

Those who possess Wisdom often find themselves living in fear of being or appearing to be foolish, which they see as negating their greatest gift. When, on the other hand, they lean into these fears, surrendering to the fact that no one can always see the higher truth, the world opens to them. By your willingness to look and even *be* foolish at times, you create space for everyone to show up exactly as who they are.

This helps us all get over ourselves a little more quickly. Rather than striving mightily to arrange our lives so we are never caught with egg on our face, your modeling reveals that there is space for all of it. We no longer need to find the "higher truth" of having stepped in dog poo. We can laugh, feel frustrated or whatever, and move on easily to what's next.

We no longer need to find the "higher truth" of having stepped in dog poo.

In this way, you hold the potential for all of us to discover Wisdom in each moment. This Wisdom exists not only in the transcendent, but in what *is* on the most human level possible.

The Wisdom you bring exists in the crying of a child, the hurt of a spurned lover, the words of the Hebrew and Christian bibles and the Koran, the divine way in which life unfolds, and everything in between. You are the possibility of unselfconscious Wisdom in every moment and every emotion.

Common Experience Coming of Age

Growing up, you probably felt more comfortable with adults, who—at least some of the time—saw the world through a broader scope. You may have been labelled precocious, cheeky, or pretentious by some because of your desire to elevate the conversation, and by others as cold, distant, and stuck up.

When you found yourself feeling foolish about something you did or said, you berated yourself: *You should have known better*. This is a painful experience for anyone, but for someone who embodies Wisdom as their very nature, it creates an existential kind of pain.

Wisdom

COMMON SHADOW ASPECTS:

- Self-Satisfied and Oblivious
- Foolish and Ignorant

Consequences of Owning Your Gifts

Owning your gifts may alienate you from others or make it tough for them to feel your empathy. You're fantastic at helping people reframe and see the silver lining in a given situation, but sometimes what's called for isn't a brilliant explanation but straight up empathy—simply feeling what the other person feels.

When you're unable to let yourself feel pain, sadness, or failure, you lose the ability to truly empathize. You tend to be there *for* people rather than *with* them.

Shadow Aspects

Over-Expressing: *Self-Satisfied and Oblivious*

The over-expressing aspect of Wisdom's shadow aims to diminish the opportunities and places where feeling and looking foolish can show up. As part of this, you feel a growing need to reframe everything in a positive light and continually grasp for the higher truth of the moment. You forget that living fully sometimes includes blundering into a lamppost with no higher meaning to be made.

You feel a growing need to reframe everything in a positive light and continually grasp for the higher truth of the moment.

This shadow leads you to avoid the intimacy and vulnerability that come with sometimes being every bit as foolish as the rest of us. Because playing a big game and truly putting yourself out there requires you to confront your fear of looking foolish, something you're unwilling to do, you achieve your aims by inadvertently constraining the size of your impact in the world.

Because you would rather make a wise observation than dive into challenges, people find themselves less interested in having a relationship with you. People wonder why they feel alone in your company.

Obvious (But Ineffective) Fix: Play the Jester and Join the Party

Frustrated that people experience you as aloof and removed, and tired of feeling like you hover above real life, you diminish yourself and come down to live with the mortals. You minimize your insights and become reflexively self-deprecating. Rather than evoking real humility and vulnerability, however, you put on a silly mask.

Part of the ego's game here is that you go out of your way to create silliness and foolishness rather than allowing it to come naturally when appropriate to the situation. Rather than being with the abundance of all there is to experience, you end up performing foolishness.

Showing up to a game and playing with no expectation of winning is never as impactful as showing up with a commitment to win and a willingness to be with the devastation of losing. Rather than aiming towards the highest Wisdom and accepting you may fall on your face in doing so, you intentionally drive towards foolishness. This performance can come off as sophomoric, patronizing, and cynical—which of course leaves you feeling damned if you embrace your gift and damned if you don't.

Under-Expressing: *Foolish and Ignorant*

The counterpart to retreating into enlightenment is retreating from it, as you sense that your Wisdom is unwelcome or threatening to others. You diminish who you are so that they (and you) feel more comfortable.

Afraid of own your Wisdom, you come off as inconsequential and superfluous. You're less threatening now, but an element of tedium and inauthenticity creep in. You're pretending to be something you're not.

By adopting this shadow aspect, you avoid being held to the higher standard that is worthy of who you are. But you also experience frustration and resentment. People don't take you as seriously as they should or appreciate your gifts.

Blind to the fact that you are actively creating this experience, you see other people and your circumstances as the problem. You're left blind to the deeper truth: *You're* the one betraying your gift and perpetuating the situation. Because our shadows hide out in our blind spots, for the most part, you're left frustrated at the world for the way they perceive you.

Obvious (But Ineffective) Fix: Grow Up and Get Wise

Tired of playing the clown and being dismissed, you dig your heels in and decide it's time to get real, to embody your higher truth without apology. This is an earnest effort on your part, but it's also a negative reaction to how things have been going. You zero in on maintaining the look and feel of Wisdom—rather than accepting yourself as wise with all the humility that entails.

Blind to the fact that you are actively creating your experience, you see other people and your circumstances as the problem.

Maintaining this charade requires you to avoid situations that put you at risk of looking anything other than wise. You shrink your world and exclude the people in your life who see and connect with you as a little goofy.

You've missed the real problem, however, adopting a surface-level change that fails to transcend your shadow extremes. Without truly confronting your fears, this obvious fix leads you to pull back from your gift and the vitality of life. Yes, you're expressing your Wisdom—it's just that none of what you say has an impact on yourself or the world.

Creating the Breakthrough

Both your shadow aspects are about avoiding undignified situations in which your Wisdom appears to have bellyflopped from the high dive. Letting go of the need to prove you're wise every single time and accepting that you'll be a goofball like the rest of us once in a while will set you free.

Your Wisdom is always present, but embodying it fully requires trust and an acceptance of your human fallibility.

Essentially, this means relinquishing control over outcomes. You can't actually control these anyway, but true freedom emerges when you can give your absolute best *and* be at peace with the result, whether you look like a genius or a total dork.

Your Wisdom is always present, but embodying it fully requires trust and an acceptance of your human fallibility. Your Wisdom reaches its full potential when no longer held hostage by the need to get it right. Your path is about leaning into life and being okay with the resultant experience. This won't always feel comfortable, and people may sometimes laugh, but it will open up ease within you and access to your fullest experience of life.

Leading and Working with People of Wisdom

Your team members who embody Wisdom are reliable North Stars for your team. They have a natural ability to pull the team out of the weeds and to keep it focused on its higher purpose.

They may also use this ability (inadvertently) in ways that distance and separate them from their co-workers. They may hesitate to fully commit in the face of risk. When you notice them playing it safe like this, acknowledge the value of what they bring, then lovingly invite them to "get into the game" with all its struggles and setbacks. In doing so, they will connect more deeply with their team members and harness the full power of their gift.

Wisdom

COMMON SHADOW ASPECTS:

- Self-Satisfied and Oblivious
- Foolish and Ignorant

On the other end of the spectrum, your wisest team members may actively diminish their gift in favour of playing the fool. People may initially reward them for this, finding their observations funny and sometimes penetratingly on target. Over time, they'll see it as tedious and counterproductive, dismissing the person in question.

What would be risky about fully owning your Wisdom in this moment?

Your job as leader is to support them in becoming present to their impact, and to how they feel increasingly isolated and ignored, allowing them to release their clownishness and step into the influential roles they were born for.

Remember that this impulse to play the fool, just like withdrawing into high-minded observer status, is rooted in fear. When you stand for these team members, do so with a great deal of love and kindness. Remind them of their inherent Wisdom and invite them to get curious about what would have them pretending they are something else in the moment.

Practises

Notice yourself playing the fool.
If Wisdom is your gift but you find yourself clowning around, can you notice this in the moment and press the pause button?

The more often you catch yourself doing this—in the moment rather than in retrospect—the easier it becomes to take responsibility for your experience of being dismissed and to see what this might keep you safe from.

Get clear on what you fear.
When you catch yourself in those moments, pause, take a breath, and ask yourself, "What am I afraid of right now?"

Ask the question literally and specifically, not rhetorically. Is it a fear of looking stupid or fallible if you turn out to be wrong? What would be risky about fully owning your Wisdom in this moment?

Once you have the answer, share it out loud with the person in question. This might sound something like, "Oh, I just noticed I went off the goofy end with that comment. I think I'm afraid of not being taken seriously. Let me put it differently..."

If the thought of this feels uncomfortable, good! That's how you know you're practising something new.

Catch yourself retreating to the bigger picture.
Notice the ways in which you retreat into Wisdom to remain unruffled by the world. See if you can catch yourself "reaching for the higher truth" rather than being with the reality of having, say, tripped over your own feet.

Once again, ask yourself what you're afraid of in that moment. What potential outcome are you are avoiding? Remember that this practise isn't about fabricating feelings. Rather, it's about seeing how you avoid certain feelings and how you dodge the experience of being fully present to the reality of the moment, whatever that may be.

COMMON SHADOW ASPECTS:

- Self-Satisfied and Oblivious
- Foolish and Ignorant

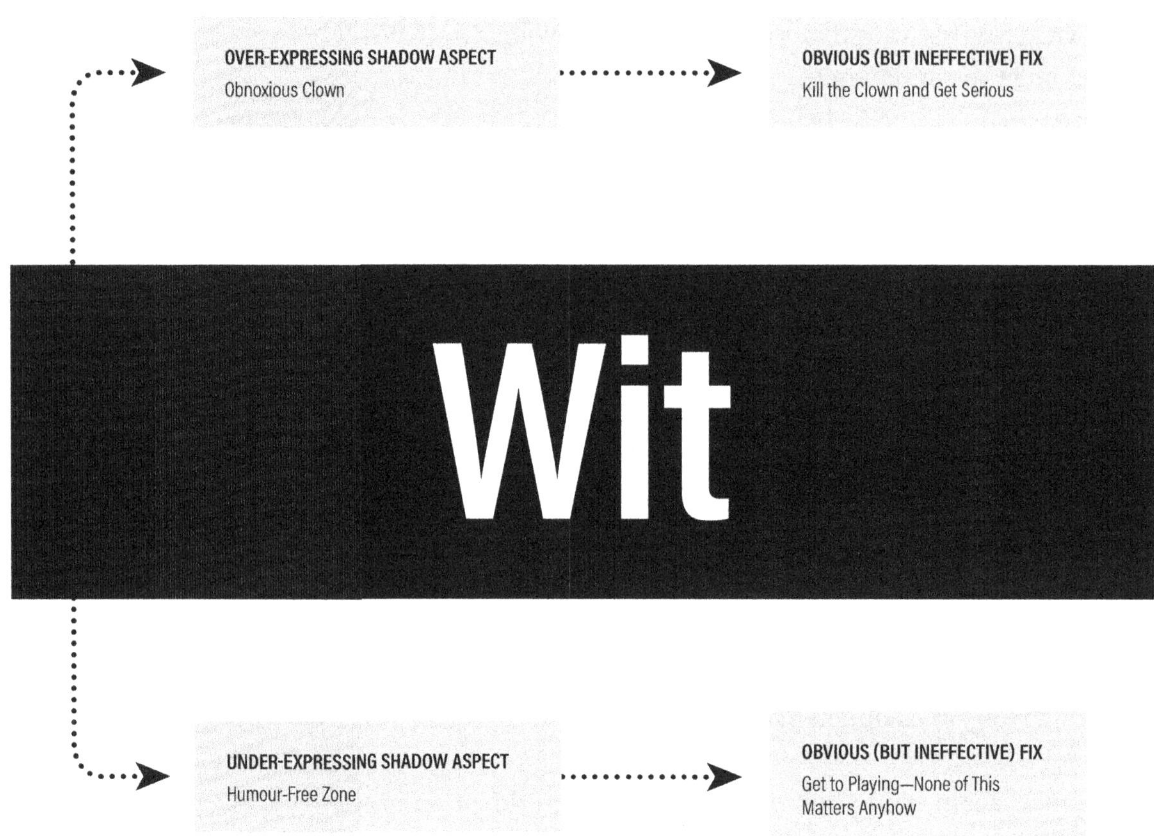
OVER-EXPRESSING SHADOW ASPECT
Obnoxious Clown
OBVIOUS (BUT INEFFECTIVE) FIX
Kill the Clown and Get Serious
Wit
UNDER-EXPRESSING SHADOW ASPECT
Humour-Free Zone
OBVIOUS (BUT INEFFECTIVE) FIX
Get to Playing—None of This
Matters Anyhow

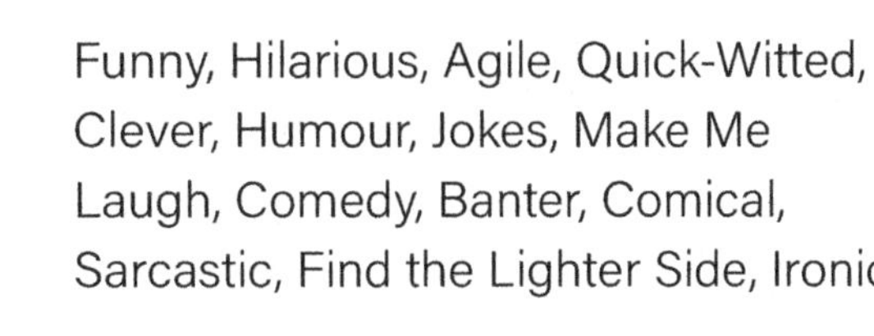

Funny, Hilarious, Agile, Quick-Witted, Clever, Humour, Jokes, Make Me Laugh, Comedy, Banter, Comical, Sarcastic, Find the Lighter Side, Ironic

The Quality

Your Gift

Everything is funnier and invokes more laughter when you are around. You're a magnet for fun and the lighter side of life, and there is simply no place that can contain you. Generating delight and play in every space you enter, you bring levity to each moment.

Wit is not merely about cracking wise and making jokes. Wit is the gift of agility and perspective—the ability to reframe and recontextualize a conversation or event such that we think about it differently. This is the heart of most good jokes—a reframing of the circumstances in a way that tickles the brain.

Consequently, your gift allows you to come up with creative solutions to problems that otherwise seem intractable. You can be masterful in tense situations, lightening the mood with a deft joke, and effective in negotiations. Your gift ensures that you are never without words and can talk your way out of anything. People cannot help but like you, allowing you to make friends of those who would otherwise be your enemies. Perhaps the greatest gift of all: In your presence, everyone becomes funnier. You are the gift of laughter, agility, and play.

COMMON SHADOW ASPECTS:

- Obnoxious Clown
- Humour-Free Zone

You are never without words and can talk your way out of anything.

What is Predictable

Life, of course, isn't all laughter and play; rather, it is the sum total of every possible human experience. Predictably, you find life's more serious moments harder to remain present to and retreat to the lighter side of things. When what the moment calls for is seriousness or gravitas, your inability to sit in these spaces leads to you force a shift in energy that isn't always helpful or welcome.

When someone brings a heavy energy into the space, you may be unable to resist poking their buttons or highlighting the absurdity of their approach. There are times and places where this is appropriate, but it's reflexive behaviour for you rather than something you've chosen. As a result, some will see you as obnoxious—like the kid in the back of the classroom making *sotto voce* jokes that undermine the teacher's authority. Others will decide you're in avoidance, unable to handle tough conversations or situations, and write you off.

You may get stuck in cool, ironic detachment, or decide to embody the clown, poking fun of things at the most inopportune of times and making yourself the object of ridicule.

Finally, in the face of withering criticism that your Wit is unwelcome and unprofessional, you may grit your teeth and become deadly serious. You don't have much practise with this, and as you attempt to lead powerfully or hammer home a point, you may come across as heavy-handed and ponderous—and get negative feedback for that.

You're left completely frustrated with both approaches, and this becomes the conundrum you can't seem to solve.

What is Possible

When you recognize that Wit is present and available to you in every moment and untether your gift from *always* needing to provoke laughter, you provide this energy to the rest of the world. Wit is the magic of the ever-changing energy in the universe. Even the wave-particle duality of light is an example of Wit. Our universe is continually shifting and changing, appearing one way one minute and another way the next.

As you do the work to open your heart and reduce your reactivity, you learn to poke people in the ribs gently enough that it becomes a gift to everyone.

As you deepen your capacity to be with *all* aspects of life rather than just those that feel pleasurable and fun, your Wit and your leadership become more meaningful. Being able to reframe the existing context is a potent tool. When you drop the need to reframe things towards a certain agenda—say, getting a laugh or impressing people with how serious you are—and can simply shape the conversation in whatever way best serves the moment, you become a transformational leader.

Those with Wit can quickly deliver a sharp rebuke when they feel wounded. This facility may lead you to cut people to ribbons before they (or you) know it's even happened. As you do the work to open your heart and reduce your reactivity, you learn to poke people in the ribs gently enough that it becomes a gift to everyone.

Finally, it can be difficult for those with Wit—who often self-identify as the "funny one"—to allow someone else to be the catalyst for laughter in a given moment. When you release your need always to be the funniest person in the room, you laugh more easily at yourself, and call forth the humour that's latent in all of us.

COMMON SHADOW ASPECTS:

- Obnoxious Clown
- Humour-Free Zone

Common Experience Coming of Age

You may have been the class clown and popular at parties. You wriggled out of trouble and tense situations with your sense of humour. You may also have been tough to pin down and prone to boredom in classes and situations that weren't fast paced enough to keep you entertained. To create a little excitement when you could no longer sit still, you may have become a distraction and a troublemaker. Your mental agility might also have made you something of a chameleon—identifying what people required of you and showing up that way.

Your mental agility might also have made you something of a chameleon—identifying what people required of you and showing up that way.

Consequences of Owning Your Gifts

Your ability to get a laugh, seemingly at will, probably led some people to see you as flippant, uncaring, or checked out, and to stop taking you seriously. As a result, you feel left out when you want to matter—failing to see that you're the one giving away your power when you routinely fall back on humour to be safe and liked.

Shadow Aspects

Over-Expressing: *Obnoxious Clown*

When things felt heavy growing up, you cheered people up and brought levity to the moment by using humour. As this stopped being a choice and became automatic, the over-expressed aspect of your shadow was created.

You rely on laughter to disconnect from anything that makes you uncomfortable—not just heavy conversations but intimacy more broadly and moments when you feel especially powerful but can't resist the urge to dissipate that tension. You're still everyone's favourite funny man, but your experience of life may wear a little thin, lacking as it does the anger, sadness, and, above all, *connection* that anchors others to their humanity.

By virtue of your ironic detachment, you become impervious to the world at large. Nothing can truly impact you because it's all a joke anyhow. While there's safety in this approach, you notice that you don't seem to achieve that much in your career or have a meaningful impact as a leader. But, hey, it's all a joke anyway, and if nothing really matters, you can joke about that, too.

Obvious (But Ineffective) Fix: Kill the Clown and Get Serious

Frustrated by a sense, especially as you get older, that people look to you for laughter but not much else and painfully aware that you aren't building anything meaningful, you reluctantly give up being the soul of Wit that comes so easily and get down to the hard, serious work of creating a meaningful life.

You claim power and chart a head-down course of action that will lead to results. You're committed now, no longer scattering your energy in quips and funny stories. You've taken off the clown nose, finally, and you like the determined face you see in the mirror.

Well, mostly. Life does have more meaning these days but at the expense of joy and play. Over time, things start to feel relentlessly heavy. You've run low on the daily laughter that used to be so refreshing and energizing.

You find yourself asking, "Was getting results really worth the sacrifice?" But there's no good answer. One way or the other, a critically important part of you goes unexpressed.

COMMON SHADOW ASPECTS:

- Obnoxious Clown
- Humour-Free Zone

Under-Expressing: *Humour-Free Zone*

Growing up, you heard repeatedly that "just being funny" wouldn't get you very far and that smart alecks were simply unwelcome. You learned to turn the volume way down on what once came naturally and without effort.

Growing up, you heard repeatedly that "just being funny" wouldn't get you very far.

Not surprisingly, you have trouble summoning your gift when it would help you assume power, have a difficult conversation, or any other situations in which your natural gift was squelched. You manage, nonetheless, to get things done and to be respected as a professional—albeit one who's a bit heavy to be around.

Ironically, you find yourself yearning for better work-life balance and a sense of ease once in a while. "If only I could have more laughter and joy in my life, things would be better." The problem isn't lack of balance, however. It's that you divided yourself into two different people, only one of whom shows up at work. It all kind of works, and you can point to the results you're getting. It's just hard to get too excited about those results when things generally feel kind of gray and lifeless.

Obvious (But Ineffective) Fix: Get to Playing—None of This Matters Anyhow

You're reliable to create results and your life looks pretty good externally. But, internally, your experience is one lacking in color and feeling excessively heavy. In the areas of your life where the under-expressed aspect of your shadow plays out, you miss the belly laughs you used to experience.

Anytime we split ourselves into different personalities for different parts of our life, we diminish our capacity for full expression.

You decide to hell with it and seek to bring back lightness and play. You may attempt to bring in more humour, lighten the mood, or layer some kind of mirth-making over top of the underlying weightiness that lies within your heart.

Alas, you haven't dismantled the underlying story that enjoying Wit and achieving results are diametrically opposed. If you lean back towards play, you will necessarily reduce your impact and the hard-won respect you've earned from others. You decide to go for it, anyway, making a wisecrack as you do—but knowing deep down you're back to the unsolvable conundrum.

Creating the Breakthrough

A central paradox for those with Wit is that life can be simultaneously mundane and exhilarating. This usually leads them to retreat entirely into playful mirth or to split themselves into two distinct personalities: One part that crushes Wit to generate impact and the other part that is fun and playful.

Anytime we split ourselves into different personalities for different parts of our life, we diminish our capacity for full expression. Being playful with friends but deadly serious at work means you're holding part of yourself in check all the time, which is exhausting and draining and leads to burnout.

A deeper experience of mirth *is* available to you, but only when you accept on some deep level that yes, life is meaningless and worthy of being laughed at—but also seeing this as an invitation to create the meaning you choose.

Your breakthrough path comes from simply holding the heaviness you sometimes feel rather than escaping it with a flip comment. The more you can be with the lows in life, trusting that they are temporary, the richer your capacity to experience the highs. At times, this may feel like you're restricting your mental agility, but in doing so, you discover that structure and restrictions can set you free. As you learn to feel greater ease with the full spectrum of your emotional and mental potential, notice what else shifts over time.

Wit

COMMON SHADOW ASPECTS:

- Obnoxious Clown
- Humour-Free Zone

Leading and Working with People of Wit

Your team members with Wit reliably lighten the mood and keep things playful. They excel at reframing traditional perspectives, and their innate ability to see things in new and surprising light opens possibilities that may otherwise have been dismissed as impossible.

You're not trying to fabricate something that isn't naturally there. Instead you're creating a deeper awareness of when to ease up on your gift and when to allow its natural expression.

Take notice of the places and times these team members use their Wit. Laughter makes for an easy out when leadership opportunities show up in the form of tough challenges. These moments ensure they're well-liked but are essentially escape hatches. When sitting in the heaviness is what's called for, your Wit-type team members are no-shows.

When you notice this happening, invite them gently to set the quick jokes aside for a while (learning to calibrate their gift will take time). Encourage them to use their mental agility instead to identify solutions. If they resist, reassure them that this isn't permanent and that they're free to deploy the lighter side of their gift in other arenas. Help them understand that Wit is just one aspect of who they are as a human being and as a leader and that this is a chance to strengthen underutilized muscles.

Finally, be on the lookout for team members who have a great sense of humour but show up instead as grim and burdened. Invite them to rediscover their lightness, at least some of the time. Stand for their ability to generate Power *and* Play, simultaneously.

Practises

Notice yourself using laughter to escape.

Wit is such a powerful escape tool. Everyone loves to laugh, and it's hard to criticize someone who enables us to do so. Your place of growth isn't about criticizing yourself for the laughter you create but about getting present to what you're avoiding. What *don't* you want to feel or be with those moments? For bonus points, practise setting aside the playfulness and relaxing into what comes up.

Are you using humour for yourself or others?

Humour for your benefit is generally a means of ensuring that you're well-liked, included, and safe. Using your humour for others means that it adds to what is in the space, and flows naturally out of the moment, rather than being shoehorned in to meet your own needs.

You may find yourself pushing back on this distinction, arguing that humour serves everyone. Sit with it, anyway, until a deeper understanding emerges—probably one having to do with quick benefits in the moment versus those that are longer-term and meaningful.

Notice the struggle between Power and Play.

Where and when does Play go out the window? What are your reasons for deciding that Wit won't serve and should be held in check? Recognize that these moments aren't necessarily opportunities to inject more fun. You're not trying to fabricate something that isn't naturally there. Instead you're creating a deeper awareness of when to ease up on your gift and when to allow its natural expression.

COMMON SHADOW ASPECTS:

- Obnoxious Clown
- Humour-Free Zone

SECTION

THREE

How to Practise

HOW TO PRACTISE

IN SECTION ONE, I laid out the model and framework for this perspective on humans, how we became who we think we are, and leadership. In Section Two, I laid out twenty-five individual qualities of being, to give you a place to begin understanding who people (including yourself) are, underneath the strategies we adopt from our fear.

In this section, I'll provide a guide to how you can put what you've learned into practise in the real world, with a set of eight practical How-To chapters. I'll also distinguish some of the terms we've laid out and provide some specific practises.

Distinguishing "Practising" and "Life as Normal"

Before we even get into the specifics of how and what to practise, it's important to distinguish the concept of a "practise." For the most part, we relate to the things we take on in life like we do a to-do list. There are neat tidy checkboxes, and once we've finished or accomplished the action, we can check it off and be done with it.

Before we even get into the specifics of how and what to practise, it's important to distinguish the concept of a "practise."

This is a very human approach to managing the busy-ness that is our daily lives. By checking something off, we can say, "I've done it" and then move on. We don't have to mentally keep track of it, and we can get back to doing everything else that needs to be done. With just a little more time, maybe we can get it all finished and then, finally, we can have peace (or binge-watch the next season of that TV show).

This approach also provides us with the opportunity to get back to "life as normal."

"Life as normal" is the way you've been living life up to this point.

"Life as normal" is the way you've been living life up to this point. From "life as normal" you know what to do, you know what you're right about, you know what you're wrong about, and you know what you don't know. "Life as normal" includes the automaticity (and comfort) of your shadows as well as the complaints that accompany the expression and impact of those shadows in your life.

"Life as normal" is cloaked by a veil of automaticity. For the most part, our shadows are invisible to us—they lie in our blind spots. We may vaguely be aware of the fact that our shadows show up from time to time (and generally judge ourselves and others for this behaviour) but that is generally the only extent to which we can perceive them. Instead, our cognitive bias has us see the world through the lens of our shadows—like a fish seeing the world through water rather than seeing the water itself.

"Life as normal" is not the path to breakthrough. The practises we offer in this book are designed to get you out of "life as normal." Doing so will be uncomfortable. Like going to the gym and lifting weights, the practises will put stress on you, initially, as they force you to leave the comfort of your homeostasis and develop new capacities. Your comfort and safety will not want you to practise. Practising is anathema to your comfort and safety because it moves you outside of "life as normal" and into the scary unknown—which is what your shadows are designed to protect you from.

The upshot of this is that it's really compelling to simply try to "get your practises done" or find shortcuts to them. You can shortcut practises any number of ways.

Rather than actually going out and taking on the practise, you could instead visualize doing them from the comfort (and safety) of your chair and "life as normal." You could take on a practise a single time, and then check it off your to-do list.

"There, I did it. I noticed a time I did that thing. Done."

When given a practise to notice yourself doing something, like, say, closing off from people in conversation instead of making the effort to catch yourself in the act and notice it as it's happening, you could simply scan your thoughts for the times you already know you close in conversation. Then, you could nod your head, resting secure in the fact that you "did" the practise and move on to whatever is next.

If you're scanning your thoughts for where you already know you do something, there can be nothing new discovered from this approach. We will come to what it means to discover something shortly. For now, it's worth considering that all these approaches that allow you to "get done" something you're practising are self-defeating for someone committed to breakthroughs in their lives and leadership.

These approaches are like going to the gym and lifting a weight once, then dusting your hands and patting yourself on the back. Exercise, lifting weights, and practises are not a one-and-done kind of thing. They're an ongoing, day-to-day practise. This is what distinguishes a practise from homework, tasks, chores, jobs, or anything else that can be neatly crossed off your to-do list.

Exercise, lifting weights, and practises are not a one-and-done kind of thing.

Distinguishing "Discovery"

Many of the practises listed in this book are practises in noticing something. The intention of practises related to noticing is that you *discover* something new about how you show up in the world.

The dictionary definition for *discover* is (the emphasis is my own):

> 1. *Find (something or someone)* ***unexpectedly*** *or in the course of a search;*
> 2. *Become aware of;*
> 3. *Perceive for the* ***first time.***

Discovering something new through a practise in noticing will require you to put energy into the practise. You won't discover something new, simply by thinking, "Oh, yeah, I should practise that." What you seek to discover is hidden by the automaticity of your shadows and "life as normal."

Instead of really discovering something, most people take on a noticing practise one of two ways:

1. Accidentally notice something, and then let that be enough; or
2. Look to what they already know

The first approach lacks any intentionality, and it relies on hopefulness that you may just randomly see through the veil of automaticity that surrounds most of our daily lives. You can take this approach, but it lacks the intention of leadership, and at best, is kind of like hoping you'll suddenly see something new in your actions.

This is distinct from creating an intention to pierce the veil of "life as normal" so as to actually discover something. In order to breach the automaticity of "life as normal," we often need to create structures to pull us into lucidity and check in with ourselves. Creating these kinds of structures helps jog us out of the automaticity that keeps most of "life as normal" obscured.

The second approach—looking to what you already know—precludes you from any opportunity for discovery. By looking in the areas where you already know you do something, there's nothing new to be discovered. Sure, you may "know" that when people do X, you do Y, but "knowing" this fact is never the same as discovering it while you're doing it in the moment.

Knowing is distinct from discovering.

Knowing is distinct from discovering.

The intention of a practise in noticing is to catch yourself red-handed, as it were. To stumble upon the fact that you are acting out the very thing you are trying to notice and to realize you weren't aware of what you were doing until this very moment.

When taking on practises around noticing, create structures to support you jogging yourself out of the automaticity of "life as normal," and practise in order to discover something new rather than to affirm something you already know.

Distinguishing Responsibility from Blame and Getting Responsible For Your Impact

A number of sections in this book talk about getting responsible for your impact. Before we talk about how to do that, we need to distinguish *responsibility* from *blame*.

Blame

Blame means that I was wrong for my choices, decisions, and actions. When operating from a context of blame, the best things get is that someone other than you is at fault for how things went. In a context of blame, people have only a few (narrow and limited) options.

Blame means that I was wrong for my choices, decisions, and actions.

The first option is to defend ourselves. No human wants to be wrong, and so when people ask, "Who's to blame for this?" (whether or not they actually use those particular words), the natural instinct is to explain why this isn't on you. I'm not to blame. No, sir! Not me.

Even better than not being to blame for something is to have the blame fall on someone else. If someone else is to blame, then obviously it's not you, and so more's the better. Passing the blame to someone else then becomes our second option.

The third option is to simply fall on our sword and writhe around. We are (courageously?) willing to accept the blame for what we have done and will flagellate ourselves accordingly. The approach to self-flagellation kind of makes sense in as much as you can at least anticipate and, to some extent, control the lashes you are receiving when you are the one doling them out.

For many people, it's easier to punish and condemn themselves than it is to have someone else do it, so when options one and two fail, heaping blame and repudiation on themselves becomes the third option.

These are the limited choices that blame leaves us with. Not a lot of options for leadership in any of this. In terms of our own mental wellbeing, the best option is to either ensure you never make a mistake (and thus are never to blame) or get really effective at finding fault in others.

At worst, you can get really effective at lashing yourself (so that no one else bothers trying) and promise that you'll never make the same mistake twice.

Blame is one of the biggest barriers to responsibility. In fact, blame destroys the possibility for responsibility—and responsibility is the domain of leadership.

Blame is one of the biggest barriers to responsibility. In fact, blame destroys the possibility for responsibility—and responsibility is the domain of leadership.

The trouble with blame is that it doesn't allow any space whatsoever for learning or growing from our mistakes. Because we find the experience of being wrong so repugnant, the only choice we have available is to avoid it at all costs. When something goes astray, we don't have the capacity to take a look and see how we might have contributed (i.e., have been responsible) to what happened. Instead, we scurry to explain why we had nothing to do with what happened and how it's not our fault.

Responsibility in this context becomes a binary on or off switch. Either it's my fault or it isn't. And because I have a vested interest in it not being my fault, there is no access to responsibility.

Without access to responsibility, my power (i.e., my ability to affect a particular situation and cause a particular result) is hamstrung. The only real time I could change what I did is when I'm at blame for how it went. Otherwise, I did everything great and there's not much for me to look at other than how I let this other person over here screw it all up. Oof.

On the other end of the scale, when I'm busy self-flagellating, there's not much room for me to hear anything about my impact or how I showed up. Because I'm so busy making myself wrong (and loathing myself for it), there's no space available to look at how I created this. Instead I must do my penance until I can stop, and then I can move on to never making the same mistake again.

Leadership is not about making a mistake once and never again. Imagine trying to ride a bike from this ridiculous approach. And yet this is how we hold ourselves and others as we go into the world and attempt to lead.

As you do your work and support others in their own, be on the lookout for blame and making ourselves and others wrong for the choices we made. When we find ourselves in a context of blame, the work is to recognize and distinguish this fact and then get back over to responsibility.

Responsibility

The capacity for responsibility is what gives a leader access to their power. The more a leader can take responsibility for, the more they have the power to change. If I can see a way in which I contributed to how things went, then I have the ability to make a different choice next time and cause a different result.

Contrast this with a leader who insists there was nothing they could have done differently ("It was out of my hands!"). This leader is powerless. Because of their inability to see how they could have contributed to the way things happened, they have no option but to hope for a different result next time and to lay blame on those that were responsible. While blame is the refuge of the powerless, responsibility is what gives the leader access to power.

The capacity for responsibility is what gives a leader access to their power.

Because every interaction or relationship with someone involves both parties, any particular leadership dynamic provides an opportunity for the leader to be responsible.

It's important to note here that taking responsibility can feel like a burden at times. Leaders, especially early on in their development, wonder why they have to always be the one looking on their side of the fence. Can't they just be right about the other person being a dingus this one time?

This experience is very human and shouldn't be derided. It's understandable to want a break from responsibility. Taking ownership means that we then have some work to do. It means setting aside the default context of blame that is largely pervasive in modern society and choosing a different way of showing up to the table.

Choosing outside of the default context requires effort and energy, especially as you, and your team, are learning to develop these new muscles. Have space, love, and compassion for yourself and those you are leading as you deepen your capacity to take more and more responsibility for the world as it shows up around you.

Here are some examples of taking responsibility for something, on varying degrees of gradient:

Lenny is frustrated that his friend, Rebecca, doesn't treat him the way he feels a friend should. Around other people, Rebecca puts Lenny down and makes fun of what he's up to in life.

- Initially, Lenny is insistent that this is all on Rebecca for not honoring their friendship. After taking a look with his coach, Lenny can see that he can be responsible for the fact that he tends to make fun of what he's doing for a career, frequently complaining about it when Rebecca is around, which would subtly encourage her to do the same.
- Lenny can also see that rather than address this with Rebecca, he finds it more comfortable to go along with her jabs. Doing so gets him out of the discomfort that may come from having a more intimate discussion with Rebecca.

Gladys is frustrated that her staff don't seem to show up and put themselves into the space.

- Taking a look at how Gladys is showing up, she can see that she tends to fill space when there is "dead air" in the room. Doing so also provides Gladys with a degree of comfort because then she doesn't have to sit in the awkward silence that would otherwise ensue.
- Gladys notices that she has some judgment of the people that tend to shy away from taking up space and, as a result, is unwilling to hold herself back when there is space available. Consequently, Gladys sees that she herself is unwilling to

sit back quietly when no one else is stepping into the space. Gladys sees that she's subtly trained her staff not to step into the space, knowing that if they wait long enough, Gladys will step in and then the staff don't have to be with the discomfort of leading and holding the room's attention.

Arnold has gone away for a vacation, only to return home and see that someone has broken into his house and robbed him.

- Without condoning the actions of the burglar, Arnold is committed to taking back his power and so takes a look through the lens of responsibility.
- With support, Arnold can see that he had boasted about his vacation for a couple of weeks prior to leaving. Looking back over his social media accounts, Arnold can see that in the weeks leading up to his vacation, he posted excitedly about his travel plans and where he'd be going along with photos of his neighbourhood.
- Finally, Arnold can see that in the months prior to his departure, he had been posting photos about the new TV, sound system, and computer he'd bought for his house and accepted a number friend requests from loose, mutual acquaintances.
- Arnold doesn't hold himself to blame for any of this nor does he diminish the burglars' culpability for their actions. Instead, he gains access to his own power by seeing how he might have contributed to the break-in and could choose different actions in the future.

The last example is an important one because people will tend to relate to this as "victim-blaming." It's not Arnold's fault that he was robbed, and no one should have to live their life planning around this. Notice how quickly we've fallen back into the context of blame and how perfectly this demonstrates the challenge to take responsibility. "It's not my fault, and I shouldn't have to be responsible" would be a perfectly reasonable answer for Arnold to provide here.

Being a leader is not about being reasonable.

But being a leader is not about being reasonable. It is about creating something greater than ourselves and striving beyond the immediacy of our human reactions. Arnold doesn't *have* to do anything. But if he is committed to leadership in all areas of his life, then looking through the lens of responsibility will give him access to have things go differently in the future, should he choose (rather than simply hoping that the same thing doesn't happen again).

Having distinguished responsibility from blame, we can now talk about the stages of leadership.

The First, Second, and Third Stages of Leadership

Our capacity for leadership tends to move through three main stages of practise.

The first stage of leadership is often focused on controlling yourself and the world around you. You manage other people's feelings, you try to avoid making too big a splash, and you try to be nice and neat and tidy.

And, on top of that, you get annoyed with people that aren't reciprocating the same thing. When people show up in a way that upsets you, you judge them for it, expecting that it's their job to manage themselves so you don't have to feel that way.

In essence, you relate to the world and expect others to relate to you through the same lens—that of the first stage.

At this stage of practise, the game is about other people. How do I avoid upsetting them? How do I make sure they like me? They should change their behaviour, etc.

To talk about responsibility and impact with someone operating in the first stage of leadership can be sticky. Because their own expression is so wrapped up in managing how other people feel, it's hard to be responsible. Instead of being responsible for their impact, you end up with something much closer to co-dependence and enmeshment.

The second stage of leadership is a breaking free from all of this control. Instead of controlling yourself and managing the world around you, you decide, "Fuck it!" and stop censoring and controlling yourself. You show up, as you are, because that's what's real for you.

At the second stage, when other people show up in a way that you find obnoxious, rather than insisting they be different, you simply remove them from your life. You close off to them, block them, or avoid them. In a sense, you are sovereign. You be as you be, you let others be as they be, and you go about your life.

Instead of controlling yourself and managing the world around you, you decide, "Fuck it!" and stop censoring and controlling yourself.

At this stage of practise, the game is really about you (or *me*). I'm not willing to censor myself. My own expression is what matters.

Just like in the first stage, your expectation of how others show up reflects the stage you're operating in. Because your outlook is now a function of being your own person and doing what you see there is to do, you also expect other people to conduct themselves the same way. If what I do offends you, then it's on you to choose to walk away from me. It's no longer on me to conduct myself in such a way that it doesn't upset you.

The shift from the first to second stage is often challenging and energizing. To finally free ourselves from the shackles of managing everyone else's feelings creates a great deal of freedom. This is also the stage of practise where many people stall out. A lot of pop-psychology, positive affirmation, and modern self-help is focused on getting people to this stage and then ending there. (It's important to note here that the shift from first to second stage is still growth. It's just that we're aiming for something beyond stopping at this point.)

The third stage of practise is a shift into *responsibility*. At this stage of practise, the leader is still committed to expressing themselves, but they are also present to the impact of how they've expressed themselves. Even though they may be bored in a meeting, they have the capacity to ask themselves, "Hey, does yawning loudly and proclaiming that I'm bored serve what we're trying to create here, or would that actually shut people down more?"

The third stage of practise is a shift into responsibility.

At this stage of practise, the leader develops not only responsibility but also the ability to calibrate how they show up and, in doing so, can manifest the greater purpose they are committed to. At this level of leadership, the game is about whatever the leader is committed to that is bigger than themselves.

This provides the leader with a commitment beyond mere self-expression in the moment. If staying quiet while someone else speaks, even though the leader disagrees, is what will create the result they are committed to creating, then the leader is capable of doing so—not as a concession or something they tolerate but as an action that genuinely empowers them and sets them free. The leader is empowered in this choice because it moves the world closer to the commitment the leader is.

At the third stage of practise, the leader's being is given to them by something greater than themselves.

At the third stage of practise, the leader's being is given to them by something greater than themselves. (Think of Gandhi's commitment to the British departing India, Mandela's commitment to the end of Apartheid, and Martin Luther King's commitment to the end of segregation as examples.)

The third stage will often occur wrong to those practising in the second stage. Rather than being able to see the deeper purpose the leader is committed to, those at the second level of practise will likely relate to this ability as co-dependence, people-pleasing, or a form of censorship—basically a step backwards into the first stage rather than a transcendent step into the third.

Unlike the myth of being "woke," like it's something you either "are" or "are not," you don't "arrive" at the third stage and then stay there. You will perpetually and perennially be in and out of these stages. In one area of your life, you may be comfortable and capable of operating with a third stage level of responsibility while in other areas, you may reserve the right (unconsciously) to hang out in the first.

Whatever stage of practise you are in is great. None of these are better—simply milestones along the journey. You can't leapfrog these stages. The only way forwards is to move through them.

HOW TO CREATE AND USE STRUCTURE

WHEN WE USE the word "structure," we're referring to anything that provides a degree of solidity to the chaos that is our daily lives. Our lives already contain a tremendous amount of structure. Some simple examples of the structure in our daily lives include:

The clocks and calendars we are surrounded with

Although nature doesn't divide time up into discrete chunks or the passing of time into discrete days, weeks, months, and years, we do. This structure allows us to make plans with one another, create meetings (and show up on time), produce something in a given amount of time, and work towards meeting deadlines that we have agreed to rather than simply getting around to things "when we feel like it."

Our legal system

Left to our own devices, we would probably, generally, try to be good to our fellow man, cooperate with one another, and be fair with each other. But without laws there would also be a great deal more anarchy, vigilantism, and rule according to our whims rather than according to a set of laws applied equally to everyone. Our legal system structures the way we show up in our life. It provides a skeletal structure to the way humans operate collectively.

A chair

A chair supports you in a particular position. It allows you to rest parts of your body and remain upright while you conduct certain tasks. The structure of the chair makes this possible while simultaneously taking away the options that would be otherwise available. If you wish to lie down, you will need to get out of the chair. The structure of a chair does not allow for that. This doesn't mean a chair is bad. It simply means that the structure of a chair is designed to support you sitting rather than lying down.

Every human being has their own unique relationship to structure as a whole.

Every human being has their own unique relationship to structure as a whole. For the more mundane examples, you may be completely unaware that these provide structure to your life. It's rare that we think about a chair the way I've listed here.

You may relate to structure as an imposition and something that takes away your freedom. And on some level, you would not be wrong about that. A chair, after all, does take away your freedom to lie down. But the chair takes away this freedom in service of your commitment to something else—being able to sit while working on whatever you're working on. This is the nature of structure. It removes aspects of our freedom in service of our commitment to something other than "leaving all of our options open."

On the other end of the spectrum, your relationship to structure may be such that your focus for transformation is almost entirely on structure. Rather than getting clear on the breakthrough you're here to create in your life and your leadership, you are more inclined to put your attention on the structure first and foremost. You may create rules, practises, and projects that are all replete with structure. This isn't necessarily bad, but when someone asks, "Why are you doing that?" you realize that your answer to this question is more of an afterthought. Simply creating the structure seems like enough.

The purpose of structure, in the context of this book, is in supporting you to create breakthroughs, to support you in piercing the veil of "life as normal," and to have you practise something that you may otherwise have resistance to.

Having resistance is natural and human. If you don't experience a degree of resistance when taking on a practise, you would probably be better served by aiming for something edgier. Your resistance is your compass, and these practises should inherently be pushing you out of your comfort zone—which will naturally drive up your resistance.

Having said this, your resistance will show up in a multitude of ways and may not always be what you expect. Sometimes, resistance is active. Active resistance, for example, would be when you are committed to doing something but continually find yourself procrastinating, avoiding, and putting off. You are clear what there is to do, and you are clear that you are resisting doing it.

Passive resistance is the more insidious form of resistance because it looks like it's outside of your control and not your fault.

Other times, your resistance may be passive. Passive resistance looks more innocent than active resistance does. An example of passive resistance would be simply forgetting to take on what you declared you would practise. It would include finding yourself too busy throughout the week and ending one more week not having had the chance to practise. Maybe you really intended to practise, but the time you set aside just happened to be the time that your sister called you, and she really needed your help and support, and so you just didn't get around to practising.

In all these forms of passive resistance, what is happening is that the scary action (practising) ends up being at the effect of the circumstances of your life. You would definitely practise if only you weren't so busy, happened to remember, didn't have people needing your support, etc.

Passive resistance is the more insidious form of resistance because it looks like it's outside of your control and not your fault.

We are not interested in fault here. We are interested in deepening your leadership—and part of being a leader is doing what you said you would do, regardless of the circumstances that show up.

In order to overcome your resistance, passive or active, you will likely need to create structure to support you.

The single best structure to overcome your resistance is usually hiring a coach. The financial investment alone calls forwards your commitment. Paying money alone won't usually be sufficient (buying expensive exercise equipment does not necessarily make you exercise for longer than the two months of novelty it provides). However, the benefit of a support structure like a coach is that each week you show up to the calls and share what you did and did not take on in your life and then have a conversation about what would support you in not getting stopped the way you did.

That being said, just because a coach is usually the most powerful structure, it isn't the only one. Below are a bunch of examples of structure that may support you to overcome your resistance and continue practising.

Study groups and accountability partners

Meet with someone or groups of people weekly, share what you're committed to doing, and then share what you did and did not do the previous week. We are often far more reliable when we are holding a structure in partnership with someone else. A study group provides the added benefit of giving you the reflection of more than one person, to help check against your ego's blind spots.

Make public declarations and follow-up by sharing how they went

Making public declarations about what you will take on (and following up by sharing how they went) will hold your feet to the fire. Accountability works when you are willing to account for what you said you would do. What this means is that you own what you did and did not do. Both sides of this structure must be present for this structure to work.

Create deadlines and be specific

Committing to do something in the "next while" doesn't put any end to your practise and thus makes it impossible for you to hold yourself accountable to it. If you are intending to take on a particular practise, be specific about what you will be practising and by when you will have completed the practise.

Schedule time to practise

If you're anything like me, you have great intentions about practising, but the moment you set this (or any other) book down, those intentions vanish into the fog and busy-ness of daily life. Specifically set aside time in your calendar to practise whatever it is you intend to practise and then hold that time as sacred. If you intend to practise emotions on purpose, do not wait until you "feel angry enough to practise." By the time you reach that point, you will no longer have the consciousness to pull yourself out of your automaticity. Instead set aside time every morning to specifically take on this practise and be unflinching in your commitment to practise at that time.

Create reminders and alarms

Because passive resistance helps us get out of doing something uncomfortable by simply forgetting, it is one of your ego's favourite tricks. Create reminders and alarms to jog you out of "life as normal" and bring you back into awareness of you as you go through life. Regular reminders on your phone can be a great way to check in with yourself and continually practise as you go about your day.

Because passive resistance helps us get out of doing something uncomfortable by simply forgetting, it is one of your ego's favourite tricks.

Track your progress

When taking on daily practises, it can be powerful to track your progress on a calendar, or something similar. Did you take this practise on today? If so, make a checkmark on that particular day. Doing so allows you to see your progress and gets you into "streaks." Seeing that you've practised four days in a row makes you more likely to avoid breaking your streak and to continue the practise into the fifth day.

HOW TO GET PRESENT TO YOUR IMPACT

GETTING PRESENT TO your impact requires a willingness to hear how the way you've shown up has affected someone else.

There are a few things that typically stop us from getting present to our impact. We'll look at an example first, then talk about the barriers in the way of getting present to our impact, and, finally, how you can practise doing so.

Getting present to your impact requires a willingness to hear how the way you've shown up has affected someone else.

Let's say that I have some feedback to provide my direct report, Laura, on the way she's showing up as a leader. I could do what is typically done and have this conversation after the fact, or possibly delay it until we have a feedback session. Laura will get my feedback far after the moment has passed and, at best, can try to apply that feedback next time she happens to catch herself doing whatever she did. Unfortunately, since most growth lies in our blind spots, it's a little bit of a setup for Laura since she's unlikely to be able to see her own blind spots. That being said, providing the feedback after the fact is always more comfortable because it allows me to avoid the intimacy of the moment including Laura's own discomfort as she receives my feedback.

Instead, in service of having a bold conversation to support Laura's breakthrough and giving her the opportunity to address how she's being right now, I choose to provide her with the feedback in the moment.

"Laura," I interrupt. "You're doing really great. I appreciate what you're providing. And I have some feedback on your leadership. May I provide it to you?"

Laura nods her head, and I continue.

"I notice that your body posture is telling me to dismiss you. The way you're holding yourself suggests that I don't really need to listen to you or that you may or may not have value to bring, but I shouldn't get my hopes up. Who I know you to be is Leader, Power, Commitment, and Brilliance—and your body language is incongruent with that. So, could you please take a breath, remind yourself that you are valuable and have a tremendous amount to provide this room and then stand accordingly?"

Laura does as I ask and carries on with the meeting. At the end of the meeting, Laura comes to me and asks to share how that was for her. When I agree, Laura shares that I left her feeling small and diminished.

So, given this example, let's talk about the barriers to getting present to my impact in this scenario.

The first barrier is our tendency to hold our focus on the intention behind our actions rather than their impact.

In this example, my intentions were to relate to Laura as the leader she is, trust that she doesn't need coddling, and to provide her the reflection that will allow her to address the way she is showing up in the moment rather than six months after the fact. My intention is to be in service of her breakthrough in "Leader."

I could argue against Laura's experience, sharing that that was not what I intended (defending my intentions), and that the reason I chose my actions was in service of her breakthrough. But all this does is shift the attention away from my impact to my intention. Instead of owning my impact, I instead defend my intention and refuse to move off that position.

The second barrier is our tendency to make what is happening entirely about the other person. Instead of owning that how I delivered my feedback left Laura feeling a certain way, I put it all on her. There's no impact for me to own—the reason she feels small and diminished is entirely Laura's to own.

While there is almost certainly something for Laura to own in how she's listening to me, there is also absolutely something for me to own about the fact that this was the impact I left her in.

The third barrier is our reserving the right to not take responsibility until the other person has done so. Instead we keep our attention on how this is the other person's stuff to own and maintain that position. In this sense, I'm not really willing to look on my side of the fence because all my attention is on how Laura always relates to herself as small and diminished, and so, of course, she's going to hear my feedback through that lens.

As leaders, we have to be willing to be the ones that go first. This means modelling responsibility and ownership, free of the need for the other person to do the same.

The challenge for each of these three barriers is that they are not inaccurate. You likely do have positive intentions. When we create a negative impact on someone, it is rarely because we intended to do so. More often than not, humans are kind, open-hearted, and want to do right by each other.

Because every interaction with someone involves two people, whatever impact occurs will always include some of their stuff. But it will also include some of your stuff. And finally, because you read books like this one and are probably committed to the work of leadership, you're going to be able to see a great deal over there on the other side. The trouble is that until you take ownership for your side of the fence, you won't be able to get present to the impact you've had.

As leaders, we have to be willing to be the ones that go first. This means modelling responsibility and ownership, free of the need for the other person to do the same.

Having laid out this litany of caveats, we can now actually talk about how you get present to your impact.

In reality, getting present to your impact is really easy. It's everything we put in the way that makes it challenging.

When you wish to learn about the impact you've had, you simply need to ask someone, "Hey, what was the impact I had on you there? How did I leave you?"

And then listen.

The hardest part is listening. In order to really get your impact, you must set down your need to defend your intentions, to point to how this is the other person's experience or that this has nothing to do with you.

You must listen and take in everything the person shares with you as absolute truth. Because to them it is.

Notice whatever shows up for you as you practise this. Do you have a desire to argue? Does your body language close? Does your breath get short? Do you wait for them to finish so you can explain? Do you interrupt them so you can apologize? What can you catch showing up for you?

All these things are in the way of truly getting present to your impact. The work of leader is to ask for, listen, and receive feedback about our impact from those courageous and kind enough to share it with us.

Once the person has finished speaking, repeat back what you heard, and ask if you got it all.

You may feel ashamed or embarrassed, especially if part of your impact is something you are especially committed to not creating. That's okay. Part of our growth requires a willingness to be with that which we do not love about ourselves. (Learning to love these parts is a large part of our transformation as leaders.)

Once you've really gotten your impact, we can begin moving to cleaning up your mess.

HOW TO CLEAN UP YOUR MESS

NOW THAT YOU'VE read about getting present to your impact, it's hopefully clear that you will predictably be making some messes. Regardless of your best intentions, regardless of how hard you try to do good in the world, and regardless of how vigilant you are, you will have an impact, and sometimes, that impact will land poorly on people.

Cleaning up your messes is not about making yourself wrong for what you've done. It's not about falling on your own sword or expressing dismay at what a loser you are. These approaches are more about admitting guilt for your sins than they are about cleaning up your messes.

Cleaning up your messes is not about making yourself wrong for what you've done.

Cleaning up your mess is about releasing the significance and corresponding defensiveness that we have around our own impact, so that we can leave people whole, complete, and clean in our wake.

Imagine that you are in someone's house, and while you are sharing an exciting story, you swing your arm to make a point and knock a glass of milk on the floor. You could spend your time insisting that it's not your fault because you were just telling a story, and you didn't intend to knock anything over. Or you could spend the next thirty minutes verbally haranguing yourself and explaining to your host what a loser you are and how this always happens and so on.

Neither of these choices does anything to clean up your mess. While you are verbally denigrating yourself, your host's kitchen still has milk and broken glass on the floor. Cleaning up your mess means letting go of the significance of the impact, so you can simply get it. And once you've gotten it, doing what needs to be done to set things back to whole and complete.

It's okay that you've spilled milk on the floor. You're human—not perfect. But you still need to clean up your mess.

Leaders that are capable of cleaning up their messes this way grow tremendously. The act of learning about your impact helps you become more responsible for how you show up in the world. In cleaning up with people, you leave them enrolled in coming along with you. People are left in the experience that you are committed to something more than your own comfort or righteousness (even if the cause you are righteous about is a worthy one).

Most people want to rush to the amends so that they don't have to be with the uncomfortable feeling of hearing about the mess they've created.

Cleaning up your mess first requires a willingness to be present to your impact. Once you've done that, the remaining steps are validation, empathizing, and amends.

Most people want to rush to the amends so that they don't have to be with the uncomfortable feeling of hearing about the mess they've created.

Resist this urge. Doing so has you skip over the actual steps to cleaning up, and there are no shortcuts in this work. By being willing to sit in the discomfort, you develop a muscle in your ability to hear about all of your impact. This capacity to receive feedback and learn about the impact you are having will serve you in becoming ever more responsible and potent as a leader.

Once you've heard everything the person in front of you has to share, validate what they've shared. Repeat it back to them to make sure you've got it all. Then, empathize with what they're experiencing. Release your own position and get over on their side so that you can really, truly understand where they're coming from.

Empathy requires releasing our own position. This means we do not listen and respond from a position like, "I understand why they feel this way. If I was ignorant and uneducated, I would feel the same way." This stance isn't true empathy. It's you holding on to your own position and then trying to explain why the other person feels the way they do from where you stand.

Real empathy is more like, "This makes complete sense. I can absolutely see how what I did left you feeling like I didn't care and was callous."

Once we've empathized with the other person, our last step is to make amends. What do we need to do to clean this up?

Typically, an apology is the beginning. If the way I left Laura was feeling diminished and small, I can apologize for that. It's absolutely not what I'm committed to and certainly not what my intention was, but I can totally get that that was the impact all the same. And I can apologize for that impact—without making it mean something significant about me (like, "I'm a shitty leader").

Once you've apologized, the last step is to check in with the person and ask, "Is there anything else you'd like or need from me to clean this up?"

You have to acknowledge and find your own willingness in this last step, and this is partially why it's so important you work with your own coach. There will be a distinction between your own level of comfort and a particular boundary you may have when it comes to cleaning up.

Early on in your work, the simple act of apologizing for your impact may feel like a breach of your boundaries. Left to our own devices, our boundaries can become excellent reasons to avoid ever stretching beyond our own capacity. The support of a coach can help you distinguish between discomfort and losing access to your own sovereignty.

What are you willing to do to clean up this particular mess and leave the person in front of you whole and complete? For the most part, people will make reasonable requests of you to clean up, especially when you've gone to the effort to truly get them and empathize with how you left them.

HOW TO BE WITH SOMETHING

MANY PRACTISES IN this book speak to being with something. Being with something stands in contrast to suppressing, wallowing, and reacting to that same thing.

You can be with anything. You can be with someone's discomfort, sadness, or anger. You can be with your own discomfort, sadness, or anger. You can practise being with your fear or the rage that someone feels while in traffic. You can be with a conversation about politics, the lack of money in your bank account, or the fact that someone has done something you believe is wrong.

Being with something stands in contrast to suppressing, wallowing, and reacting to that same thing.

The practise of being with something is actually incredibly simple. Like most of these practises, the challenge is less in the practise itself and more about what we put in the way of it.

"Being with" is the simple act of sitting and being with something without needing it to change, without needing anyone or anything to be different, and without doing anything to avoid having to be with it.

Here are some of the many ways we avoid being with something:

Trying to fix or change it

This is one of the most common approaches that has us avoiding being with something or someone. As a simple example, imagine someone sitting down beside you who is having a crappy day. You try to help them by reframing their situation and having them see the silver lining.

Rather than simply being with someone having a crappy day, you are attempting to fix their perspective, so they have a different experience. This allows you to avoid being with someone else's crappy day, their negativity, or whatever else it is that you are unable to be with. It also gives your ego a boost, leaving you feeling like you've made a positive difference to this person by "helping" them with their bad feelings.

WAYS WE AVOID BEING WITH SOMETHING

- Trying to fix or change it
- Avoiding it physically
- Avoiding it mentally
- Anger, judgment, and condemnation
- Suppression
- Reacting and wallowing

Avoiding it physically

Rather than simply being with something, another common solution is to avoid it altogether. Often, we avoid things physically. In the previous example, instead of reframing things so that the person beside you has a different experience, you instead simply "cut out" negative people in your life. People having bad days? No, thank you.

You'll physically avoid people that show up in a particular kind of way (whatever there is for you to practise being with, typically), and your own tendency to do the same things will remain in your blind spot.

Avoiding it mentally

You can also avoid being with something mentally. Perhaps you cannot be with conversations about politics, and so when you are at the dinner table and the conversation shifts in this direction, you remain physically present but check out mentally, occupying yourself with your own thoughts or tuning out the conversation.

Anger, judgment, and condemnation

One of the ways we avoid being with something in both ourselves and others is through anger, judgment, and condemnation. Rather than sitting with something and letting ourselves be with everything that is driven up, we zealously attempt to eradicate it. We get righteously angry and demand that the particular behaviour or circumstance be stamped out of existence.

Although the tools used are a little different, this is not that much of a shift from the first example. Instead of using positive reframing, you're using righteous judgment. In either case, your inability to be with something, means that you automatically (that is to say, as a reaction and without any choice on your part) must change it.

There are many, many, many more ways in which we avoid being with something, and we could continue drawing out this list for days. Rather than do that, we'll finish up here by pointing to the two main ways that people avoid truly being with something.

Suppression

Suppressing whatever is showing up is the most common way to avoid being with something. We can suppress ourselves by refusing to feel something altogether. If you've ever met someone who told you they "just don't get angry/sad/afraid," you can pretty much guarantee there is a degree of suppression going on for that person since anger, along with sadness, and joy, and fear are fundamental aspects of what it is to be human.

It's important to note here that you may not even be conscious that you are suppressing something (that's part of what makes it so effective). It doesn't occur to us like we are actively getting angry and then stuffing that down. Once we've practised suppressing something long enough, it becomes automatic. We no longer have to take a conscious role in doing so. As soon as the stimulus of anger/sadness/etc. shows up, we unconsciously and automatically react by stuffing it down.

On the surface, what we're left present to is the fact that we "just don't get angry/sad/emotional/etc."

Consequently, if this is the main way you avoid being with something, you might argue, "Well, I just don't ever feel that way" when you read a practise to be with something in particular. You may even begrudgingly agree to take on a particular practise, only to come back next week and insist, "I just didn't get angry/sad/etc. so there was no opportunity to practise."

Your practise starts when you release the story that you "don't ever feel that way." Instead a more powerful context for you to step into would be, "I do feel this way from time to time. I'm just not aware of it." And then ask yourself how you might practise from there.

If you were to step into that context, you might start to create a practise for yourself of noticing what you do to avoid feeling angry. Or perhaps you begin your practise from the context "I get angry, but I've gotten really good at hiding it. My job is to spot it." And then be in the practise of noticing whatever clues and hints might surface to lead you back to the human experience you are having.

We can only be with what we can distinguish.

We can only be with what we can distinguish.

What that means is that as long as you are unaware of yourself doing something, you have no capacity to be with it. You will avoid or attempt to change that behaviour in others while continuing to be oblivious to the times when you yourself act this way.

Reacting and wallowing

Suppression grants us the ability to operate over top of something. As an attorney, I suppressed much of what I felt, allowing me to operate purely from a cold, rational, logical headspace (the shadow of Brilliance provides a great description of the way I showed up at this point in my life.)

Suppression is effective because it creates the experience of being above something. The thinking is often something along the lines of "Anger is an unproductive emotion, so just don't have any." Simple, right?

If suppression allows us to avoid something altogether, then wallowing and reacting is about diving in headfirst and drowning in whatever it is that we cannot be with.

When we wallow or react to whatever it is we cannot be with, the experience tends to be dramatic and overblown. There is a lot of outrage, anxiety, catastrophizing, indignance, and, again, righteousness.

Wallowing in whatever is showing up is the act of making something meaningful and real. It's not simply that someone in a country on the other side of the world is doing something cruel; it's that we must mount a campaign to do something about it. We must stay up late at night worrying about it. We must shift every conversation towards this important topic and rally everyone else to our same cause (until we've got a new cause).

From the incredible meaning that is attached to that which someone cannot be with, their reaction is a given; it is automatic. When we have no capacity to simply be with something but rather make it meaningful and get swept up into it, we lose access to ourselves. Instead of remaining sovereign and in integrity to ourselves, our values, and our leadership, we become automatons, reacting to the stimulus of the moment.

When our tendency is to wallow in whatever we cannot be with, reaction becomes inevitable. If we have no capacity to be with what we perceive as selfishness, we won't simply shrug our shoulders when someone shows up selfishly. We will attempt to address it. Maybe we give them a piece of our mind. Maybe we double down on our own efforts to be generous and kind. Maybe we write angry letters to the local newspaper calling out that person that did that thing that one time.

All of these leave you reacting to what you cannot be with rather than simply being with it, and continuing on with whatever you are committed to as a leader.

Two Sides of the Same Coin

On the surface, each of these approaches could not occur more differently than one another. Those operating from the suppression side will judge the wallowers and "reactives" as foolish, dramatic, and out of control. Those operating from the side of wallowing and reacting will judge the suppressors as cold, out of touch, and aloof.

In fact, both of these approaches to avoiding being with are two sides of the same coin. By judging the other side of the coin, we can avoid being with the fact that fundamentally we are unable to be with something and instead think to ourselves, "At least I'm not like that."

We'll use the inability to be with anger as an example to illustrate these two different sides of the same coin.

On the suppression side, we have Reggie. Reggie has stories that "Anger just isn't productive. And it's harmful. I choose not to be angry." When someone around Reggie gets angry, Reggie energetically closes to them. He might attempt to placate them, but on another level, he retreats up into the safety of his head and rational analysis. He might flatly respond to this person, explaining why their anger doesn't make sense, and attempting to use logic to allow the person in front of them to escape their anger the same way Reggie does.

When Reggie himself gets angry, he heads it off at the pass. Rather than feel his own anger, he thinks about it. He analyzes and rationalizes his anger, effectively disconnecting from his feelings, and, once again, retreating into his own head. The experience people have around Reggie when he is angry is a little like being around a cold, ruthless sociopath. They can tell, on some level, that he's upset, but he remains flat, cool, and collected.

The experience people have around Reggie when he is angry is a little like being around a cold, ruthless sociopath.

On the wallowing and reacting side, we have Betty. Betty also has stories that "Anger is harmful. It's wrong. We shouldn't be angry to people; we should be nice to them." When someone around Betty gets angry, she takes it personally. Someone else's anger is not simply someone being angry. It is a meaningful expression about who Betty is as a human being.

Betty spins on the other person's anger. She thinks about it, worries about it, asks herself if there is something wrong with her. Betty herself may get angry back at this person, furious that they would direct anger towards her. Betty may start posting on social media that people shouldn't get angry for no reason and create a group for people dedicated to bringing cheer into the world rather than anger.

When Betty herself gets angry, she is swept up in it. She has little ability to discern that her anger is about herself and instead feels righteous and indignant about the person, event, or circumstance that drove up this anger. Betty may even experience boldness and empowerment from the fervour provided by her anger.

Both Reggie and Betty lack an ability to simply be with anger without having it move them off the natural, full expression of themselves. Reggie was not born a robot, and Betty was not born righteous and dramatic—they both simply learned to show up these ways in the face of what they cannot be with as a function of their shadows.

For Reggie, practising being with anger would involve allowing himself to feel and experience his own anger without doing anything with it—and when present to someone else's anger, to stay open, connected, and present rather than retreating into the comfort and safety of cold, hard logic.

For Betty, practising being with anger would involve allowing herself to feel and experience her own anger without doing anything with it. Rather than acting on her anger or making it meaningful, Betty's job might be simply to acknowledge, "I'm angry," and then sit in that, separating her anger from all the meaning she subsequently attaches to it—and when present to someone else's anger, rather than reacting to it, staying open, connected, and present with the human being in front of her.

For Betty, practising being with anger would involve allowing herself to feel and experience her own anger without doing anything with it.

It's important to note here that neither what Reggie nor Betty does is wrong, bad, or "should" be changed. This book is not about condemning patterns of behaviour and insisting you make changes because what you are doing is wrong.

The point is that for both Reggie and Betty, there are aspects of their leadership that will remain forever out of their reach because of their inability to be with anger. Their reactivity to this particular stimulus ensures that they will be operating "on rails" as soon as it shows up—Reggie, through the cold, hard world of analysis (leaving people feeling ungotten and unheard) and Betty, through the righteous indignation and dramatic angst of making things overly meaningful (leaving people swept up into her tornado).

Whatever you are practising being with throughout this book, you can always begin your practise by first noticing how you avoid being with that particular thing.

HOW TO PRACTISE WITH EMOTIONS (YOUR'S AND OTHER'S)

EVERY HUMAN BEING is raised with a different (and often complex) set of relationships to the varying emotions that make up our day-to-day experience being a human.

For some people, we are trained that anger is unacceptable. It is violent, unproductive, and harmful. For others we may be trained that sadness is weak and ineffective and gets you belittled. For others still, we may learn that being overly joyous will get you dismissed or related to as childish.

Your training can come in all manner of forms. You may learn a particular relationship to anger because that is what one of your parents modelled. If we see our father shouting and yelling in the car when people cut him off, we learn that anger is something to be sprayed around. If you get angry, it's okay to let it all out, kind of like an unmanned fire hose, provided the only people in the car with you are your family members.

Or, you may have learned the opposite. From having a mother that got angry and yelled at home, you were left scared and often walking on eggshells. In this situation, you may have learned (or concluded) that anger was unacceptable and never had a place. You made a promise that you would never cause the harm that your mother caused.

Our training comes in a wide variety of forms, and the important thing is that you came by your relationship to your emotions honestly. That is to say, there's a good and valid reason that you ended up the way you did.

This is the best place to end this particular inquiry. We could get really curious about why you formed the particular relationships you did, what the exact moment was that triggered your training, and all of that. This kind of inquiry is often more the domain of therapy, though, and here, we are more interested in having you move forward rather than casting your gaze backward.

In order to do so, you're often best served by acknowledging that you came by the relationship you have to each emotion honestly and then moving on to distinguishing what that relationship is so you can begin to work with it.

Given a relationship to any particular emotion, we don't usually have much facility with that emotion. Throughout the practises offered for various ways of being, you'll see suggestions to take on practises like, "Owning your anger" or "Practising sadness on purpose."

The starting point for working with your emotions is recognizing that you will not, by default, have much facility with the emotions for which you have a disempowered relationship.

The starting point for working with your emotions is recognizing that you will not, by default, have much facility with the emotions for which you have a disempowered relationship.

Let's use anger as an example. If I've learned that "anger is bad" broadly speaking, then my capacity and range of expressing and experiencing my anger will tend to be very binary.

I'll stuff and suppress my anger as long as I can, and it will tend to surface as a blowup. I occur meek and obsequious most of the time until I can't hold it in any longer. Then, my anger explodes like a volcano finally blowing its top. I rage and let it all out, and upon relieving the pressure, double down on the story that anger is wrong (now, predictably, with proof of that fact, given my recent blowup).

Or perhaps, because expressing it outwards is unacceptable, I deliver all that bile and rage inward, berating, haranguing, and loathing myself for who I am and how I show up.

When I talk about having a limited facility with anger, this experience I've just described is what I mean. Your capacity to be with, experience, and express anger (yours and others) is limited to all-on or all-off. This makes anger (in this example) especially problematic. Rather than being able to experience a degree of my own anger and then get clear on what I might need to do to move through it, I have only two tools at my disposal.

Emotional responsibility begins with the capacity to recognize when a particular emotion is present for you and being willing to own this fact.

When anger starts to show up, I have to suppress and deny its existence, insisting that it not be present. The only time I can really "work" with my anger is once it's become too much for me to continue stuffing down. At this point, I don't have any capacity left. I'm full, and the only option I have is to blast it everywhere, like a star going nova.

For someone with the relationship we've just laid out for anger, you can guarantee that they will show up the same way with any employee, partner, friend, etc. that they are supporting. If your relationship to anger is that it has no place at work, then you will have zero capacity to be with someone when they are having their own experience of anger. Just like you do internally, you will subtly (or overtly) push them towards stuffing and shutting down their own anger, continuing the cycle, and ensuring that your blind spots are borne out organizationally.

Learning to develop emotional range is about changing our relationship to our emotions, such that we have a wide variety of facility and range we can work with—both in ourselves and others.

In order to create this shift, you need to create an ability to be responsible for your emotions. Emotional responsibility begins with the capacity to recognize when a particular emotion is present for you and being willing to own this fact.

Because of the negative relationship people tend to have with particular emotions, they lack the capacity to even recognize their presence. Rather than thinking, "Oh, I'm getting angry, and I'm stuffing that down, trying to make it go away," their experience is more like, "I'm not angry. What are you talking about?"

Distinguishing

Before we can be responsible for anything, we have to be able to see it. If my tendency to steal money from people lies in my blind spot, and thus I have no awareness of it, being responsible for it is impossible.

In order to begin practising emotional responsibility, you must start by noticing when you are angry, sad, joyous, or whatever emotion you are practising with.

In order to begin practising emotional responsibility, you must start by noticing when you are angry, sad, joyous, or whatever emotion you are practising with. Insisting you don't get angry, etc. simply keeps this in your blind spot.

You can begin by looking for whatever version of a particular emotion you are able to distinguish. Perhaps instead of anger, you are more present to mild, low-grade frustration. Perhaps instead of sadness, you are more present to resignation. Shifting your context from "I just don't get [emotion]" to "I just am not good at recognizing when I am [emotion]," will give you a different lens through which to look and begin to recognize your emotional range as you move through it.

Experiencing

As you start to recognize the hints of a particular emotion, the next step is the practise of experiencing that emotion.

There are many ways to resist experiencing your emotions. One of the most popular (and effective) is to *think* about your emotions rather than to *feel* them. This involves doing things like asking yourself, "Why am I sad?" or "What is making me sad?" This inquiry is then just a quick jump to "Well, that doesn't need to make me feel sad..." and then reframing things so that you don't have to be with your emotion. In just two short moves, we've managed to avoid being with our emotions once again.

These kinds of inquiries allow you to bypass the actual feelings associated with a particular emotion and instead go on a chase for meaning and significance. Why you are feeling the way you do is irrelevant in this practise. What matters is that you *do* feel the way you do—and that you currently have a limited muscle in feeling that way.

Instead, the practise is to distinguish how you are feeling and then *allow yourself to feel that way*. When you notice that you are feeling sad, let that emotion wash over you. Notice when you get into analysis and set those thoughts aside. Notice where you feel your sadness physically. What's the experience in your body? Practise sitting with that physical feeling without doing anything about it.

Expressing

Once you can distinguish and experience your emotions, the final step is practising the expression of them. Emotions are energetic in nature, and energy works by moving. Like a river flowing, when we don't block our emotions but allow them to run free, they change and morph as we move through life.

You've almost certainly noticed this tendency in babies and toddlers. They experience one emotion, express it, and then very quickly move on to a new one.

When we have limited or no facility to experience and express a particular emotion, it's like we dam the river. The water backs up behind the dam, flooding the lands behind it, and letting only a minuscule trickle through. Like the lands behind the dam, you end up drowning in your blocked emotions, believing you are actually keeping them at bay, but really suffocating under them.

Emotions must be expressed one way or the other. Even if we suppress a particular emotion, it will still find a way out (perhaps through explosive road rage or passive aggression). In order to develop someone's leadership, we are interested in the responsible expression of emotions, so that they can move through you rather than getting blocked and causing problems.

Being responsible for your emotions means that you are able to distinguish them, experience them, and then express them in a responsible manner. Responsibly expressing your emotions means that you are responsible for their impact, allowing them to move through you without derailing what you are committed to. Doing so frees you up and allows you the gift of the entire emotional range of a fully expressed human being.

As a leader, I want to honor my anger while simultaneously letting the person in front of me know that the anger actually has nothing to do with them.

While our emotions are always true, in the sense that what we are feeling is real, the meaning we have attached to our emotions is usually made up. I might experience anger because someone made a mistake, but this does not mean the person is wrong for the mistake. As a leader, I want to honor my anger while simultaneously letting the person in front of me know that the anger actually has nothing to do with them.

In this instance, I might say, "Hey, I'm having some anger show up. I'm clear it's not about you, but I can also tell I need to move it through my body. Can you give me five minutes?"

This is an extreme example, but it models the responsibility we are talking about. The leader is present to what is going on in their body and recognizes that they need to address it rather than operating over top of it. They let the person know that this is not about them and that they will be right back.

The best way to practise expressing your emotions on purpose is to set aside a consistent, dedicated time to actually practise expressing a particular emotion. If you are practising with anger (as an example), you might set aside two minutes each night to practise the physical and verbal expression of anger.

In order to be responsible, you would want to make sure that those around you understood what you were doing, and that this was not about them. You might check and make sure that the room you are practising in has the door closed and the windows shut. And if you're worried about sound travelling, you may put a pillow over your face so that your screaming doesn't carry into the other room.

People will create all manner of excuses to avoid practising this way.

The first excuse is that, when they set a time like this, they simply don't feel that particular emotion.

Of course, you wouldn't. You've spent a lifetime shutting down this emotion. You've dammed the river of this particular emotion and are simultaneously drowning in it while unable to recognize its presence.

If you are willing to empower the practise and channel the emotion anyway, the trickle will start to grow, and soon you will start to see what is there to be released. Practising this way may require that you "force" or "fake" it for a while. Give it the space to show up—and it will.

The second excuse is that it feels unnatural doing this.

Of course, it does! What's natural has been shutting down, stuffing and suppressing this particular emotion. What feels natural is "life as normal." Transformation rarely, if ever, feels natural at first—it's about growing beyond your existing range. If you want to transform and cause transformation in others, you must be willing to hang out in the places that currently feel unnatural to you. Feeling unnatural is a compass for your growth.

Creating breakthroughs is not free—it is about leaning into and confronting our fear.

The third excuse is that you have roommates or family members or neighbours or people that might hear you practising.

Then, practise responsibility and let them know.

"Hey, I'm really committed to creating a breakthrough around my anger. To do that, I'm going to be practising something. It feels a little silly to me and also a little scary. What that means is that for two minutes, I'm going in my room, closing the door, and yelling into a pillow. I don't think you'll hear me, but just in case you do, I want you to know nothing's wrong. I'm just practising."

The content of the excuses is never really the issue. What these excuses really provide is a reason not to do the thing that is scary and uncomfortable. If your relationship to anger is as we've described above, your friends, family, and neighbours would be overjoyed to hear that you are committed to creating a breakthrough.

But creating breakthroughs is not free—it is about leaning into and confronting our fear.

So, practise.

HOW TO FORGIVE

MANY OF THE ways of being listed in this book have forgiveness as part of their path to transformation and freedom. Forgiveness provides access to freedom. It releases you from the burdensome energy that you have been holding over someone—be it another person or yourself.

We always take the poison that we feed the rest of the world. What this means is that someone who is unable or unwilling to forgive others is doing the exact same thing with themselves. "I forgive but never forget" is often code for someone misunderstanding how forgiveness works.

An inability to truly forgive leads to resentment. When I feel wronged by you, and you or I or both of us step over this fact, my feelings cannot be resolved. The hurt and upset that I feel has no way of being completed, so, it festers. Over time, this leads to growing resentment.

An inability to truly forgive leads to resentment.

The metaphor I like to use for the way we have learned to do forgiveness is imagining that you have a backpack on your shoulders and are on a long journey. Every time you experience a perceived hurt, transgression, or wrong, it's like a hot coal that you pick up. You stuff the hot coal in your backpack, where it no longer burns your hand, and you continue on your way.

Because the hot coal is insulated by the fabric of your jacket and your backpack, you don't feel its impact too much. But it remains there—adding to your heat and the weight you carry with you.

Rather than really forgive someone, instead we simply set aside what we believe was wrong, pushing it down and putting it somewhere where, for the most part, we can ignore it.

As time goes on, the number of resentments, grievances, and woes we carry with us increases, and our ability to move freely becomes slowed and hindered to a greater and greater extent.

In order to really deal with this burden we are carrying with us, we must stop walking, sit down, and put our hand into the backpack. We have to reach in and grab a single hot coal, which causes us pain and may burn us temporarily. We have to look at that particular coal, as we hold it, and really let ourselves feel it in its entirety. And only once we've done all of that can we set the coal down and stop carrying it everywhere with us.

We avoid and resist doing this for a number of reasons.

First, it takes time to work through the resentments we are holding on to. Over time, we simply get used to the added burden we are carrying, and so, we are unable to really feel the impact our inability to forgive is having on us. We carry the added weight, having long forgotten the freedom we once had. And so, living the busy lives we do, forgiveness seems like a luxury of time we cannot afford. We don't have time to slow down—we have shit to do. And this resentment isn't really causing me any problems, anyhow. "It's only an issue with that jerk that did that thing that time. I definitely don't have it show up anywhere else in my life."

Second, to some extent, it's human nature to be a little vindictive. If you hurt me, it's natural for me to want you to feel the same pain back—that would make us even. By holding on to this resentment I'm carrying, I get to hold something over you. Even if you never get karmic retribution for the hurt you caused me, I get to energetically punish you on some level.

Third, because we aren't aware of what it costs us to hang on to our resentments and because we are living busy lives, we tend to be more present to what it will cost us to really forgive than we are to what it will provide us. Rather than get clear on the freedom that is available on the other side of forgiveness, our focus is on the time we don't have that we'll have to spend sitting down and working through something.

Built-up resentments, over time, end up controlling your life.

These built-up resentments, over time, end up controlling your life. You avoid people that seem at all similar to the previous person that hurt you. You hold over yourself the same things you hold over other people, eliminating your ability to play, be spontaneous, and experiment as you live into your life (because those things might lead to causing the same hurt you are unwilling to forgive in other people.)

The practise of forgiveness involves four parts:

1. A willingness to release our resentment;
2. Expressing all the energy that we have been holding onto;
3. Taking responsibility; and
4. Opening our hearts back up to love.

Willingness to Release

At the end of the day, forgiveness is a choice you have to make. If you are unwilling to let someone off the hook, then you yourself will forever remain on the hook, hanging on to this energy and reserving the right to stay resentful.

When practising forgiveness, you want to really check in with yourself if you are willing to release this energy and the resentment you are holding over someone. You want to ask this question and really sit with it rather than saying yes cursorily so that you can "get on with the practise."

You are best served by slowing way down and really checking in with yourself. "Hey, I've been holding this over someone, and letting go may not be easy. It's costing me something to maintain this resentment, but I'm getting something out of it. In service of really freeing myself,am I willing to forgive them?"

Your willingness doesn't mean you magically forgive them in that moment. There is still work to be done. Your willingness means that you are willing to do that work.

Absent your willingness, you can go through the motions of forgiveness without achieving any of the desired shift in your being—without experiencing the freedom of forgiveness.

Expressing the Energy

This is the portion of forgiveness that involves you taking out the hot coal and really feeling it burning your hand.

Your work at this stage is to express all the emotional and energetic content around this particular resentment. This is a solo practise. Spitting hot fire into the face of the target of your resentment might feel good in the short term, but it will do very little in terms of your work. Instead, sit down and really allow yourself to verbalize or write out or express in some other manner what you feel as you sit with this particular resentment.

If you are taking on forgiving someone else, then remember what they did and how you feel about it. If you are forgiving yourself, then remember what you did and how you feel about how you showed up.

We are not looking for you to be "responsible" here. This is not the time to say things like, "Well, Bruno did those things, and I hate him for it, but I recognize he was just doing his best, so it's actually okay." This would be an example of you being unwilling to fully express your own resentment.

So, express. Give yourself permission (and be a demand) for the most honest expression of your resentment and emotions surrounding this particular resentment. If you are unable or unwilling to fully express your resentment at this stage, the remaining parts of this practise will be unsuccessful.

At the end of this part, you should feel like there's nothing left you have to give. Like you've let it all out, and, to some extent, are drained or wrung out like a cloth.

Taking Responsibility

Responsibility provides us access to our own power, and what we have power and ownership over, we can do something about. When we practise taking responsibility, we can start to see how something wasn't entirely someone else's fault and see that we were as much a part of the puzzle as anyone else.

Responsibility provides us access to our own power, and what we have power and ownership over, we can do something about.

Once you've fully expressed all your energy around a particular resentment, you want to begin taking ownership for your role in what happened. What can you be responsible for? How did you contribute to the resentment you are holding on to?

If you have not fully unloaded and expressed the energy in the previous step, it will be almost impossible to take responsibility.

When you find yourself stuck at this point in the practise, you're often best served by going back and seeing what else there is for you to express in terms of your energy and emotions surrounding the particular resentment. Then, come back to taking responsibility.

Opening Your Heart Back Up to Love

The final part of forgiving requires opening our heart back up to love. Finding our way back to seeing the greatness on the other side of things rather than their shortcomings.

When we grow resentments, our focus becomes myopic, zeroing in on the downfalls and foibles in the other person. From this place, it's hard for them to ever get out of the hole we've put them in. We relate to everything they do going forwards through the lens of our judgment.

If someone never paid me back the money I lent them, I might listen to every future request they make through the lens of "Well, this person's a deadbeat, so what's really at play here?" Even if they were to try to pay me back, I might receive that payment through my judgment, thinking to myself, "Sure, they're paying me back, but they're a deadbeat, and I know that. So, what's the catch here?"

By opening our hearts back up to love, we connect over there with the greatness, the light, and the leadership that is inherent in every human being.

In order to do so, you practise getting present with and acknowledging the greatness that is in the other person and in yourself. What can you acknowledge in them? What is it that you love about them? What do you admire about this person and delight in getting to be with? How about yourself? What do you admire about yourself? What can you acknowledge yourself for in terms of how this all went?

You can practise seeing and acknowledging someone's greatness in the broadest, most general context, or you can do so through the lens of this particular resentment. If you truly let everything fall away, what can you see about who they are as a being of light that showed up here?

As long as we are holding on to resentful energy or unwilling to take responsibility for our role, it is challenging to open our heart back up. Indeed, we've got a vested interest in not doing so—to open your heart is to be vulnerable and put yourself at risk. So, if this final part of forgiving feels challenging, it may be a sign that there is more for you to express and release energetically or to take responsibility for.

Practising forgiveness in this way takes time and demands something of you. It is not "free" or "default" to forgive in this manner. The default for most of us is to hang on to our resentments, growing ever more righteous about them, in an attempt to avoid being burned a second time.

The leader practises forgiveness. Not just for the other person, but for themselves. Set yourself free.

HOW TO PROVIDE FEEDBACK

Many of the sections in this book devoted to leading people require providing feedback.

Providing feedback is uncomfortable. People, including yourself, will have a relationship to giving and receiving feedback. Whether it's positive or negative, someone's relationship to feedback will dictate the experience they have throughout the process of giving and receiving it.

Some of the more common relationships to positive feedback are:

- Positive feedback is just filler before the negative feedback comes, so wait for the other shoe to drop.
- Accepting positive feedback means you're arrogant or getting cocky.
- You shouldn't need positive feedback; you should just do a good job.
- Yeah, you're saying these nice things about me, but I need to focus on improving, so let's hurry up and get to the areas of growth.

Providing any kind of feedback, positive or negative, is going to bump into someone's existing relationship to receiving feedback.

There are many more disempowered relationships that exist around positive feedback. The point here is that providing any kind of feedback, positive or negative, is going to bump into someone's existing relationship to receiving feedback.

And further, you also have your own relationship to feedback, which will dictate how you provide it. If you believe that giving negative feedback is unkind and people hate receiving it, then you'll provide this kind of feedback in such a way that tries to manage or compensate for your belief.

Maybe you provide negative feedback by surrounding it with effusive (and inflated) praise. And when someone has a reaction to receiving it, you jump to make them feel all right and loved.

The point here is not that you do something wrong when you give feedback but rather to illustrate how much "stuff" is in the way of directly providing feedback and consequently, why it tends to be done so poorly.

The last challenge is that because providing feedback is generally required in any position of leadership and because our relationship to feedback remains largely invisible to us, we can't see any of this. Instead, like many people when it comes to their own leadership, we have a vested interest in our belief that we're pretty good at it—and maybe just need to touch up a few areas.

Instead of coming to this section holding sacred the belief that you're "pretty good at this," do your best to bring a beginner's mind. What if you know nothing about providing feedback, and there was the opportunity here to completely transform how this aspect of leadership goes for you?

The most effective way to provide feedback begins first by distinguishing what you yourself have in the way of doing so. You can do so through the following exercise:

Start by writing down all of your beliefs about feedback (both positive and negative). Here are some prompts to spur your thinking:

- Feedback is...
- Getting feedback means...
- People giving feedback are...
- If you're getting feedback, that means that...
- If you're giving feedback, that means that...

The most effective way to provide feedback begins first by distinguishing what you yourself have in the way of doing so.

Once you have a list of at least ten items, then you can begin writing down the actions you take as a result of these beliefs. Here are some prompts to support that:

- What do you do as a result of these beliefs about feedback?
- How do you manage these beliefs when you don't have any choice but to give feedback?
- What do you do when you are receiving feedback as a result of these beliefs?
- What do you do when you are giving feedback as a result of these beliefs?

The combination of these two lists provides you with your current relationship to feedback. This won't magically change that relationship; taking that on is deeper work better served in the container of a coaching relationship. What this will provide you is some clarity for your own innate bias and how you will get in the way of providing people feedback flatly.

Here are the steps to providing feedback directly and artfully:

1. Ask permission—in the moment.
2. Acknowledge who someone is and ascribe positive intention.
3. Speak to the impact they are having.
4. Check in to see if they're present to this, and, if necessary, remind them they've done nothing wrong.
5. Invite them to take another swing.
6. Bring love.

Ask Permission

Asking permission to provide feedback does a few things. First, it gives the person about to receive feedback the reins of control. They get to say yes or no. Your job at this point is to honor what they respond with. If they are a no, then follow up with them after the fact.

Second, when we ask someone permission to provide feedback, they listen differently. We are priming them to listen in a particular way, and, because they have given their permission, they are better able to receive what we provide.

When we ask someone permission to provide feedback, they listen differently.

"Steve, I'm going to interrupt you for a moment. I have some feedback on your leadership. Would you like it?"

We want to ask permission to provide feedback in the moment. This is the best time to provide feedback. It will give people the opportunity to immediately address what is happening and to ask any questions they may have about it. Imagine a squash coach that was giving feedback to their player on their forehand swing but only did so three days after the game. The player is going to improve far more slowly than if they were to get that feedback right after they've made the swing.

Acknowledge Who Someone Is and Ascribe Positive Intentions

The relationship most of us have to receiving feedback is that it means we're not good enough, and we're doing something wrong. You want to be conscious of this listening before you speak and adjust your own speaking accordingly. As a starting point, we want to honor what is going well and the greatness of the person in front of us. For more on reflecting someone's greatness, see the following section.

Feedback is most powerful when you can tie it back to who someone truly is as a leader (that is to say, their being underneath what they are doing). This provides an opportunity for them to see the incongruity between what they're doing and who they are.

So, we begin feedback by acknowledging who this person is. We do so simply and cleanly. We don't inflate it, and we don't need to make it long or overly effusive in an attempt to "pad" what will follow. Be genuine in your acknowledgment, and let it be enough.

"Steve, I love your commitment to excellence and how clear it is you want this project to be more than something we just shuffle together and shove off our desks. And what I notice is that your commitment to doing things right here seems to have you cutting people off and trying to force things to go a certain way."

Speak To the Impact They Are Having

As leaders, our intentions matter but especially important is the impact of how we are showing up. If my intention is that everyone feel loved and understand we're on the same team, but my impact is that certain people feel ostracized and bullied, then it doesn't much matter how well-intentioned I am—there's something for me to take on.

By reflecting the impact someone is having, we take it out of the realm of arguing about their intention and can allay some of the predictable defensiveness that shows up when we receive feedback.

"While I trust this isn't your intention, Steve, I notice the impact in the room is that some people are shutting down, and most people are just nodding their heads and going along with you at this point."

Check In to See If They're Aware and, If Necessary, Remind Them They've Done Nothing Wrong

Our impact tends to hide in our blind spots, and, consequently, we have judgment about it and ourselves as it is made apparent to us. This is the point where you want to check to see if the person you are giving feedback to is present to their impact and to remind them they've done nothing wrong.

Good feedback comes from a neutral, clean way of being; if we are piling on our own judgment and making the person wrong, that will add to the judgment they are already dumping on themselves. Your job as leader is first to do your own work with your own coach or leader, so that you can release any right/wrong energy you may have prior to giving this kind of feedback.

If we are piling on our own judgment and making the person wrong, that will add to the judgment they are already dumping on themselves.

"Steve, are you able to see what I'm pointing to? Are you present to that impact?"

"Yes, kind of. I notice people feel less engaged, and it's making me frustrated, and then I'm trying to push us harder."

"Great! Nice noticing. So, first, you're not doing anything wrong here. That reaction makes complete sense. And it seems like that isn't the impact you want to be having. So, take a breath, and give yourself and your team a bit of space."

If you check to see if the person present is aware of their impact, and they are not or argue with you, you can also draw in the rest of the room in support of them.

Throughout this process, it is important to remember that you are not trying to prove a point. You are trying to serve the person for which you are providing this feedback (by helping them grow their leadership). You do not seek feedback from the room to make them wrong or prove yourself right. You seek it so that the person you are supporting can start to see their blind spots.

"Steve, are you present to this impact?"

"I really don't see it."

"Okay, great. I totally get that. Let's check in with the room, so you can see what I'm pointing to. Who would be willing to share about the impact of Steve's being right now? Please, speak to me when you do so rather than to Steve."

Sheila puts up her hand.

"Great, Sheila. What's the impact?"

"Well, I volunteered a suggestion, but then Steve kind of moved past it quickly and almost in a clipped manner. So, then I figured what's the point? Why bother sharing if we're just going to get through this?"

"Great, thank you, Sheila. Steve, can you get that that is part of the impact you're having?"

"Yes, totally. But it's not what I want to be creating."

"Of course not! It's clear that what you want to create here is team and commitment. Your impact is out of alignment with your intention. So, no harm, no foul. This is actually a beautiful opportunity to realign yourself and your leadership. You're doing great work here, Steve."

Invite Them to Take Another Swing

Once someone is present to their impact, there is an opportunity to have another go. Remember that your job as leader is not to have them do it perfectly after they get your feedback; it is simply to have them adjusting and taking the next step towards their leadership and breakthroughs.

So, offer the person receiving feedback the opportunity to take a breath, remind them they're doing great (just by virtue of the fact that they are hanging out with you in this conversation, they really are!), and then invite them to take another swing.

"Okay, Steve. Clear on the impact you're having and don't want to create?"

"Yes."

"Great. You're doing really great work here. Thank you for modelling leadership for all of us. So, will you take a breath, maybe shake yourself out, and then take another swing?"

Steve takes a breath, closes his eyes and shakes his arms before coming back to present.

"Okay. Thanks everyone for sharing how that was landing. Let's try again. I really do want to hear your ideas, and I'm a little nervous about our timeline. I really want us to make this happen, and I think that's having me rush through this. So, let me slow down, and let's hear what you've got."

Bring Love

This last aspect of providing feedback is not really "last," sequentially speaking. This is a reminder that both giving and receiving feedback are acts of courage. They are operating in the face of our fear and our need to perform. This is why we tend to procrastinate, delay, and avoid giving feedback in the moment (when it is most effective). Remember to bring lots of love to this process as you walk through it.

Both giving and receiving feedback are acts of courage.

Bringing a lot of love does not mean you heap praise filled with superlatives on top of someone or that you spend fifteen minutes telling someone how awesome they are before giving them the feedback that really matters. Love is most effective when you trust it—and yourself—rather than trying to aggrandize it. It is often our efforts to go "above and beyond" sharing how much we appreciate someone that leaves them feeling like you're fluffing them rather than genuinely acknowledging them for their greatness.

HOW TO REFLECT AND ACKNOWLEDGE SOMEONE'S GREATNESS

THE PRACTISE OF reflecting someone's greatness is perhaps the more important practise for a leader.

The philosophy and model of this book and its approach to leadership is predicated upon the premise that we are born as light and learn to cover our light over in order to survive and thrive. To reflect someone's greatness is the act of seeing beyond the foibles of their humanity and ego—their shadows—to the truth and light that exists below the surface.

Because leadership exists beyond the edge of our own comfort, the act of leading and developing leadership in others and ourselves will, by definition, be confronting. When confronted, we naturally shift into the behaviours dictated by our shadows. We close our hearts and where we're left is present only to the impact of our shadows rather than the greatness beneath.

The act of leading and developing leadership in others and ourselves will, by definition, be confronting.

For example, as I've described above, someone who possesses the quality of Commitment, when confronted, may show up as flaky (the under-expressing aspect of their shadow). During these times, they will be much more present to this way of showing up than they will to the underlying truth of the Commitment they are. And predictably, so will you as their leader and the person supporting them.

To reflect someone's greatness, we acknowledge them for the greatness underneath whatever may be showing up in the moment—especially when what is showing up are their shadows. What can you acknowledge the person in front of you for? When you slow down and ask yourself the question, "What qualities does this person bring into the room?", what are you present to?

This question doesn't require long periods of thought and notetaking. This is a question to be answered in the moment from your heart. The more you can leave your brain out of the equation, the better. Once you've answered this question, the next step is to acknowledge what you see verbally.

If you are unable to receive acknowledgment for your own greatness, you will be forever stymied in your attempts to provide that same gift to others.

Imagine Tom, a leader, has just asked Regina to stop helping other people, so that she can take on the work that will cause her own breakthrough (rather than staying safe by taking care of other people). Regina is frustrated by this as she believes her generosity is a good thing. Seeing her confrontation, Tom acknowledges both it and Regina's greatness.

"Regina, I want to acknowledge you for your courage and your generosity. I'm clear that what I'm asking you to do is challenging, and I know that a lot of our team would really love to have your support. Your generosity is a tremendous blessing on this team—really, on any team. And having said all that, I'm also clear that it requires a lot of courage to set down that generosity, temporarily, so that you can create breakthroughs in new areas. Thank you for how you're showing up."

Seeing and reflecting someone's greatness can at times be effortless and easy and, at other times, challenging and hard. Reflecting someone's greatness is challenging in two main ways. The first challenge is our own confrontation.

The more confronted someone else is, the more their shadows will be apparent and the more you will have to look past or through in order to get present to their greatness.

Being with someone who is confronted *is confronting*. The more confronted you are, the more your own shadows will be in the way of your ability to see the greatness over there. Assuming that you are immune from this fact sets you up to be oblivious to your own shadows and their impact. Instead when you notice someone is confronted, consider that you too are confronted and are best served by slowing down.

If you notice that you are unable to get beyond the impact of someone's shadows and simply cannot get clear on the greatness in the person across from you, you may be served by pausing and taking on some of the other practises listed above first (releasing emotions, noticing what is showing up for you, forgiveness, etc.).

The second challenge is rooted in our fear that we will do it wrong. We have been trained that acknowledging someone in this manner is phoney, insincere, manipulative, or simply scaffolding to be put in place so that we can then share with them the "real" truth (which is typically some piece of feedback about how they suck or are being shitty). Because of this training, we either avoid giving acknowledgment altogether, or we artificially inflate it in an attempt to compensate.

Neither of these approaches is helpful. Instead when reflecting someone's greatness, the practise is to trust yourself. Trust that what you see is sufficient. And trust that the gift you have to offer (in your reflection and acknowledgment) is exactly that: A gift.

The art of reflecting and acknowledging greatness is a practise. You may not get it right the first time, and you may feel clumsy and unnatural in your attempts. Don't let that stop you from continuing to practise. As you continue to shine light on the greatness you see in others, you will discover the power and potency that comes from giving someone the gift of being seen for the totality of who they truly are rather than how they are being in the moment.

Finally, be in an ongoing practise of asking for acknowledgment. Ask it from your coach or leader regularly. When taking on something especially confronting, practise courageously reaching out to people and asking them for a reminder of your own greatness.

This is not being weak, needy, or cloying. This is being courageous in the practise of leadership, by doing your own work first—even, and especially, when it's uncomfortable.

SUPPLEMENTARY MATERIAL

ACKNOWLEDGEMENTS

Who Do You Think You Are? is not a model I created out of thin air, but rather an integration, adaptation, and elaboration of other models. All of this work is done on the shoulders of giants, and I would be remiss if I didn't acknowledge those that came before me.

The model underpinning *Who Do You Think You Are?* is an *ontological* one. Ontology is the study of *being*—what is it that makes you *you*, and me *me*? What are the qualities that distinguish you and me from each other and from everyone else?

And, most importantly to this book, how do we distinguish those qualities, and then draw them forwards in service of leadership?

The Old Masters

The earliest conversations about ontology were started during the antiquities by philosophers and scholars like Plato and Aristotle. As you can tell, this model is not a new one, not by a long shot. Part of the challenge of an ontological underpinning is that, to some extent, our *being* is that which is felt and experienced rather than something that can be scientifically codified and then proven.

Much of the early discussion around ontology is rooted in metaphysics—questions and debate concerning the nature of reality and what we can and cannot actually know about reality. This doesn't tend to have a lot of bearing on this book and doing deep ontological work with someone, but all the same, it's important to point out how far back this work can be traced.

Zen

At the heart of much of the ontological approach to relating and working with people is Zen. Much of Zen practise is focused on giving ourselves an experience of being with something, noticing what that drives up, and then practising being with instead of reacting to the thing in question. At its core, this is all the ontological approach ever is. Noticing what we cannot be with in life and then getting supported to practise *being* with that thing. In many ways, I would describe the work I do as facilitated Zen.

Alan Watts and Werner Erhard

Alan Watts was a luminary that lectured and spoke often on Zen in a way that allowed the Western world to receive, understand and integrate it into our lives. Alan Watts was a huge influence early on for Werner Erhard, who, in many ways, is the godfather of modern ontology.

Werner Erhard created EST (Erhard Seminars Training), which later became Landmark Education before he left that work and moved on to create what was next. Werner Erhard really opened the realm of accessing transformation through our *being* and supporting people not just to think about who they are *being* in the world but to directly create and step into that experience *in the moment*. This is really the heart of transformation.

While having insights and developing an understanding of yourself, your fears, what stops you, and what makes you great is all fine and good, the needle doesn't move until we shift from awareness into action. Werner's seminal work in ontology moved a lot of the conversation out of mere awareness into transforming the way people live their lives.

Much of my lineage is rooted in Landmark and the profound work being done in that structure.

Accomplishment Coaching

Accomplishment Coaching ("AC") trained me in much of my early understanding of ontology. Through their work, I was supported not only to learn who I truly am but also to distinguish that from my shadows and live my life beyond their safety. This was not the conclusion of my training but really, the beginning—you never actually conclude the work of developing your being. From now until the day you die, there will always be new edges for you to lean into—new edges where you are not yet fully expressed.

In my training with AC, I learned how to see the *being* in other people, and slowly, how to distinguish it. Over time, I worked in their leadership track and eventually was leading the same rigorous coach training I had undergone myself, training other people to see being and distinguish it.

During this time, most of my work in ontology was in the application of it—seeing what was showing up in someone else, distinguishing it, and then working with it to move them forwards in their lives.

After I moved on from leading AC's work, I continued to work with people in this way and began to develop a model for what I was seeing and how it showed up, ultimately arriving at the model in this book.

It is to AC that I owe the largest debt of gratitude. Without their work, nothing would likely have changed very much. I would have continued along the predictable path I was on, being brilliant but arrogant, charming but closed, and sharing a lot of content that had a small impact. AC opened my heart and showed me my soul—and showed me the soul of the rest of the world. Their work is life-changing and transformational. If there is anyone considering coaching as a career, I cannot evangelise AC's training enough.

The Individuals

In addition to those that came before me, there are a lot of people that supported me along the journey to creating this body of work.

To Mum and Dad, thank you for standing by and loving me every time I made a decision that went against what you thought might serve me best (as well as all the decisions I made that you thought were great!). Thank you for offering your wisdom and releasing your attachment to how I chose.

To Bay, my wife, thank you for the countless conversations while on walks, going for drives, eating meals, and everywhere else in our lives that led to the writing of this book. You are my source, inspiration, and heart.

To Adam, Deb, Jolynne, and Rachel, thank you for the coaching over the last decade. As I shared, all this work has been discovered, and that discovery came into being through my work with each of you.

To Christopher, Jodi, Kerry, and Denise, thank you for the support and development of my leadership. As I deepen my own work and develop the leadership of others, I'm often present to how much trust is required. Thank you for trusting me each step of the way.

To Michelle, Rodney, and Christine, thank you for being my contemporaries, friends, and colleagues. To look back and see where we were when we first met in San Diego, it's hard to believe where we are today. Each of your wisdom is present in these pages, mostly as a function of the ways you've touched me through our friendships.

To all of my clients, the members of the Forge, and those that have worked with me in some capacity, thank you for showing up and bringing whatever there was to bring. The discovery of this work is often a function of the courageous work you bring for us to take on in our conversations. Your willingness to show up, speak your truth, and then trust me to support you is what has led to this book.

To everyone I've mentioned here, and all of those I haven't—I love you. Thank you.

ABOUT THE AUTHOR

ADAM QUINEY IS an executive leadership coach specializing in working with the Smartest People in the Room. A former software developer and attorney, Adam's learned the hard way about the costs that come from keeping your heart safe and chasing after external rewards to feel whole and complete.

From love, Adam is Connection, Passion, Presence, Wit and Brilliance. From fear, he is awkward, robotic, apathetic, irrelevant and arrogant. He's learned to embrace all these parts of himself, and works with others to do the same in their own lives. Living with his beautiful wife and their two dogs (one of which is a cat) in Victoria, B.C., he is a man on a mission to bring the world to a more inspired and fully-expressed place.

Adam has led coach and leadership training internationally, and supports his clients on the journey to live and lead from head, to heart, and ultimately, to soul. He is the co-founder of The Forge, a transformational group for coaches and leaders worldwide, and runs a boutique coaching practice with clients from around the world.

During his spare time, Adam is a dancer, a musician, an artist, a lover of video games and dogs, and immersed in his own transformational work.

For more about Adam, visit www.AdamQuiney.com

GO DEEPER THAN YOU CAN GO ALONE

THE FACT: YOU'RE too smart to be helped.

You operate at an incredibly high-level of functioning. Most of the world doesn't understand you. They can't.

You try to share your life with them, and they'll tell you why you're so fortunate. They'll pass off what you're feeling, telling you you're just trying too hard.

"You should just slow down and enjoy life."

Thanks...

Everyone around you is either envious or excited about what you've created. No one really understands your situation, because they can't. They see the benefits of a life where your throttle is all-on or all-off, but not the costs.

I work with people like you. Leaders who have achieved success and exposed the myth that doing so leads to happiness. Leaders that awe the people around them, but know deep down there's more to life than this.

We work together to uncover the very patterns and habits that have led to your success—and to see how they are now what holds you stuck. We transform the way you show up in your life, developing you as a leader that lives from your deepest truth. A leader that models not only success, but adventure, excitement, happiness, daring, and passion.

Most of my people seem to have three stages to the journey their souls have chosen:

Head-based brilliance—Owning the brilliance you are, instead of pretending it's not there, or fighting to prove its there (why are you fighting to prove it? We're all aware of it. Just trust it.) Simply owning that you are the smartest person in the room is the first step of your growth.

Heart-based brilliance—Starting to let go of the need to look or be smart, trusting it's there and fine, and dropping down into your heart. In doing so, discovering that access through heart provides a great deal more brilliance into the world, and into every space you find yourself in. The story about people being stupid, morons, etc. falls away and instead a new muscle is developed allowing you to see, evoke and *cause* the brilliance in everyone and every space.

Soul-based brilliance—The shedding of reliance on your intellect to move you through the world. Completely embracing flow, and spirit, and trusting that you are divinely guided, and from that guidance, here to guide others the same way. Releasing knowing how it will go. A life of complete freedom and ease, and a dropping away of "needing to make things work." Releasing the struggle and concerns that you will somehow screw things up or wind up unable to recover from your failings.

Wherever you find yourself on your journey is perfect.

To learn more and apply, visit
www.AdamQuiney.com/work/

LEADING WITH PEERS

BE A PART of an exclusive group of coaches and leaders, committed to the deepest work possible: creating their own transformation and deepening themselves in service of others.

We get it—there are a lot of programs out there promising you not only the skills, tools and techniques needed to become a successful coach or leader, but also promising you'll be rolling in cash, wearing sequin jumpsuits, and riding peacocks off into the sunset.

The Forge isn't that program. If you're anything like us and our tribe, you've probably been seeking for a while. You care about people, you care about this work, and you're committed to leadership (yours and others). You want the best—you want training that wows you and leaves you a different human.

And, like us, you've probably found that it's challenging to find that kind of training. There's lots of good training out there. Training that provides you tools, gives you a taste of being on your edge, and leaves you feeling incredibly inspired. But it's rare to find training that leaves you a different human being.

The Forge is that training. Training that will not only deepen your ability to transform others, but to do so by transforming yourself.

The Forge creates a powerful, loving container, in which your transformation can unfold. There's nowhere to hide, and nowhere forward but through. Learn how to be with all of what shows up in life, so that you never again need to wait for something to pass before you can show up powerfully and create your life the way you want.

The Forge isn't a conversation about coaching and leadership. It's a conversation that *causes* coaching and leadership. Rather than learn new ways to talk about leading, you will discover the art of coaching and leading in a way that will have it ingrained in the marrow of your bones.

Move beyond thinking about and trying to figure out how to use coaching and leadership techniques. The Forge will leave you in mastery of these art forms, such that they will be using you.

You will not leave The Forge knowing about coaching and leadership. You will leave being a coach and being a leader.

To learn more about The Forge, visit:
www.evergrowthcoaching.com/the-forge

CREATE MORE THAN SIMPLE INSPIRATION

AFTER YEARS OF attending intensives, seminars, and workshops, we often found ourselves getting one of two things: inspiration and insight that seemed to fade as we re-entered the "real" world, or formulas to be applied, which didn't move us further on the dial towards the experience of life we wanted to be having, or the results we wanted to create. Sometimes, the inspiration created by the people we saw and their success stories made it seem like we were even further away from the success we wanted to create for ourselves.

Hearing stories of other people's success can be inspiring, but sometimes the gap between where they are, and where you find yourself can be daunting, especially if you're not sure of the work to be done to bridge the distance.

You may have experienced the same things we have: that insight, on its own, without action attached, tends to be toxic. It doesn't create results, or lasting transformation; it's simply interesting, and in the short-term, inspiring. But then, eventually, it becomes one more measuring stick, up to which you aren't living. And when that happens, that measuring stick conveniently becomes another stick with which to beat yourself up.

On the other hand, while collecting formulas and recipes for success feels good, it turns out that a lack of information is rarely what keeps us from creating the lives we want. If it was, Google would probably have set millions if not billions of people free by now. There always seems to be one more funnel, one more leadership hack and one more recipe to follow—and then you'll have what you want.

THE Intensive is the genesis of our insight, and us modeling our work. Creating what we see is missing in the coaching and leadership space, and supporting other coaches and leaders to do the same.

You're not interested in pretty good.

You're interested in **great**. You're interested in shattering paradigms and stretching way out of your comfort zone, because that's what you want to support other people to do, and you're clear that you have to do your own work first. THE Intensive is an opportunity to do exactly that. We will teach you new concepts, while supporting you in using them to step beyond your comfort. Instead of simply learning more information, you will step through your own transformation and actually experience the power of your deepest work.

The promise of THE Intensive is that you do not leave the way you came in. You leave having *transformed*. You don't need to remember the information and techniques your head is filled with—the shift has already happened internally by the time you leave. You return to the world, and rather than trying to remember what to do, you simply *be* it.

To learn more about THE Intensive, visit
www.evergrowthcoaching.com/the-intensive

APPENDIX A

INTERACTION WITH OTHER MODELS

PEOPLE ARE OFTEN curious about how this model and ontology in general interact with concepts like the polarity of divine masculine and feminine, our Zone of Excellence and Zone of Genius, and other models. Here's a rough framework for how each of these things fit in with each other.

Aiming for usefulness rather than correctness

In the context of a model for leadership and how people operate, what makes it valuable is not whether it's true or false. What matters is whether or not it *supports you* in accomplishing what you want to accomplish. That is the only criteria you really need to evaluate a particular model, at least one designed to enable your leadership and that of others.

There is no scientific proof that ontology and the model laid out here are valid. In fact, they are *inherently unscientific* because they are unprovable and unfalsifiable. They have to be; they are based not on empirically gathered and rigorously tested data. They are based on our *experience* of something.

How could you even test that? How would you test to see if a rock is a rock? You could test to see what the underlying minerals are, but then what if the rocky thing is not made of those particular minerals you tested for? If you get down to the lowest level, you will discover that the rock isn't even a rock—it's a set of atoms and below that, electrons and protons and so on and so on.

Who Do You Think You Are? is rooted in our fundamental experience of someone and the fundamental experience they bring with them into every space. This isn't something tested. It's something experienced.

Even worse than that, everyone experiences people through their own lens, and so, we can't even guarantee that two people will report the same experience of you. Notwithstanding, if we were to ask a multitude of people what shows up when you do, I guarantee we would get a wide variety of answers with a humongous amount of overlap. While the experience will not be identical, it becomes clear very quickly that your *being* is always present regardless of who you're with.

So, the bottom line is this: Relax.

If this model works for you, then great. Use it until it doesn't. If it doesn't work for you, use a different model.

Zone of Genius

The concept of your Zone of Genius (and the corresponding zones of Incompetence, Competence and Excellence) grew out of Gay Hendricks's book, *The Big Leap*. Gay describes the Zone of Genius this way:

> *In this zone, you capitalize on your natural abilities which are innate rather than learned. This is the state in which you get into "flow," find ceaseless inspiration, and seem to not only come up with work that is distinguished and unique but also do so in a way that excels beyond what anyone else is doing.*

Because most of our world functions around what we are *doing*, we tend to put our attention there. Consequently, people look at these zones (and try to figure out what theirs are) by looking at what they *do*.

We'll ask questions like, "What do I do that no one else can do?" and "What do I do that is so effortless I'm not even aware I'm doing it?"

I assert these questions are traps. They immediately narrow your scope down to the world of the doing and completely eliminate the deeper, ontological picture (that is to say, the picture that looks at who you are *being* in the world).

Here's one example of the kind of question that leads you in this direction. "What sucks away all your energy? What do you avoid doing? Those things fall outside your Zone of Genius." (This question is from Dan Sullivan's book, *Unique Ability*, another book focused on this concept.)

It seems like a great question since if you avoid doing it, it *must* not be part of your Zone of Genius. Whether or not Gay intended people to look through this lens, I invite you *not* to.

Being drained is not a function of the circumstances of your life, the people you're around, nor the thing you're currently doing. It is a function of who you are *being* while you do those things.

Being drained is the result of resisting the expression of your truest self. A function of forcing yourself to show up in a way that is incongruous to who you are. While we think our resistance is related to the task in front of us, the person we are talking to, or the experience we are having, the deeper truth is that your experience of being drained comes from holding and expressing yourself differently when those particular circumstances are present.

Your Zone of Genius is simply a function of your particular essence—your unique way of being. When you are coming from this place, you are operating from your Zone of Genius.

Let's imagine someone named Reginald who is brilliant but struggles to own his Brilliance powerfully. When he finds himself around people that don't share the trait of Brilliance, Reginald tends to dumb himself down (basically being condescending and a little manipulative even if it's intended from kindness).

It's predictable that Reginald will experience his time around these people as draining because he is resisting simply owning the Brilliance that he is. This is the same way it would be draining for me to walk around on all fours when my body is designed to be bipedal. Reginald will conclude that being in situations like this one must be outside of his Zone of Genius and then correspondingly arrange his life so that he doesn't need to spend time with people like this.

Breakthrough!

Except it's not. Reginald is just contracting from life and granting more power to his story that he can't be with certain aspects of life. In reality, Reginald's Zone of Genius is always available—provided he's willing to let other people have their own experience (which may include feeling awe or even some intimidation in the presence of his Brilliance fully expressed).

Your Zone of Genius is never a function of what you are doing. It is a function of who you are being while you do whatever is in front of you to do. The gift then is that your Zone of Genius is *always* available. The bad news of that is that when confronted with a task, person, or circumstance you don't like and find draining, your job is not to turn away from it, citing it not being in your Zone of Genius as the reason but rather to lean in and ask yourself, "How could I face this circumstance in my life from my deepest, truest ways of being?" This question will deepen your ability to live in your Zone of Genius.

Who Do You Think You Are? will point you to your Zone of Genius. The hard part is choosing to be and express these parts of yourself in the areas where you have learned they are not welcome.

For a deeper dive into the concept of your Zone of Genius as well as your Zones of Excellence, Competence, and Incompetence, check out the book *The Big Leap* by Gay Hendricks.

Polarity, Divine Masculine, and Divine Feminine

In divine polarity, the terms masculine and feminine are used not to describe a gender but to describe two forms of energy that are ever-present in the universe. You could call these energies Order and Chaos, Light and Dark, Positive and Negative (like the poles on a battery), or Masculine and Feminine.

Men tend to embody more of the masculine energy, and women more of the feminine, but there are no rules. Everyone possesses some amount of masculine energy and some amount of feminine energy. The same holds true for transgender individuals, individuals that don't identify with any particular gender, and any other kind of category you care to put yourself or someone else in. For some people, these two energies tend to be fairly balanced, but for most of us, our energy is a little more closely aligned in one way or the other and often, aligned with our gender.

The Masculine energy is that of resting consciousness. It's the void, the nothingness into which the entirety of existence and creation are poured. Without a void—a container, so to speak—there would be nothing to hold the energy of creation. That container is the Masculine energy. Masculine energy tends away from relationship and towards solitude, resting consciousness, and nothingness.

The Feminine energy is that of love and light. It is the energy of creation—the universe expanding, the stars being born and then being blown apart in a supernova and everything else in between. Feminine energy is the energy of creation and destruction and the love and feeling of everything in life. Feminine energy tends towards relationship, often feeling a pull to gather life towards it rather than towards the solitude that is the realm of Masculine energy.

Who Do You Think You Are? points to fundamental, underlying ways of *being* in the world that you innately exude. It's not necessarily something you do but something you *are*. There are an infinite number of ways to express any particular way of being. You can express any particular way of being while embodying Masculine energy or Feminine energy (or whatever combination you choose). Let's use the being of Love as an example.

If you embody the being of Love, you could express that by baking someone cupcakes, praising and acknowledging them for who they are, making love with them, the way you look into their eyes, or the way you relate to them when they're showing up from their fear.

None of these approaches are the *right* way to express love. And if all you ever did was express love in these five ways, you would be limiting your expression. There are an infinite number of ways that you can express your particular essence; trying to figure out the right way or following a script is ultimately self-limiting.

Someone could express the Love they are by simply witnessing and watching someone with deep admiration. They could sit, watching their partner, and appreciate everything about them—from the way their hair curls, the mole on their cheek, the curve in their back. Very little is actually said and yet the person witnessing is expressing Love. This would be an example of embodying the Masculine energy while expressing Love.

Alternatively, someone could express Love by providing a great deal of attention to their partner. They could make them lunches, write them notes, and send them text messages to let them know they're thinking of them. This would be a more active, more creative expression of Love, and thus an example of embodying the Feminine energy while expressing Love.

There's no *right* way to express your being, nor is it better to embody a Masculine or Feminine energy. What matters here, at least as far as this book is concerned, is that your *being* exists underneath the energy you embody.

For a deeper dive into the divine masculine and feminine check out David Deida's books, *The Way of the Superior Man* and *Dear Lover*.

Three Principles, Philosophy of Mind, and Health Realization

The Three Principles ("3Ps") are a philosophy of mind, thought, and consciousness, initially conceived by untrained philosopher, Sydney

Banks (he related to himself as a "Theosopher".) 3Ps was built on earlier bodies of work called the Philosophy of Mind and Health Realization.

The fundamental tenet of these philosophies is that there is an innate wellbeing that we all possess, and this is our default experience of life. What tends to move us away from that experience of wellbeing is our thinking. While thinking happens naturally and automatically, the problems begin when we begin to believe our thinking as opposed to distinguishing that there really isn't any reality other than the one created by our thoughts.

Expanding on these philosophies would take much more time and explanation than will serve here. The main overlap between these philosophies and *Who Do You Think You Are?* (or ontology in general) is that of the innate state of wellbeing.

What 3Ps would refer to as your innate state of wellbeing is what I describe as your light—the qualities of being that you possess and embody innately. Your light is always available, regardless of what you are doing, who you are with, how frightened you feel, or anything else. You are always able to access these ways of being. That is not to suggest that you won't experience resistance or fear in the process of getting back to yourself. In fact, you've trained yourself over many years to show up from your shadows. Because you've relied on these shadows to get through life and succeed in situations that otherwise are uncomfortable or frightening, letting go of them and returning to a defenceless state will be scary and naturally drive up your resistance.

Nonetheless, your light, or, as put in the 3Ps, your innate wellbeing, is always your default state and always available.

The main divergence between this model and 3Ps is that in 3Ps, you ultimately learn to relate to everything as simply fabricated and that there is no reality, no underlying self—there is only what you actively create.

This is similar to holding a rock in one hand and a feather in the other hand and noticing how they are both ultimately a collection of atoms. There is no actual "rock" nor an actual "feather." That's all made up, to an extent. Actually, 3Ps will go one step further and hold that even the atoms and electrons are made up and more Thought.

However, if I throw the rock at a window, it will have a different effect than if I throw the feather at the window. At least within the realm of Thought (as the 3Ps approach puts it), these items have distinct qualities.

It is these qualities that *Who Do You Think You Are?* points towards. You can argue that we're all stardust or all made up of thought, but at the same time, you yourself have a unique way of being that I and the world around you experience. We are attempting to work with that being, and so, combine both the spiritual nature of existence with the humanity of it (rather than simply bypassing the humanity altogether).

For a deeper dive into the Three Principles, check out Michael Neill's book, *The Inside-out Revolution* and Sydney Banks's book, *The Missing Link*.

StrengthsFinder

The StrengthsFinder approach touches, to an extent, on many of the qualities of being listed in this book.

The core concept of StrengthsFinder is that much of the management or leadership in the workplace is focused around supporting you in taking on the areas that you are not good in—places where you are weak, in the theory that developing that makes you more rounded. StrengthsFinder turns this on its head by saying that, actually, we should be identifying people's strengths and putting them into positions that are best served by those strengths.

There is a truth and a fallacy to this approach. The truth is that people who innately are Connection will likely do better in jobs that involve a lot of connection rather than jobs that involve sitting at a desk all day long. I will come to the fallacy shortly.

StrengthsFinder's categories tend to capture specific aspects of someone's underlying *being*. For example, one of the five strengths listed in my StrengthsFinder profile is Discipline. The description for this trait is "People who are especially talented in the Discipline theme enjoy routine and structure. Their world is best described by the order they create."

Looking at *Who Do You Think You Are?*, this is in part due to my Brilliance and corresponding love of breaking systems down into individual pieces and then optimizing from there as well as the shadow of my Passion, which at times can lead me to feel compulsive, out of control, and obsessive. By creating discipline, I learned how to tame and manage the part of myself that at times felt unsafe.

There are times when my ability to create discipline is really a reflection and expression of my deepest self. There are other times when it's a reaction to my fear, and, in fact, encouraging me to continue bringing more discipline would actually move me away from my fullest expression.

Is StrengthsFinder wrong because of this? No, it's not wrong, any more than *Who Do You Think You Are?* is right. They are simply models and different ways of looking at the world and the people within it. The thing I find is missing from StrengthsFinder is that it does not distinguish our essence from our shadow or survival mechanism and, consequently, can reward the very thing that is blocking your next stage of leadership. However, *Who Do You Think You Are?* can be overly broad and difficult to operationalize, especially early on in your working with them.

These are the trade-offs that come with any particular model.

For a deeper dive into StrengthsFinder's strengths-based test, check out the book *StrengthsFinder 2.0*.

Myers-Briggs

The Myers-Briggs typing approach is based on a quiz and then determination of your personality into one of sixteen types. The underlying assumption of the Myers-Briggs Type Indicator (MBTI) is that we all have specific preferences in the way we construe our experiences, and these preferences underlie our interests, needs, values, and motivation.

The MBTI was created out of the speculation that humans experience the world using four principal psychological functions—sensation, intuition, feeling, and thinking—and then classifying people into one of sixteen categories reflecting those functions.

People can use the MBTI to relate to themselves as a fixed object. When someone identifies themselves as an Introverted type (The I indicator in MBTI types), they conclude that it's simply always going to be challenging for them to be in large groups or situations that would demand socializing. When someone identifies themselves as a Perceiving type (the P indicator in MBTI types), they conclude that they will *always* see rules and deadlines as flexible and thus should not be beholden to them.

However, this falls down in the face of developing someone's leadership. What do we do in a situation that demands someone empower and work with deadlines and rules? You may argue that the leader should then hire someone else to do this, but what about the situation where that is not an option? Delegating a task elsewhere is fine, but it simply pushes off the need for the leader to develop the breakthrough themselves. What about when they need their direct report to get responsible for rules and deadlines with their team? How can you develop this ability in someone else when your only ability is to delegate and avoid confronting it?

While *Who Do You Think You Are?* describes your essence underlying everything, the MBTI can, at times, describe the manifestation of this essence—that is to say, the way you act out in the world as a result of who you are underneath.

Part of the MBTI description for Extraverted types includes "could be described as talkative, outgoing" and Introverted types "could be described as reserved, private." However, both of these are reflected in the shadow aspects of Connection.

Because the MBTI test often involves binary answers to questions ("Is your idea of a great Friday night to stay home and cook a lovely meal or go out for a night on the town with friends?"), it often forces people out into one of the two opposite poles of the same underlying way of being.

MBTI tends to capture more of the surface layer that reflects the underlying essence (which is what *Who Do You Think You Are?* points to.)

Enneagram

The Enneagram is an ancient typing system that remains relevant today. Composed of nine distinct types along with a slew of "wings" and other factors that make those nine-types more malleable, your Enneagram type describes the following:

1. What you learned growing up earned you value (in the form of love, recognition, safety, etc.).
2. What you learned was unsafe and required you protect yourself from.
3. What you learned to listen and look for as a consequence of the first two bullets.
4. How you learned to act as a result of the first three bullets.

The Enneagram is closer to the model laid out in this book and ontology in general than most of the other typing approaches because it speaks more to our ways of being first and foremost, than to our doing.

Who Do You Think You Are? tends to put more attention on the individual elements of someone's light that make up the person in front of you. Sometimes you'll be present to someone's Brilliance, other times the awesome Presence they cast.

You could think of the Enneagram as describing certain types of material (e.g., rocks, water, skin, trees). *Who Do You Think You Are?* is a little more like the periodic table of elements, pointing to the actual atoms that make up whatever particular material you have in front of you. An Enneagram type-7 will often have both Brilliance and Wit as part of their qualities of being, but many other Enneagram types will also have those same ways of being.

For more on the Enneagram, check out Don Richard Riso and Russ Hudson's book, *The Wisdom of the Enneagram*, and Clarence Thomson's website, http://www.enneagramcentral.com.

APPENDIX B

QUICK REFERENCE GUIDE

THIS REFERENCE GUIDE is a duplicate of the one at the start of Section Two, and is intended to provide an easy place to access when you're flipping through trying to find a particular quality of shadow aspect.

QUICK REFERENCE GUIDE

QUALITY OF BEING	SHADOW ASPECTS + THEIR OBVIOUS (BUT INEFFECTIVE) FIXES	
	Over-Expressing Shadow Aspect *Obvious (But Ineffective) Fix*	**Under-Expressing Shadow Aspect** *Obvious (But Ineffective) Fix*
ADVENTURE page 74	**Treacherous, Careless and Irresponsible** *Get Real and Knuckle Down*	**Controlling and Controlled** *Make the Dramatic Leap*
BRILLIANCE page 86	**Condescending and Skeptical** *Sell Your Ferrari and Become a Monk*	**Dense and Manipulative** *Trade in the Dunce Cap for a Mortarboard and Gown*
CHAMPION page 98	**Zealous Taskmaster** *Stop Caring So Much — People are Gonna be People*	**Pessimistic Cheerleader** *Rally the Troops — Guys, We Can Do Better!*
COMMITMENT page 108	**Enslaved Tyrant** *Chain Yourself to Being Unchained*	**Flaky Hummingbird** *Suffer Your Way to Transformation*
CONNECTION page 120	**Superficial and Exhausted** *Withdraw From the Exhaustion*	**Shy and Isolated** *Force Yourself To the Party*
CREATION page 132	**Unmanned Firehose** *Lock Yourself Down With Structure*	**Narrow-Minded Drone** *Become a Bull in a China Shop*
CURIOSITY page 144	**Fence-sitter** *Throw Curiosity Out the Window — It's Time To Make Things Happen*	**Rigidly Following Rules** *Slow Down, Let's Just Chill Out Here*
EASE page 156	**Vague and Non-Committal** *The Dude Gets Real, and Life Gets Heavy*	**Overly Significant** *Let Go of Commitment and Chill Out*
GENEROSITY page 168	**Martyring Doormat** *It's Time to Get What's Yours*	**Selfish Zealot** *Stop Keeping Track...*
GRACE page 178	**Haughty Spectator** *You Can't Beat 'Em, So Join 'Em*	**Profane and Plebeian** *Rise Above It All*
INTEGRITY page 188	**Tyrannical Dictator** *You Only Live Once, So Start Living*	**Oblivious Hypocrite** *Get Right and Live Straight*
JOY page 200	**Obnoxious Child** *Get Serious and Put Away the Toys*	**Pit of Despair** *Just Have Fun — Nothing Matters Anyway*
LEADER page 212	**Leader of Followers** *Let Other People Lead*	**Follower of Leaders** *Step Up — It's My Time*

QUICK REFERENCE GUIDE

QUALITY OF BEING	SHADOW ASPECTS + THEIR OBVIOUS (BUT INEFFECTIVE) FIXES	
	Over-Expressing Shadow Aspect *Obvious (But Ineffective) Fix*	**Under-Expressing Shadow Aspect** *Obvious (But Ineffective) Fix*
LOVE page 224	**Cloying and Suffocating** *Just Stop Caring So Much*	**Cruel and Heartless** *Become a Being of Pure Love*
MAGIC page 234	**Escapist** *Hang Up the Wizard Robes*	**Jaded and Mundane** *Paint Outside the Lines*
PASSION page 244	**Compulsive and Obsessive** *Throttle the Compulsion*	**Apathetic and Bored** *Get Swept Away in the Passion*
PEACE page 256	**Rigid Buddha** *Begin the Season of Yes!*	**Frenetic Problem-Solver** *Embody the Irrefutable No*
PERMISSION page 268	**Sloppy, Swampy and Messy** *Button Things Up and Get Real*	**Censored and Censoring** *Put an End to the Apologies*
POWER page 280	**Irresponsible Monster** *Cage the Monster*	**Tamed Lion** *Unleash the Beast*
PRESENCE/RADIANCE page 290	**Obnoxious Diva** *Give Other People All of the Space*	**Elephant Behind a Blade of Grass** *Take Up All the Space You Need*
PURPOSE page 300	**Purposeful Fascist** *Turn Off the Purpose and Pour Another Glass of Wine*	**Listless Freedom** *Roll Up Your Shirtsleeves and Get Shit Done*
SPIRIT/DIVINITY page 312	**Spiritually Bypassing** *Abandon God and Walk with the Mortals*	**Faithless Cynic** *Ladle on the Piety*
UNITY/ONENESS page 322	**Indecisive and Frozen** *Stop Soft-Pedalling and Take Action*	**Righteous Crusader** *Give Up the Fight and Hold It All Sacred*
WISDOM page 334	**Self-satisfied and Oblivious** *Play the Jester and Join the Party*	**Foolish and Ignorant** *Grow Up and Get Wise*
WIT page 344	**Obnoxious Clown** *Kill the Clown and Get Serious*	**Humour-Free Zone** *Get to Playing—None of This Matters Anyhow*

INDEX

D

E

F

L

M

N

O

P

R

S

Made in United States
North Haven, CT
09 November 2022

26468816R00248